Photo: Christian Raby, Paris. Pictured: Michael Simpson & Barret O'Brien

Afterlife

GHOSTLY COMEDIES

PLAYS BY

ROSARY HARTEL O'NEILL

VOLUME 3

iUniverse books may be ordered through booksellers or by contacting:

iUniverse
1663 Liberty Drive
Bloomington, IN 47403
www.iuniverse.com
1-800-Authors (1-800-288-4677)

ISBN: 978-1-4620-5753-5 (sc)
ISBN: 978-1-4620-5754-2 (ebk)

Printed in the United States of America

iUniverse rev. date: 04/19/2012

For plays held by Samuel French: Licensing Fees are payable one week before the opening performance of the play to Samuel French, Inc, at 45 West 25th Street, New York, NY 10010. Please visit their website at www.samuelfrench.com for performance rights applications and licensing fee payment.

Book Design: Karen Engelmann I www.karenengelmann.com

AFTERLIFE

GHOSTLY COMEDIES
PLAYS BY
ROSARY HARTEL O'NEILL
VOLUME 3

DEDICATED TO:

All dreamers of an asthetic bent and their
champions, like my husband Bob
and my children
Rachelle, Barret, Rory, and Dale.

BRAVO!

Special thanks to Midwives
Karen Engelmann, Jim Bosjolie,
Tonda Marton, Ken Dingledine,
and Lysna Marzani.

ROSARY HARTEL O'NEILL

ROSARY O'NEILL'S THIRD VOLUME OF PLAYS
certainly provides ample evidence of the playwright's
versatility and artistic fertility.

As our resident dramatist, our 112 year-old institution
is so proud we have this gifted artist at this period of
world history that has never needed more the power of
theatre to confront, alert, and awaken.

O. Aldon James
President, National Arts Club
New York, NY

ROSARY O'NEILL TRIUMPHS AGAIN in this, her latest anthology of theatrical offerings! Her frank look into the human soul draws the reader and audience into a world otherwise only imagined...supplying us with complex glimpses into the lives and inner turmoil of these characters. Three of the plays that make up this book deal with legends and icons of the silver screen...Marilyn Monroe, James Dean, and Montgomery Clift. All of these actors, while achieving screen immortality and becoming fixtures in pop culture, suffered with their own private demons, and their lives ended in tragedy. Beyond the glitter and the spotlights, Rosary has delved into their personal psyches, tearing away the gloss to reveal the turmoil they endured. While doing so, she has made each icon more approachable and human...forcing us to examine more closely the real people behind the masks. The human condition is a constant throughout time, and with her marvelous style of writing, she has once again breathed life into these celluloid giants, offering an intimate look into the emotions that they certainly felt... The second play deals with a topic that anyone from Louisiana can relate to...hurricanes. Having her beloved New Orleans ravaged by hurricane Katrina, Rosary pulls from deep personal emotions for this play. As anyone from Louisiana can tell you, you cannot imagine the fear, horror, and finally the sadness that accompany these catastrophic events!

Having had the honor of being allowed to direct two of her works (BLACKJACK, THE THIEF OF POSSESSION, and THE AWAKENING OF KATE CHOPIN), I hold a personal connection to these marvelous literary works, and to their creator, Rosary O'Neill, whom I am proud to call my friend! Read these plays... contemplate them, and enjoy them. Rosary is a playwright of amazing depth and sensitivity. Welcome to her characters and their lives and their worlds...beautiful, poignant, but ultimately each one fatally flawed.

DAN FOREST
Director, City Park Players and Spectral Sisters,
Alexandria, Louisiana

TABLE OF CONTENTS

THE PLAYS

ROSARY HARTEL O'NEILL

INTRODUCTION / VOLUME 3

My father was born in 1904. If he were alive he would be 107. I've had 2 lives, one in New Orleans and one in New York. I returned here mid-life to pursue a girlhood fantasy. I'd studied with Uta Hagen (the legendary actress of HB Studio) and Herbert Berghoff the genius director from whom HB Studios gets its name. Back then; I wanted to be a famous actress; now I wanted to be an acclaimed playwright. Superlatives dominate my vocabulary.

Catastrophe and miracles spurned my relocation. A divorce, death of both parents, and the exodus of my adult children had left me bereft. For 15 plus years, I'd been producing theatre (as founding artistic director of Southern Rep) and teaching college (as the second female/full professor at Loyola University). In 2001, the American Embassy awarded me a 5-year Senior Fulbright Drama Specialist appointment to teach and have my plays done in Europe.

Living in New York, I could travel abroad easily. Was fate pushing me from New Orleans? I must confess that two of my four children were studying in New York so my flight was partly nest-driven. But I believe in signs. I'd met a scientist on a Southwest plane en route to a writer's conference at Sewanee. He said, "Move to New York. I can't think of a playwright, not in New York."

I resisted the exodus (not knowing the seed of Katrina was growing in the universe.) How could I write like a New Yorker? I wasn't "emerging," young, or fresh. At my daughter Dale's high school graduation tea, when I suggested to some mothers that I might leave for New York to be a published playwright, one mom said, "Do it for all of us." Shortly before Katrina hit, I sold my memories and moved from 4000 sf in New Orleans to 400 sf in Manhattan. I later married the clairvoyant scientist.

So how would I find an identity in this new place? I was born and raised in New Orleans. All my family lives or is buried there. It sounds weird, but I used to find comfort driving past the cemetery where my ancestors rest. I felt lucky to have been raised in and work in the city of my birth.

I signed on for playwriting workshops in NYC and met students from Russia, Georgia, France, South America, India, China, Romania, Africa, Germany, Canada, England, Iran, the Ukraine, et al. All of us were immigrants weaving our lives into tapestries for others. The vitality of New York excited me, and I joined the ranks of the carefree, nomad playwrights who delight in The Big Apple.

But along with pluses came minuses. I was warned that plays about New Orleans were considered "folksy" or regional. I'd better keep my hopes low since I'd never be published unless I was produced on Broadway. But, disaster created an opening. After Katrina, the same dismissed plays became important, politically sensitive, cutting edge. Samuel French, Inc., the leading publisher of plays worldwide, licensed all my work in 2 anthologies. (A Village writer friend declared, "Rosary this is huge.") The only price I paid was losing my past.

All the times I lived in New Orleans and on the Gulf Coast, I only evacuated once--drove to Dallas and then the hurricane spun around and didn't hit. Back then, hurricanes were American girls like Betsy. As they increased, they became bisexual and international: Andrew, Camille, Jose, etc. I moved to NYC, and Katrina annihilated New Orleans. Overnight, the world of my childhood was gone.

But New York is generous to orphans. And other artists are bountiful. In mourning after Katrina, I agreed to go to Loren Kaplan's screen writing and playwrights workshop. He said I didn't have to write a word, could just attend; sometimes artists are too low to do a thing. I could just listen and watch. With that permission, I developed my hurricane comedy, BEHIND CUT GLASS.

Upstate, another friend (David Greenan) introduced me to Gary Schiro, who toured my plays throughout NY with his Hudson Opera House troupe. Still other friends brought me to The Norman Mailer Institute (Norris Mailer), Actors Studio (Brian Delate), Harlem Writers project at Columbia University (Joyce Griffen), HB Studios (Julie McKee), International Women Writers Guild (with mentors Kathleen Spivak and Hannelorre Hahn), the Virginia Center for the Creative Arts (Suny Monk) and the Virginia Playwrights and Screenwriters initiative (Boomie Pedersen). Fellowships at these places helped me develop MARILYN/GOD, JAMES DEAN AND THE DEVIL, and MONTGOMERY CLIFT AND THE ALL GIRL FAN CLUB.

The National Arts Club (the leading institution for artists) in NYC, Aldon James, president, championed me and I went from Louisiana misfit to playwright-in-residence. That club of generous strangers, now friends support-ed the rehearsal and mounting of all of my work. New art has always been the lifeblood at the National Arts Club. And I am pleased to trickle into the mix.

HEARTS and my other card plays (published in Vol. 1) were all produced in staged readings there. Lesson learned: patrons champion itinerant writers all over New York.

I'm living in NYC and again it's a recession. Is adversity following me—or could victory be nearby? But I have completed 6 more plays--all ghostly comedies. Why ghostly? In all these plays, an apparition or some spirit guide arrives at a time of great calamity. I was blessed to leave New Orleans, before New Orleans left me. But she is a guardian angel, looming behind me.

CUT GLASS is a post-Katrina expansion on my one act WISHING ACES (Pub. in vol 1). I wanted to bring in a whole kaleidoscope of New Orleans characters, boatmen, hunters, Beau, the hero might reckon with on his flight. CUT GLASS can be done "operatically" with over 24 actors or downscaled to five. A barometer inspired it.

It was nearing August 29th one year after Katrina hit, I was fearing bad weather in New Orleans and remembering my parents once had a wall barometer a ruler's length that predicted storms. It would say, "Fair, rainy, stormy, hurricane." And when the dial went to hurricane, we left their "big house" on the Gulf Coast by Cadillac for New Orleans. Despite plenty of electronic warning, Katrina's 40-foot waves leveled the mansion (my parents actually called it that.) Of the 500 beachfront mansions only 5 remain.

CUT GLASS led me to write other scary comedies. In MARILYN/GOD, drugs and exhaustion have made their inroads into Marilyn's sanity. In the last moments of her life, Marilyn faces God, and she must audition for heaven. Voices of dead celebrities (personified or not) from the other side push her to sing, dance, and act her way through the golden gates. Terrified she tries to stop the audition, but too much time has passed and she can't go back to earth.

Marilyn had a premonition of death. There's evidence she called her psychiatrist many times during her final days. Jimmy had no warning. He hit the road and it was cool like 70 degrees with the slight feeling of autumn in the air. It'd gotten chilly on the highway at dusk. He went in T-shirt and light jacket unprepared for what he was to confront on the Highway of Death. Speeding in his convertible, he didn't worry about rain. It was California after all and a rural highway. There was no sign for Jimmy except he hadn't seen a car in a long time and one was due. In JAMES DEAN AND THE DEVIL, Jimmy storms his way down a chaotic highway to discover he is dead and must break out of hell.

Like Marilyn and Jimmy, I can't go back to my earthly haunts in New Orleans. But I'm alive. I still wear sunglasses year round. But in NYC it's because of the traffic and dusty streets as opposed to New Orleans' glaring sun. In NYC when you wear sunglasses people stop and ask, "Are you somebody?"

I walk down Broadway and recall Marilyn, Jimmy, and Montgomery walked these streets to the Actors Studio. I pass brownstones, taunting me to capture their stories, much like the mansions and alleys in New Orleans called me to pen theirs.

Since WISHING ACES was performed at the theatre I founded (Southern Rep in New Orleans), I've always written a play with a lead for my son, actor Barret O'Brien. When he got into the acting program at Yale he told me, "Ma you don't have to write for me anymore." I wrote MARILYN/GOD for one woman and voices and after that he said, "Never do that again."

So I wrote JAMES DEAN AND THE DEVIL, MONTGOMERY CLIFT AND THE ALL-GIRL FAN CLUB and perfected HEARTS: THE KING OF FOOLS for him.

To me writing is like one big crossword puzzle--finding the word for the slot for the character for the time and keeping the reader and myself from being bored. When I write for particular actors, I see them in the roles and that helps me be specific.

In HEARTS, dying artist Rooster chooses to leave the home of his boyhood and claim his talent. After a face altering accident, movie star Montgomery Clift must choose retirement or advancement in film with a compromised face.

Katrina made me interested in orphans, the dispossessed, those of uncertain backgrounds. Monty, Jimmy, Marilyn all fought to be legitimate, real New York artists, accepted for their talent despite their backgrounds.

My great grandfather Jacob Malter was a Civil War orphan reared by a Yankee soldier who happened to drive by and see him sobbing in a gutter. Does that bind me closer to the famous dispossessed icons?

Buddhists say the one thing certain in life is impermanence. I have felt this deeply and been enriched by it. Little deaths provide an opening for the new and the wonderful to slip in and lighten the soul. Part of me is in that cemetery in New Orleans but a bigger part is dancing with death and creating ghostly comedies.

ROSARY HARTEL O'NEILL
NEW YORK, NEW YORK
MARCH, 2012

ROSARY HARTEL O'NEILL

THE PLAYS

BUNKY: BARRET O'BRIEN   IRENE: JANET SHEA

Hearts:
THE PRINCE OF FOOLS
A PLAY IN TWO ACTS

DR. CLEANTH (Nicknamed CLAY) RICHARDS. 40+.
An ethnic psychiatrist, attractive. Clay is a solitary woman,
sensitive but remote. She keeps her thoughts close to her
vest and brightens her suit with a paisley bow tie, which
she continually adjusts. Clay's advice is grounded in ratio-
nality, making her manner ceremonial and stilted. A general feeling of rejection grounds her actions.

ROOSTER (Nicknamed Roo) DUBONNET. 31.
A painter: sallow cheeks, big eyes, wayward hair. Rooster
has pushed himself beyond reasonable limits in his pursuit
of art and family approval. He is critically ill from a virus,
which makes his skin break out in a rash from the heat.
The disease gives Roo a distinct nonchalance, the charm of
the damned.

IRENE (Nicknamed Mimi) SONIAT DUBONNET. 60+.
Mother to Rooster, she looks forty-five. Irene is blandly
miserable, because of her failing eyesight, but she refuses
to wear anything but prescription, rose-colored sunglasses.
She walks with a limp because she has stumbled into
several walls. Even so, she redefines the word style—in
her wide-framed sunglasses, Chanel dresses, and flawless
makeup. She is one of those striking women—nerves of
steel, iron lungs, sharp as a tack—who has nothing to do
but protect her grown children, and she watches them like
a dog guards her bones.

BUNKY DUBONNET LEGERE. 22.
Irene's grandson and Rooster's nephew, admitted into
Tulane University because of family money. Bunky dresses
in jeans and boots because they make him feel special, and
most of his friends are a lot smarter and younger. His life
goals are vague because he puts off thinking about them.
Bunky's consuming interest is singing the blues at parties.
He will go beyond rational limits to have fun—postponing
studying until absolutely forced to do so. Bunky has an
alcohol problem. When he drinks, his personality changes
into an exaggerated gaiety and a hair-trigger rage.

JASMINE RUSH. 38.
Adopted daughter to Irene Dubonnet, and Bunky's step-
aunt. She speaks with an affected west Texas drawl. A
former hand model, Jasmine is poised with all ten fingers
to climb the social ladder. Like a peacock, she is always
preening herself—adjusting an eyelash, puffing her hair,
buffing her rings. Jasmine has uncalled-for flashes of jeal-
ousy during which she refuses to calm down. Materialism
invades every aspect of her life, compelling her to marry
rich, no matter the price.

SHEILA FITZGERALD. 28.
An artists' agent, with a passion for things of the spirit.
Sheila attracts others with an ephemeral vitality that
reminds one of a butterfly. Her gentleness is matched by
delicate features: porcelain skin, peaches-and-cream com-
plexion, and graceful hands. When Sheila smiles, she laces
her fingers through her hair, which ripples and tumbles
around her face.

SETTING

The day room of a Garden District mansion,
New Orleans, Louisiana.

ACT ONE. The day room. Valentine's Day.
Late afternoon.

ACT TWO. The day room. The Bacchus Parade.
Mardi Gras. Late afternoon.

ACT ONE

SETTING: An antebellum mansion in the Garden District, New Orleans, Louisiana. We are in the day room overlooking a rose garden. There is a day bed with cushions so soft they invite sleep, and wind-up toys everywhere: racing cars, trucks, planes, an electric train. Paintings of toys in various stages of completion are placed about. A life-size inflatable doll of Edward Munch's "The Scream" stands center. The effect is of a boy's dream, the actual furniture being less important than the wonder created. A hood resembling a castle drapes a cage of doves. A snow parrot guards the rear from a coop like a Chinese house.

AT RISE:

SOUND: It is raining quietly, one of those late afternoon showers that New Orleans is famous for. Moisture chills the air, preserving the five o'clock cocktails: mint juleps in red glasses, candy hearts, and Valentine cups.

LIGHTS: A mysterious light. The glare casts shadows through the bluish-white blinds. Lights fade up on ROOSTER DUBONNET asleep on the day bed. Center stage is an angelic creature, SHEILA FITZGERALD, surrounded by whirling, rotating toys. SHE moves as if part of an apparition.

SOUND: Footsteps approach from offstage. SHEILA leaves. ROOSTER pulls back the curtain from his day bed. CLAY RICHARDS enters with a medical case. ROOSTER flicks on the tape deck by remote control.

SOUND: A symphony by Gorecki fades on.

CLAY: What's your fever?

ROOSTER: You can't expect me to remember all that.

CLAY: Your relapse began when you returned to your mother's.

ROOSTER: Sssh, doc! I love this symphony. It expresses a truth about "la condition humaine."

CLAY: Roo, this is serious.

ROOSTER: I don't care. As an artist, you focus on the hours you have to peak. The rest's going to your room.

CLAY: Oh, come on.

ROOSTER: I'm a prince, and this is my castle. It's not a real castle. It's a house in the Garden District—

CLAY: You're full of anger—

ROOSTER: But it's a kingdom where fantasy reigns and toys are celebrated—

CLAY: Anger's got to express itself somewhere.

(HE picks up a car and races it.)

ROOSTER: I ordered this hot rod from the *Palais Royal* Shop in Paris. I believe some toys have souls, don't you. You can trust a toy.

CLAY: You're living with people you don't feel close to.

ROOSTER: Ha! I've a Civil War mentality.

CLAY: A mother who's nicer to strangers than she is to you.

ROOSTER: I like being kicked around. We live like lords here! *(Laughs)* The cavaliers were remarkable for their affection for their castles. I've a sumptuous life —

CLAY: Replete with its small kindnesses and cruelties.

ROOSTER: The past isn't dead, Clay. It exists in our blood in the things we are heir to—in decades of wealth, passed from one generation to the next. I'm the big brother of the dynasty.

(SOUND: BUTLER shrieks, "Where's the maid? Where's the maid?")

ROOSTER: My parrot, Commander Butler. *(To the bird)* Now, now, Butler; No one's going to catch me and send me away.

CLAY: My grandma wouldn't let a bird inside the house. Said they were harbingers of death.

ROOSTER: Butler's jealous. He doesn't like your tie because it's the color of passion, and he wants it all for himself.

CLAY: You need adult activities!

(SOUND: The parrot screams, "Where's the maid?")

ROOSTER: Butler's seen too much. Too many people cried back here. You can feel the grief in the walls, and you wouldn't want to walk around here alone at night. ...Sometimes we make it to the slave quarters, where my nephew lives ... You can stir up a racket, run around nude, and nobody will bother you.

CLAY: *(Fingers her tie, with a twinge of panic)* Remember when you flew me to Ensenada ...When you had that episode. We went walking by the water. Counting the seagulls. Stirring up the sand. Hypnotized by the lapping of the waves. *(A silence passes between them.)* You began painting again. You'll never leave your mother without feeling guilty. But no one can live with one foot stuck in the present and one in the past.

(IRENE DUBONNET enters, wearing pink sunglasses and yelling off-stage at her chauffeur, HUCK. Her eyes are going, and SHE has difficulty adjusting to the change of light. IRENE leaves the door open.)

IRENE: Huck! Lock the gates. Load the rifles. Huck! It's a trick to scare off burglars, Doctor.

ROOSTER: Shut the door!

IRENE: I don't take advantage of my driver. But Huck couldn't find the Country Club!

CLAY: Where're your real glasses?

IRENE: I pitched them in the Mississippi River and started memorizing my house! It's bad enough my eyes are failing. I won't lose my looks, too. I can't believe I've to walk around looking at the floor for toys.

ROOSTER: Don't let my bird out! Shut the door.

IRENE: Rooster belongs to the International Caged Bird Society. But he can't make his parrot do a thing.

CLAY: Has Roo taken his medicine?

IRENE: I forget. He orders more and more catalogues for that bird. We must be on some master list of suckers.

CLAY: Eight pills. Four times a day.

IRENE: Butler belongs to the Louisiana Parrot Society. The membership dues are twenty-four feathers a year.

CLAY: What's Roo's fever?

IRENE: When he doesn't think about it, it goes away. That parrot's a hundred years old. He used to whistle Dixie. He was raised by a gentleman who kept his plantation up river. If you don't buy Roo everything, he thinks you're a bad mother. *(Motioning to a box of butterflies)* I ordered pressed butterflies: black and yellow, scarlet, and French blue. For Roo to paint nature … I didn't kill them, Doctor. Toward the end of its short life, the butterfly loses strength. Its wings which had carried it so easily are ragged and …

CLAY: Doesn't it frighten you a bit? That report from the Oschner Clinic. Roo's treatment is not going as planned. He's lost touch with his feelings. Epstein-Barr's a disease that …it's based on mental deterioration.

IRENE: Let's keep the topic to trivial things.

CLAY: Fine! *(Angry)* But take note. Nothing's trivial to a psychiatrist.

BUNKY LEGERE struts inside balancing boxes, flowers and a book. Midday champagne makes him defiant. The following lines overlap with enthusiasm.

BUNKY: Gifts for the queen. You can't visit Granny on Valentine's Day without bringing something. *(Reads)* The Treasury of Clean Jokes for Seniors.

IRENE: "Seniors"!

BUNKY: Hi, Doc. All the old babes are soaking up the suds …

IRENE: My grandson's referring to the champagne. Bunky doesn't understand polite conversation. The only sound he's comfortable with is a grunt.

BUNKY: Oink! Oink!

CLAY: Is Bunky going to a costume party?

IRENE: It's stress. He began with the cowboy hat when he started growing his hair. Then he went for the whole outfit. *(SHE waves off BUNKY who struts cowboy-like)* Bunky, put up the Valentine *petit fours*.

BUNKY: *(Seizing candy)* Red hots, yum!

IRENE: And check under the beds for burglars …

BUNKY: Why me? I'm young?

(BUNKY grabs a drink on the way out.)

CLAY: I don't mean to be rude, but I don't have time for small talk.

IRENE: Paper says there's a minor thug on the prowl. You've time for a killer?

(SOUND: The grandfather's clock chimes.)

IRENE: *(cont.)* Dinner's late. The new cook's probably watching TV.

CLAY: Have you been able to get Roo to eat?

IRENE: Not much. When his fever rises, I sleep in the chair. I cool his hands and forehead with alcohol until it falls.

CLAY: Tell me what you feel, not what you do.

IRENE: I feel that psychiatrists are quacks. Psychiatrists can't fix anything. They just jabber away.

CLAY: The report says Roo's condition comes from emotional shock.

IRENE: Have you ever heard of someone cured of syzofrenia or manic depression? You can't cut them out like a tumor.

CLAY: I know it is tough, but can you describe the discord in your marriage?

IRENE: Pete and I had a traditional life— No, yall just keep prescribing more visits and pills. Visits and pills.

CLAY: You'll pardon me, but I hear Mr. Dubonnet was quite the womanizer.

IRENE: Aren't they all? Yes, they say psychiatrists are the dummies of medical school.

CLAY: I was valedictorian… Did you feel sorry for Roo? Warn him not to be like his father? Roo's fixated on your past.

IRENE: Roo's a Southerner; from French aristocrats. Where are you from?

CLAY: I'm an American, yes.

IRENE: A Yankee, no doubt. The South won a spiritual victory. I remember waiting for the last Confederate soldier to die. It was broadcast on national radio. Even the North loves the mythology of the South. *(Pointing)* That's Jefferson Davis on that pedestal... We venerate the lost, here. I've financed statues of our boys across the South.

(BUNKY bursts back in.)

BUNKY: The coast's clear except for that drug addict! It's a joke! What's the deal with safety? I quote Uncle Roo, "Why has safety crystallized into the all-consuming action?"

IRENE: Bunky always interrupts me. To speak, I've got to interrupt him. It's a verbal struggle. I take the floor when I can.

BUNKY: I've this high solitary trip with my C.D.'s. I come here to find family, and it's like fending an ambush.

IRENE: That's because you don't like to put yourself out.

(Curbing his rage, BUNKY cavorts like a pirate to a dish of candy.)

BUNKY: Ho! Ho! What've we here? Candy hearts. *(Parcels out candy, reading)* Let's read our fortunes. I got, "Intrigue." Rooster, yours says,

ROOSTER: "Romance."

BUNKY: And what does Mimi have?

IRENE: "Long life"! Marvelous.

BUNKY: And for the doctor? Oh no. Too bad.

CLAY: "Lost love."

BUNKY: Don't look so serious. It's a game. *(Sings loud)* "Let's All Go Down to the Audubon Zoo... Ax for Yoo," etc.

(The following lines overlap with excitement.)

CLAY: What are you studying at Tulane?

BUNKY: Music! I figured if I'm not going to get a job after college, I might—.

IRENE: I don't know what you see in that Third-World mu—

BUNKY: You've got to go past the guitar to the banjo, to stringed and knotted sounds.

CLAY: Music relieves pain through the expression of pain.

BUNKY: Right. Blues was born in the Delta like something spawned off the floor of the ocean—

IRENE: Where will you work?

BUNKY: A Bluesman can play anywhere as long as he doesn't care about making money.

IRENE: Magical thinking! To the Romans, the Emperor Nero's playing a fiddle made him a stooge.

BUNKY: *(His eyes glassy from disappointment)* Bluesmen have been thrown out of clubs, off buses, but the hope is, "We can go over the waters, beyond the great damn …"

CLAY: Who taught you that?

BUNKY: A genius who sang on a crate. *(Howls some phrases)* "We all go do-wn to the Au-du-bon Zoo, and they all-ll ask fo yo—-ou—"

IRENE: I want to listen to something where my ears don't hurt.

CLAY: *(Chuckles)* You're prejudiced against volume!

IRENE: Because someone howls, I should listen? I wouldn't play the Blues!

BUNKY: You can't play the Blues because you have no soul. Music is dead. There're God knows how many Bluesmen living in hell in this country— ravaged by drugs, deaf from protest music. They're trying to tell white-bread Southerners that "Music's King." King of what?

(Crazed, HE heads for the door.)

IRENE: You're leaving? To meet some girl arriving half-dressed …

BUNKY: I can't take any more talks—Where you speak and I listen…

IRENE: The lower class's always been loose, but when the upper class starts, well.

BUNKY: Where you rave about how I'm doing it to you. Poor inconsiderate slob that I am.

IRENE: Bunky's yet to accumulate one semester of credit—

BUNKY: I don't regret a thing I've done. If you say something and you mean it, it makes you seem loud. Wrong even. God! Where're the Advil?

IRENE: Bertha found your report card! All F's.

CLAY: What can you expect?

IRENE: At Tulane, you want something, you work for it. In this family, you want it, you dream about it.

CLAY: You said you wanted to study music.

BUNKY: I like to sing the Blues. That's all. You think I like to rip people off, huh? I'm happy, see, and y'all detest that. You fucking resent me having fun. *(To CLAY)* Well, say something. You don't seem like a damn shrink to me!

IRENE: Bunky can use that foul mouth because somebody worked all night to support this ...

BUNKY: *(To IRENE)* And YOU. You make it clear you come first. If you don't like it, tough shit. Turn off the TV, the music, the conversation. Maybe if I do what you tell me to stop, I'll be fine. *(Apologetically)* I'm not responsible for this disposition. I was panned earlier.

(As BUNKY exits, HE collides into JASMINE.
HE slams the door, and the knob falls off.)

IRENE: Why can't anybody fix the handles?

JASMINE: *(Coquettishly)* Does Mama Dubonnet have definite opinions or what?

IRENE: I'm not opinionated, I'm just right. Doctor, you remember my adopted daughter, Jasmine Rush.

JASMINE: Hi. I love shrinks! You live near here?

CLAY: It's a house call.

IRENE: At three hundred bucks an hour.

CLAY: And yes, I live on the Avenue.

JASMINE: Yummy.

CLAY: In a garage behind a ten-million-dollar mansion. You're the family celebrity?

JASMINE: Recently flopped, yes. My last picture was a record loser. We were shooting so far beyond our means, we didn't know what our means was.

IRENE: Too bad...... Bunky's father, didn't live to bail her out.

CLAY: What're you doing home?

JASMINE: I'm marrying the richest man in Tyler, Texas. We're talking a guy who can write a twenty-thousand-dollar check and not subtract it. Purvis Axelrod.

IRENE: "Jasmine Axelrod." No, it doesn't go together.

JASMINE: Mama Dubonnet's making the arrangements for my wedding, at the New Orleans Country Club, one month from today. You have to be a member to entertain there. She's ordering me lingerie from Saks, china from Adlers. Look how nice the invitations turned out. *(Reads)* "Mrs. Peter Malter Dubonnet cordially invites you to the marriage of her daughter, Jasmine."

IRENE: It doesn't say adopted daughter, or stepdaughter. Her daughter. Well, I've got to give her away properly.

ROOSTER: For God's sake! Stop talking!

JASMINE: *(To ROO)* Either go to sleep or stay awake. But don't stay somewhere in the middle and complain about it. *(Flashes her ring)* Here's one itty bitty thing I want to show you, Doctor.

CLAY: I wouldn't wear that ring on any back streets.

JASMINE: I told Purvis, my fiancé, "I don't want much for my engagement, but I want it big and I want it real." He keeps saying, "Where have you been all my life?" and I reply, "Well for half of it, I wasn't born yet." *(Pause)* Purvis is eighty-one.

CLAY: Marry him at once.

JASMINE: He's from an old New Orleans family. Been married three times but no children. I told him I was still intact.

IRENE: Jasmine, please.

JASMINE: We're getting married at the Cathedral with the archbishop officiating. *(Eying IRENE)* It was all Mama Dubonnet's decision. The dinner for four thousand will follow at the Club! It was all Mama Dubonnet's decision! We'll honeymoon at the *Crillon* in Paris before cruising the Greek Isles.

ROOSTER: *(Mocking JASMINE)* It was all Mama Dubonnet's decision.

JASMINE: The only exercise my little man gets is to switch on the ignition, to press the air conditioner, and to dial the car phone. Without cars and the weather, there'd be nothing to talk about.

CLAY: What business is Purvis in?

JASMINE: Purvis is a third-generation screw manager! He's gone further faster than anybody! He runs the family screw business, "The House of Screws." Forty thousand feet of screws ...

ROOSTER: Can't y'all talk somewhere else?

JASMINE: There are fifty types, Italian screws, French screws. If he doesn't have it, he can get it. And now you need a birth certificate for your screw, so you can trace it back to the manufacturer. Some of 'em have viruses.

IRENE: Is there any money in screws?

JASMINE: Purvis's worth ten billion on paper. You should see his plantation by the House of Screws. Rooms and rooms of Regency furniture and ...*(Pronounces it wrong like taster)* ... tester beds.

IRENE: *(Correcting her with a long "e")* Tester. I have something scratching my neck.

JASMINE: Oh, it's a tiny, weenie laundry tag. I'll give it a good yank.

IRENE: Careful. It's my favorite blouse.

JASMINE: Oh, no. I ripped a hole. Oh! I don't think you can fix it. *(Sobs loudly)* Gosh! I ruined your—

IRENE: What's wrong?

JASMINE: There was a time when that blouse would have meant more to you than me.

IRENE: My precious! I was never that selfish. Let's go to the parlor. Make a list of everything you'll need for your wedding. I'll teach you a tune my mama taught me on the piano. "Mockingbird Hill" *(Sings like a squawking bird)* "When the sun in the—"

IRENE AND JASMINE: "— morning creeps over the hill and kisses the rosebuds on my window sill. Then my heart—"

CLAY: Mrs. Dubonnet! We have to talk.

IRENE AND JASMINE: *(Sing on)* "Then my heart leaps with pleasure when I hear the thrill of the birds in the tree tops ..."

(IRENE stumbles, then screams as SHE and JASMINE exit.)

IRENE: Why must Bertha wax every step? Someone's going to trip and sue me for a million dollars.

(LIGHTS: The sky fades to violet.)

(CLAY sinks in a chair.)

CLAY: How do you deal with difficult people? Like your mother?

ROOSTER: I picture her dead, so I can forgive her. All those years of being obeyed have turned her into a stranger.

CLAY: Your mother doesn't like relationships that're stronger than hers. But the world her posture was created for no longer exists. *(Worshipful)* You're not a boy.

(ROOSTER lifts a cigar from a box and savors it. Offstage, JASMINE bangs out "Mockingbird Hill," at the piano.)

IRENE AND JASMINE: *(Screeching)* "Tra la la. Tweedle dee dee it gives me a thrill. To wa-ke up in the morn-ing on the moc-king-bird hill—"

CLAY: Roo! Follow this analogy, but don't take it literally. Deal with your mother like a dog. If a dog does one thing wrong, you punish it. You don't stop feeding the dog, or seeing it. Just stop the behavior that brings you grief.

(BUNKY appears, balancing a bowl of shrimp, his Carnival cup, and a box of Band-aids. Mellow with liquor, HE stumbles as HE heads for the bar.)

BUNKY: Dang! You want a shrimp? It's spineless.

ROOSTER: I know a lot of spineless people so why not eat a—!

BUNKY: Shrimp prepared by *(pronounced fail)* Fayal!

ROOSTER: *(Explaining, jovially)* The new cook.

BUNKY: Her name is spelled: "F-a-y-a-l. She a reluctant member of the work force. She wants to watch TV and peel shrimp. *(Gobbles shrimp as HE refills his booze)* She's half-right. Half-left. I found her drinking wine and playing Trivial Pursuit—

CLAY: We're in a session!

BUNKY: —Fayal makes great shrimp remoulade. But I'm not attracted to her in her work mode …

CLAY: Don't you have some studies—?

BUNKY: I know I've got to grow up soon— But I'm postponing it! I've attended Tulane for six months and never been tested. …I refuse to be tested. *(Growns, desperate)* Oh my god. Fayal is pregnant. …She's three months pregnant. I want to cancel my life. I'd never actually kill myself. I want to help Fayal. But every alternative seems stupid. You think she'll abort the baby?

ROOSTER: Rich babies don't die before they're born, but in a car wreck at fifteen.

BUNKY: Fayal is so screwed up. She says she loves me, no matter what. Then she threatens to drive to the top of the Mississippi River Bridge and leap out.

(ROOSTER hands BUNKY a wad of bills.)

BUNKY:*(cont.)* Why're you sticking these bills in my face?

ROOSTER: I believe in spending money. Why leave it to lawyers who didn't like you when you were alive?

BUNKY: Fayal's moping for marriage.

ROOSTER: Do it. You want to end up like me—in limbo, suspended between youth and death ... I struck out. Had my string of broken hearts. Mama had money, the facilities, and this vacuum to be filled.

BUNKY: Speak to Fayal? Uncle Roo! Please. I need a relative, any relative to buffer the shock.

ROOSTER: Oschner Clinic says, "Avoid stress." My forté's comedy, not drama! Frankly, you don't look pitiful enough.

(BUNKY refills his "to go" cup.)

CLAY: Booze won't help, Bunky. You've got to do what's needed to pull yourself together. Go to a friend's house. Sit in the bathroom. Watch television. Something safe. I'll help you.

BUNKY: That's speculative.

CLAY: Everything's speculative. I'm as trusting a person as you'll find.

BUNKY: Once you start trusting people, then the question becomes, "Where do we stop?"

(JASMINE returns, with a yellow Post-it pad. SHE snoops about the room, sticking labels on various heirlooms. SHE hums "Mockingbird Hill.")

JASMINE: Y'all don't mind me. I'm tagging a few itty bitty things for wedding gifts.

CLAY: *(Perturbed)* How long will that take—?

ROOSTER: I'm ignoring Jasmine, so she doesn't exist.

JASMINE: I'm writing my name on what Purvis and I want. *(SHE squeals)* A sketch by Miss Irving.

(JASMINE scribbles her name on the back. ROO chugs down some cough syrup.)

ROOSTER: Take everything. I don't care.

JASMINE: I expect he'll groan for days about how sick he is. I remember the delightful cruise to Ensenada. *(Bites a tiny elephant)* Turquoise from the Ivory Coast. Do you think it's eighteen carets?

CLAY: Detach!

(JASMINE writes her name on a crystal bell.)

JASMINE: This bell was Great-Aunt Jane's. Listen to the lovely sound.

ROOSTER: Now, that I bought, myself! Get out!

(JASMINE pockets a photo.)

JASMINE: Few situations can be bettered by going berserk.

ROOSTER: What'd you just take?

JASMINE: I suppose I can have my own picture! It's not Roo's fault that his gallery in Ensenada flopped.

CLAY: I'll have to ask you to leave.

JASMINE: Only one person loved his painting, but two days later he died. He was ninety-five.

(JASMINE flounces out.)

ROOSTER: *(Hollers offstage)* Your being a thief has nothing to do with me.

(SOUND: Offstage, screaming. A door slams.)

(CLAY illuminates a Tiffany lamp.)

CLAY: Why've you stopped painting, Roo?

ROOSTER: I've artistic acrophobia. Fear of artistic heights...

CLAY: You're worried about something that doesn't exist.

ROOSTER: No the images I'm studying are realer than life itself. But— I'm losing myself in the ... the hourglass ...in the haunted blending of time.

CLAY: Rely on me.

ROOSTER: That's fine for the daytime, but at night, I'm not the author of my dreams. Something fierce is driving me! A scene I fear but am compelled to enter. Most people don't see beyond today, so for them the future's postponed. But for artists, it's 'round the bend of sleep. In my dreams, I'm like a soul searching for sight. I stare at that window bathed in light. This angel lady appears— She calls my name. Who is she?

17

(LIGHTS: Lights change into a dreamlike fog.)

(SOUND: Eerie music and echo effects.)

(SHEILA floats in.)

CLAY: You're buying into an imaginary universe. With make-believe friends.

IRENE *(Offstage): (Screaming)* Time's up. Your session's over.

CLAY: You're living with people who tell you, you can't choose…

IRENE *(Offstage)*: Huck! Load the guns and triple lock the gates.

CLAY: Draining thoughts can lead to insanity.

ROOSTER: I'm not cracking up! I'm king.

CLAY: Then start resisting! If someone's killing you, you've the right to annihilate her, even if it's your mother.

LIGHTS: Rays of lavender sunset shine through the windows.

CLAY collects her bag and exits. ROOSTER winds up a musical toy and watches it clap.

(SHEILA FITZGERALD, the mysterious figure ROO's been dreaming about, appears through the garden door. Her face beaming, SHE tiptoes about winding all the toys.)

(ROOSTER looks up, startled.)

SHEILA: Ssh! Try to be quiet at this most unquiet time.

ROOSTER: Is this a dream?

SHEILA: I love the oyster shells by the logustrum. Pearly white with purple centers.

ROOSTER: How did you get in?

SHEILA: I'm a locksmith's daughter. I've been trying to contact you.

ROOSTER: Mother answers my mail. *(Stunned by her beauty)* Who are you?

SHEILA: Sheila Fitzgerald.

ROOSTER: Are you real?

SHEILA: This looks like a holding place for heaven. Twilight tumbling through the glass—A wash of lavender on the wicker And purple dawn camellias. Violet rims their petals— (*SHEILA stretches her hands as if ascending.*) Such karma. Ooh. A full moon.

ROOSTER: Whenever there's a full moon, there's a bunch of crazies on the street...

SHEILA: A sign! Jiminy Cricket's riding my shoulder. (*SHE lifts the cricket on to her finger.*) A grasshopper was the image of immortality in Greece because he could sing.

(*SHEILA floats about, admiring objects and artwork.*)

ROOSTER: Get to the point.

SHEILA: Playthings are profuse.

ROOSTER: And get out.

SHEILA: Why do you keep so many toys?

ROOSTER: Time warp....I'm attempting to create a dream world where I can realize myself as a painter. My art is a ...

SHEILA: Soliloquy on boyhood....Misunderstood? You're searching for meaning?

ROOSTER: No. Just originality in a city of exaggeration. Once, I found the discipline, inspiration, and liberty needed to create here.

SHEILA: And now?

ROOSTER: Most people don't like my work.

SHEILA: I'm sure it has a devastating effect on them, because it is incredible. And then you do everything: oils, watercolors, pencils, pen and ink. If you show your paintings to twenty-seven people, twenty-six will exile you for whatever reason because they're jealous. And you're so ... No one warned me you'd be so ...Interesting. I don't intend to stare.

(SOUND: Birds coo.)

ROOSTER: It's doves cooing. *Blanche* and *Neige*. They won't mate while you're watching them... .The only way to become civilized is to return to the rules and ordering of nature.

(SHEILA plays with a jack-in-the-box and THEY both laugh.)

SHEILA: And play with wind up toys.

ROOSTER: You like silly things? *(HE winds up various toys.)* The bird hopping away.

SHEILA: *(Laughing)* My sides hurt.

ROOSTER: The gymnast flipping.

SHEILA: *(Howling)* I've got these pangs.

ROOSTER: The chick breaking out the egg? The spinning doll?

SHEILA: Oh no! Do you have a powder room?

(Touching "The Scream" statue.)

ROOSTER: And the *Silent Scream*. Because sometimes that's the way it is. *(Pause) Finita La Comedia.*

SHEILA: I'm an agent. Audubon Gallery. I'd like to represent you.

ROOSTER: *(Laughs and coughs)* You're in sales?—it's amateur night in Dixie. It takes me fifteen minutes to decide if I want three or four aspirins. How do you expect me to—Agents! They're everything I'm running from. Counterfeit power. The whole specter of the con men that haunt artists' history.

SHEILA: I don't have one colleague who'd do that.

ROOSTER: Working the phones like hungry stockbrokers, they'd con their own mother out of her last pair of shoes. I'm three times more likely to die from chicken pox than to hire an agent. *(Coughs violently)* Get out.

SHEILA: If you're sick, call the doctor. Get yourself fixed. *(Pause)* You're a genius. I'll make you face that.

ROOSTER: Agents love acting superior.

SHEILA: Maybe you New Orleans boys can rely on wills and bequests. But the rest of us had better hustle.

ROOSTER: A cocktail, Miss Fitzgerald? … Mrs. Fitzgerald.

SHEILA: Miss. Water with lemon, please.

ROOSTER: The first agent I talked to said, "These are highly marketable paintings, I suggest you show them to someone else." The second agent said, "I wanted to like your paintings, but I don't." The third was the cruelest. "I like the birds, the atmosphere, but there's nothing at the base of the work."

SHEILA: Agents aren't out to form an evil empire. They're just dictatorial. …Unless I enter your life, your work won't be known for twenty years.

ROOSTER: You won't succeed.

SHEILA: I have a prospect for your painting, *Night Race*.

ROOSTER: Prospects are suspect.

SHEILA: It's a museum award for a residency in North Carolina.

ROOSTER: What's the hitch?

SHEILA: You have to enter the contest. When smart people tell you to do something, do it.

ROOSTER: The smartest characters are in my paintings, and they're not ready.

SHEILA: Artists can't eliminate risks.

ROOSTER: I'm not applying for that award unless I'm sure I'll get it.

SHEILA: It's a matter of how much fear you're willing to face, and the precautions you use to counter failure.

ROOSTER: I don't want more slaps from the museum people.

SHEILA: Art's an industry run by the privileged and powerful, and to an extent the tail wags the dog. But everyone needs a guardian—And you're an angel to someone else. *(Sexually)* My mission is to realize God on this planet. A painting represents a communion of souls parted by time and space. It's a cry, reflections spilling out on the canvas. Emotions tracking through! Your soul releasing others to see the syncopation of color, sumptuousness of form, celebration of sacred and secular. Your paintings do what art was meant to do: "Carry me aloft on waves of ecstatic release."

(SOUND: The grandfather clock chimes.)

SHEILA: *(cont.)* My goodness! I'm late. *(Pause)* New Orleans is so dangerous that I've joined "Take Back the Light." It's a prayer group. We're contemplating who God is in our lives by gazing at the heavens. Dreaming our way back to Paradise. Sometimes the night sky is so saturated with stars that their combined light would outshine a hundred full moons.

(Calling back) Yes or no.

ROOSTER: *(Calls out)* Yes.

(SHEILA slips out the garden door into the pink twilight. Doves coo. ROO distances her with his thumb as if creating a picture.)

(To self) Wood lilies, moon flowers, and Sheila! Elusive Sheila. Suddenly, I'm in cahoots with a woman I barely know.

INTERMISSION

ACT TWO

AT RISE: Three weeks later. Five o'clock cocktails decorate the day room, which has been transformed into a portrait studio, portrait chair, Chinese screen, artist easel. Toys have been replaced by flowering orchids, creating a feeling of spaciousness. Gathered around a child's tea table are IRENE, CLAY, and JASMINE, who is dressed in overstated wedding attire complete with tiara and veil. JASMINE fans herself with a nosegay and protects her dress. THEY are playing the card game, Hearts. Laughter. JASMINE lets out a scream. BUNKY enters, tipsy.

JASMINE: *(Horrified at cards)* Yuck! The Black Widow.

CLAY: *(To JASMINE)* You've got to collect all these hearts and shoot the moon.

BUNKY: *(To JASMINE)* I thought Roo was supposed to be painting you?

CLAY: He's late.

IRENE: Darn! I can't make out these cards. Doesn't the doctor have any other lunes to observe?

JASMINE: You get me one real live jerk to do my portrait. I'll say, "Hot damn, let's go." Hot damn. Boy, when you learned you could say that word, it was so wonderful.

IRENE: Everything about you embarrasses me, Jasmine.

JASMINE: Men in the South treat me like a dog. Throw me a scrap. Toss me a bone! Next election, I'm voting for every female candidate. I don't care if she has six heads.

BUNKY: *(Waving his trophy)* I got Roo a snapping turtle.

(All the women scream)

IRENE: If there's anything rotten and miserable in the street, Bunky wants to take care of it!

CLAY: Bunky likes coming into the room with a rodent.

IRENE: Last time it was a big worm.

BUNKY: To unlock this turtle when it bites, you have to chop its head off. *(Demonstrates, shrieks)* POW.

(All the women scream)

IRENE: Bunky!! See if the cook's shown up. I'm existing, not living. I'd say things are fine, but they aren't. Bertha spent the day ironing. Bleach spots all over my clothes. When I ask her about it, she cries. Verma puts mismatched lingerie in the bureau drawer. She says, "Well?" I have three help. I can't have more. What with the cost of taxes and all that. So many of my maids are dead and gone.

CLAY: The western economy depends on the underpayment of minorities. It makes them feel worthless and give up.

BUNKY: Mimi's working hard to die. Let her die!

IRENE: Fine way to talk while you're drinking my liquor.

(BUNKY seizes a fistful of aspirins and some Jack Daniels.)

BUNKY: Once and a while, I pick an argument. Least, I feel like I'm alive.

IRENE: You sleep all day, and you get up looking for a drink?

BUNKY: I'm trying to numb the pain of life.

CLAY: You'll never find a real job, boozing like that.

BUNKY: I can't take a day job. Some days I don't feel like getting up. *(HE exits and yells back)* Are you on the rag, doc or what!

JASMINE: *(Shrieks, suddenly)* I got all the hearts. I won. Shooting the Moon in Hearts.

IRENE: Well, maybe now Bunky can join us for another hand.

BUNKY: I don't like cards. You've no idea who I am. I enrolled for drugs to stop depression!

IRENE: You should go to confession.

BUNKY: I've a lingering distrust of religion.

IRENE: Fourteen years of Catholic schooling!

BUNKY: All the holy figures I believed in are suspended in mid-air. Everywhere I see the family is just screwed up now in history. I'm thinking of getting a gig in a British pub. They're looking for bluesmen from Louisiana, who can get down in the trenches and SCREAM!

(BUNKY exits. JASMINE stuffs Kleenex in her arm pits. SHE paces about the room, seizing a phone directory.)

JASMINE: I'm so sick of Roo being late. I'm so sick of the lies. It's gotten so I'm so sick all the time.

CLAY: Why are you pacing?

JASMINE: I don't want to look limp in this wedding dress.

IRENE: Artists always sacrifice their family first.

CLAY: There're tons of artists in the phone directory who wouldn't abuse you. Why are you putting Kleenex between your toes?

JASMINE: *(Hyper. Yanks off her shoe)* My feet are swollen--I need a toe reduction. I just hate my toes. My second toe's too long. Purvis is mad, because I've scheduled plastic surgery. I've already had three nose jobs. I'm tired of waiting around for his approval. Purvis's got this back pain, so he can't... It's not cancer, thank God. He has to bring this "donut" pillow along to sit down. He gets these seizures. During dinner, he'll push a button and shock himself. At the opera, he shoots up in his seat. He's guzzling a quart of vodka a day. Purvis wants me to fly to South America to see some chiropractor. But I refuse.

CLAY: Why not humor him?

JASMINE: Because he treats me like a reject. We're not even married yet. This is a three-carat diamond. Purvis gave his third wife a six-carat one! "My sister wanted her to have it," he says. At our engagement party, that bitch whispers to me, "I've already had it appraised for fifty thousand dollars!" It was all I could do to stay in the receiving line, without killing her. I'm not flying with Purvis unless I get jewelry of equal value. They can put his back on ice, I don't care!

CLAY: You want the rewards of a rich marriage with none of the penalties?

JASMINE: Now that he's obtained an engagement announcement, he's blackmailing me into accepting these gross disloyalties.

CLAY: Do you love him? *(Pause)* We all gravitate toward security.

JASMINE: Purvis and I disagree because he lies, steals, and cheats. If only Purvis would lie to other people and tell me the truth.

CLAY: Action follows being. If someone lies habitually, they're a liar. *(Pause)* When you're young, there's always something new… But when you're older. In your early forties. Life becomes this bartering deal. Most men want a quick fix. Their fiancées don't admire them. So they stop caring. Adultery can be addictive.

JASMINE: Weren't you one of those privileged patients at the Fertility Clinic? I was just there for my diaphragm.

IRENE: Jasmine!

JASMINE: Younger girls always remember the old ones. I hear you've frozen parts of yourself? Waiting for a suitable partner.

IRENE: This is not parlor conversation.

JASMINE: You self-important types are weirdos!

CLAY: I don't know why I get these rashes.

JASMINE: You can't show affection, so you buy this education of the mind.

CLAY: Too much starch at the neck.

JASMINE: Eventually, it erupts, the torment that's in your life. That's why I read National Enquirer.

CLAY: Tell Roo I've gone to walk my canines.

IRENE: Why leave? Just because Jasmine hears some fool gossip . . .

CLAY: To be an effective doctor, one needs to manage one's emotions, to glide past impossible conversations. I've watched so many girls in the Garden District freeze up and die. The girls get tired of being pretty things who do nothing. *(Putting on a coat)* They acquire a weakness for cruelty.

JASMINE: Take off that coat, it makes you look Butch.

CLAY: I'll respond to that when I'm detached. *(Pause)* This is not the best time for me. My favorite dog died in June. I've a new Catahoula hound with one crystal eye and a white cross on her forehead. I call her Desdemona. My old dog Ophelia's jealous. She's in a state. I hope she doesn't drown herself by the willow tree!

(CLAY exits. BUNKY swaggers in with a bag of grass for the turtle.)

(SOUND: The phone blares.)

(BUNKY grasps it and snaps into the phone.)

BUNKY: Hello. Sounds like a cafeteria. A waiting room? You're at the clinic. Yes… yes. I'll wait for you to call.

BUNKY hangs up and heads for the door. ROOSTER and SHEILA enter through the garden. THEY float around the room, laying flowers everywhere and kissing each other.

IRENE: Why can't you enter through the front door like normal people?

SHEILA: What a lovely garden! Honeysuckle! Roses! Gardenias so sweet, you can smell them from here. And such a surprise to see the crepe myrtles in bloom. Day lilies, ginger, and…

ROOSTER: Narcissus all along the moon bridge.

JASMINE: *(Whispers to IRENE)* I need a Rolaid.

IRENE: I hope you didn't steal those from the park. Boys who destroy public property are heavily fined. ...You didn't tell me "Hello," son.

JASMINE: He's in his lover mode. He can't talk to us mortals.

ROOSTER: *(To SHEILA)* Oh look, honey, a butterfly.

SHEILA: A butterfly's really a caterpillar who let go.

JASMINE: Roo! My make-up's fading.

ROOSTER: I postponed our sitting, remember?

JASMINE: I need a virtual assistant. More and more, I'm living in betrayals.

ROOSTER: We're celebrating. Y'all are all invited.

SHEILA: Roo's won an award to paint.

ROOSTER: From the Hyde Museum.

SHEILA: A totemic place!

ROOSTER: They're been hitting on me from all directions—the phone, the front door, the FAX--

SHEILA: Roo has won a retreat in North Carolina

ROOSTER: And fifty thousand dollars— *(Ecstatic, HE waves a flurry of papers.)* This award is a great honor.

IRENE: How many artists applied, two? I wouldn't go on any vacation where you bring your own toilet paper.

JASMINE: North Carolina's bursting with nuclear waste. Before you eat wild duck there, you've got to get it tested for radioactivity.

(SOUND: A phone ring offstage.)

BUNKY *(Offstage)*: I've got it.

ROOSTER: Ma! Don't spoil this.

IRENE: Get famous later in life or you'll get bored with it.

SHEILA: Your mother will be fine, once she understands your success.

IRENE: *(To SHEILA)* Freshen up. Every time I see you, the hem's falling out of your skirt.

ROOSTER: Don't talk to her that way!

JASMINE: Once working women hit thirty, they have that disheveled look-

IRENE: Faded print dresses--

JASMINE: Hair in a desperate condition--

ROOSTER: *(Loudly)* Quiet! The retreat is mine in May and I'm going. Everyone is invited to visit.

SHEILA: Let's look at what God might want Rooster to do. When painting, Roo makes sure he knows the feeling the universe expects and he delivers it. ...Art is where the divine enters our human world. Roo sees things that only God can see. For that the mountains would be good.

ROOSTER: Ma, my artwork was selected by an impartial panel.

IRENE: Who're soliciting my donation. Painting's not my favorite charity. Jasmine's wedding costs five hundred thousand dollars.

JASMINE: Don't blame me!

IRENE: Bunky needs eight thousand for insurance --. And the archbishop's got that capital campaign. I'd like to prop your paintings up, but it would mean a misallocation of funds. Sometime, I'll outline for you how my foundation works. You want to see all the mean solicitations. Jasmine get the folder—From the Hyde Museum people-- the President, trustees, banquet committee insisting I buy tables at your award--

ROOSTER: These are form letters. It doesn't say here you have to.

IRENE: If you wait till I die you'll get everything. But keep these poor art people out of my house.

SHEILA: *(Trying to help her)* You're walking in the wrong direction.

IRENE: *(Pushing her off, stumbles as SHE exits)* Roo's upset me, so I've lost my balance. I can't see a dang thing. My eyes come and go.

SHEILA: *(To IRENE)* Don't be mad.

IRENE: I'm not mad. I'm heartbroken, but I'm not mad.

(ROOSTER looks away, as JASMINE crosses to help her.)

JASMINE: Careful, my precious!

IRENE: *(Slips as SHE exits)* Ye gods! Why must Bertha wax every room? Someone's going to slip and sue me for a million dollars. *(Pause)* Sheila come here. I need to speak to you privately.

(SHEILA exits with her. JASMINE marches to ROO.)

JASMINE: Mama's starting one of her manic modes. Soon, she'll be skulking about the parlor with a look that'll cut cement.

ROOSTER: You see a steam roller, jump out of its path.

JASMINE: The ophthalmologist's doubling her pills! You can't go now!

ROOSTER: Does somebody have to live with her?

JASMINE: Yes! An adult I'd like to stay, but Purvis and I need to go into seclusion.

ROOSTER: Hire a nurse!

JASMINE: *(Stretches her arms heavenward)* I'm an adopted daughter. You're her only son!

ROOSTER: At best, I'm excluded from any authoritative decision. Sooner or later, I must be decisive or I'm dead meat.

(SOUND: *A faraway phone rings.*)

BUNKY *(Offstage)*: *(Screaming)* It's for me!

JASMINE: Mama's eyes are going. She's insists on having my reception at the Country Club. But God knows what will happen if you move to North Carolina...

ROOSTER: Did Mama put you up to this?

JASMINE: I've no time to belabor --I've four thousand invitations to get out.

ROOSTER: I can't do your portrait, Jasmine . . . unless I stick you in hell!

JASMINE: You're jealous because I'm nice to Mama and you're not. All right! I'll tell you. I can't stay near Mama because Purvis *(Quietly)* thinks he's an alcoholic. Purvis's not an alcoholic. He just likes to drink.

ROOSTER: Purvis is eighty-one, but his liver is a hundred and seven.

JASMINE: Please. Purvis's admitting himself to a detox center in Texas!

ROOSTER: Try River Oaks. That's near the house. Then Huck could pass by every day and toot the horn

JASMINE: I haven't told Mama. They have to wait to put Purvis in detox, until his brother gets out!

ROOSTER: Some House of Screws!

JASMINE: I'll take Purvis out for the wedding day, then put him back in.

ROOSTER: *(Louder)* Some Hou-se of Scr-ews.

JASMINE: I was raised to be a good girl but the South's short on husbands. *(Yanking at her ring)* This diamond is too tight, but I'm not taking it off. New Orleans, is a party town, and the ring's got a stone like a beam.

ROOSTER: The lights are on, but nobody's home. Break off the wedding. It's a gypsy ring.

JASMINE: I'm not going to carry a lantern and dance under the moon alone. My picture is featured in the Society Section. Purvis is going ahead with this wedding if I have to drug his oatmeal to do so. If not, I'll yank his brown hair out by its gray roots. Throw him back into the night from whence he came.

ROOSTER: *(Ironic)* I'm aware of your sense of being different and needing to be perfect. I'm the safe brother for you to get real with. Purvis is a very sensitive disturbed drunk. You think if you save him he will finally love you. But he will probably just marry someone younger. The man is a quiet maniac. If he didn't have money, he'd be classified a rodent.

(JASMINE exits, screaming.)

JASMINE: Mama! Mama! Roo's being mean to me… again.

(ROOSTER sings to self.)

ROOSTER: *(Sings)* They they all went down to the Audubon Zoo and they all AWKS all ask for you. They all AWKS for you.

(IRENE enters carrying a doorknob.)

IRENE: Knobs falling off! You can't get in, and you can't get out. Bertha spent the day ironing. Bleach spots all over my clothes, and when I ask her about it, she cries. Bertha puts mismatched lingerie in my bureau drawer. She says, "Well?" I've three maids. I can't have more. What with the cost of taxes and all that.

ROOSTER: Where's Sheila?

IRENE: I warned that woman not to start meddling in our affairs.

ROOSTER: Where?

IRENE: I'm going to Dr. Paine tomorrow. I can see the outside. I can't see faces. I can drive if I go carefully. Most sons care for their mothers. You'll just march over my body to North Carolina. I don't take it personal that you don't have time. If you take it personal and you're a mother, it's four old-fashioneds in the room at night.

ROOSTER: I asked about Sheila.

IRENE: Oh, she went for a walk.

ROOSTER: What did you say to her?

IRENE: (Teasing) Nothing. She's got her Ken doll.

(BUNKY charges in. Seeing MIMI, he stops.)

ROOSTER: (Whispers) Mama's here with a black cloud over her head. Casting a pall about the room.

BUNKY: How do you feel, Mimi?

IRENE: I have no feeling. I'm just one breath short of the grave. Roo'll put me in Metairie Cemetery next week!

BUNKY: (Starting for the door) Roo, I'll be back in my quarters.

ROOSTER: Stay. Please.

(BUNKY refills his cup of liquor.)

IRENE: Why have you stopped doing Jasmine's portrait?

ROOSTER: It's a painting in search of a face.

ROOSTER: That was a hit.

BUNKY: It wasn't a hit. It was a home run.

IRENE: As soon as life seems peaceful, you start picking on Jasmine.

(ROOSTER continues sketching the toy.)

ROOSTER: I know I've made lots of mistakes in the past. Mama, for the first time in years, I'm having fun. I have tough days. But I'm improving, and it's all because of...

IRENE: Is there any sex in this? No, but it's all about it. I attempted the same thing at your age. Ha! Entertain me. Do the dance of the seven veils!

BUNKY: Sheila and Roo have a tremendous relationship --

IRENE: How long do we have to keep talking about it? The entire social season, I guess. ...I want to compliment you on your agent. That woman could con the whole family under the table sequentially.

ROOSTER: *(Sadness wells through him)* I don't know how to have a relationship and be in this family.

IRENE: Sell your things and buy a tract house! Wear Birkenstock sandals and try to look painfully thin. Ha!

BUNKY: Sheila's a Catholic.

IRENE: Will she nurse him when he collapses, answer me that.

BUNKY: I suppose so.

IRENE: Good.

BUNKY: *(To ROOSTER)* You don't have to feel bad about wanting a relationship.

IRENE: Don't slouch. Roo'a grateful to this woman for hawking his work. He's suffering because he knows... she'll never get invited into the inner circle. Well, aren't these your potential clients?

BUNKY: You peaked in elementary school, Mimi, but Sheila's very evolved.

IRENE: Stand up straight. You boys don't appreciate how society works because you've always been in it.

ROOSTER: *(To BUNKY)* Sometimes she leaves me feeling wiped out for hours.

IRENE: Soon y'all will be pawning rings on the streets for bread. All you'll have is the memory of money.

BUNKY: Roo's pouring his guts out, and you're discussing . . .

IRENE: I'm trying to maintain a thin veneer of civilization. To smooth over something rough with something refined.

ROOSTER: I want to marry Sheila.

IRENE: And you wanted to light fires at two. Take my advice, say "No," possibly with hope.

BUNKY: Sheila's pretty. Isn't she?

IRENE: Cohabitate if you must, in one of those rabbit hutches in the dark parts of town. I can float above it. I don't see most things.

ROOSTER: The family mold!

BUNKY: It's a slowly constricting straightjacket!

IRENE: *(Pointedly)* Dinner's late. Fayal hasn't shown up again.

(BUNKY retreats to the bar, to add ice to his drink. ROOSTER approaches his MOTHER.)

ROOSTER: When I was a little, I decided that I was no good. I ran to this porch when I heard you and Dad fighting at dinner, and I decided it was my fault. I did everything to distract you from hating each other. I worked myself to death as an artist to show that I was lovable. I never learned to be myself.

IRENE: Nonsense.

ROOSTER: *(Laughs despondently)* I wasted all those years proving something I don't have to prove. I am lovable. I know that you depend on me for someone to be close with.

IRENE: It's just I don't see well.

ROOSTER: To share feelings, to go places with. You're important to me. We've shared so much hell together, maybe we can share a little heaven. I need...

IRENE: You need me to leave you alone and to give you to another woman.

ROOSTER: I'm not ending our relationship, but I don't want to grow old in this house.

IRENE: What's going to happen to me? I can't make my eyes focus. I don't know who people are if they don't come up close. Or talk loud. It's all blurry.

ROOSTER: I tried to control my feelings for Sheila by willing them away.

BUNKY: Roo wants some good stuff in his life.

IRENE: Shut up.

BUNKY: She's impossible.

IRENE: I'm the one who's distressed. Whose eyes come and go. Who crashes into things.

ROOSTER: (Directly to his MOTHER) I've been practicing how to talk to you. I walk around the house, this nowhere room where I dream. I turn on the lights, try a new way. I tell myself not to feel, to think, that you'll want what's best for me.

IRENE: I don't want to end up alone in this big house.

ROOSTER: I look at the ornaments, the photographs, the relics of my youth. Important things that no longer have value. Notebooks, paint sets, "A" papers. My car collection. Everywhere I look I find a feeling. Every object has a story, every window a horizon. Each view brings back a scene from the past. When I gaze about, I'm still a boy with idle dreams.

IRENE: You were raised to think of others, not to dream.

ROOSTER: I've stared through the memories and felt grief. Opened the sealed doors of feelings. Said goodbye to all those years of my life, and let the fantasies evaporate like so much smoke. I've gone back and back through the layers of fear. Recalling girls who were too tall, too fat, or too dumb. I know no one will ever please you. So I'm just asking you—not to be cruel to Sheila.

IRENE: I don't have to accept anybody.

ROOSTER: Don't say mean things.

IRENE: If I hadn't been bossy, I wouldn't have survived. I was raised on the slow side. But I've enough of my daddy in me to make it. Don't expect me at that woman's wedding. I'd have to be really desperate or really dead!

ROOSTER: Dead! The word is throbbing in my ears. I've reviewed my life today, and it looks bleak. I've been stranded here in a warped sense of devotion to you. I'm going under, losing every chance for my future, and you haven't grown a speck. So, I'll call once a month. I'm attracted to places where people don't invade privacy. I need a sense of purpose. I want to know why I'm getting up in the morning and why I go through the day.

IRENE: I can't take another loss.

ROOSTER: I grew up in a castle with no windows. I didn't know life was available outside. You're the queen, and you don't want to admit outsiders. Listen to me. Needing to please you doesn't fade with age. But I'm declining the role of Prince Consort.

IRENE: You know I hate you for this. Get out.

ROOSTER: Once you lower your expectations of me, you'll feel better.

IRENE: Get out! Get out!

ROOSTER: You've done your big rejection number on me, and I'm alive. So I suppose I'll manage.

(ROOSTER exits victoriously. IRENE rises and starts to exit.)

IRENE: *(Stoically to BUNKY)* It's hard to find that perfect decency that's necessary to carry on. Roo's so ungrateful. He decides unwisely and dumps me with the results. Why can't he bring home something that looks good? *(SHE slips, repeating a thought)* Must Bertha wax every floor! Someone's going to trip and sue me for a million dollars.

(IRENE stumbles offstage. ROOSTER returns. BUNKY checks to make sure IRENE is gone.)

ROOSTER: Mama'll get by without glasses as long as she can, even if it means falling down a flight of stairs.

BUNKY: Uncle Roo, I hope this doesn't overload your brain.

ROOSTER: It doesn't take much.

BUNKY: I'm in big trouble, man. Fayal's at Charity Clinic. She is having a miscarriage.

ROOSTER: An abortion!!

BUNKY: She's lost a lot of blood… Don't look shocked. It's a fierce accident. An act of God.

ROOSTER: You better get to… the hospital.

BUNKY: *(Shakes his head)* I can't go. I've downed enough booze to kill a small animal. Life's miserable. God wants it that way. Come with me. I sat through your sob story, even though I was vaguely embarrassed by it.

(SOUND: Outside a crowd screams as Bacchus parade lumbers down the Avenue.)

(SHEILA rushes in.)

SHEILA: Rooster! Rooster!

ROOSTER: I love to hear you say my name.

SHEILA: They're throwing doubloons by the handful. Showers of gold. Look, I've got six pearls. Purple metallic beads and green ones with gold babies. …What's wrong?

ROOSTER: Fayal is having a miscarriage at Charity Clinic. Even if I push hard, I can't get Bunky to go.

BUNKY: *(Cracks joke)* I don't want to give up my boyhood. High status but low class. I've been to Charity many times, and it never makes a difference. *(Pause, guiltily)* Okay. I'm off. ....I suppose I can hold my feelings in. Once I loved her better than ever. I was just bad and couldn't help it.

ROOSTER: I love you, man.

BUNKY: *Salude!*

(BUNKY leaves.)

(SOUND: The Bacchus parade rumbles by.)

(SHEILA puts a necklace on ROO.)

SHEILA: Purple metallic beads and green ones with gold babies.

ROOSTER: I love Mardi Gras. These lavish stupidities. It's one of the few spots where men don't feel guilty about having fun.

SHEILA: Shall we eat nothing by candlelight with soft music?
(THEY kiss.)

IRENE: *(Offstage)* Rooster. Come here and talk to me!

ROOSTER: *(cont.)* Mama. Buzzing like a hornet at the crossroads. She's staking out her territory. That's what Southern mothers do. Rich ones.

SHEILA: I'd like to get to know your mother. But she talks around me.

ROOSTER: She's being polite. She'll be rude later.

SHEILA: Let's talk about North Carolina...

ROOSTER: North Carolina is not like New Orleans. Eventually everything that comes South winds up in New Orleans.

SHEILA: Let's talk about how it's going to be for us.

ROOSTER: When I leave here, all these rituals will be tossed away like so...

SHEILA: A small room will suffice. Someplace with light that only the two of us will see. And a tiny bookcase with old encyclopedias--

ROOSTER: I've been wrestling with the idea of turning down the award There's so much non-talent that gets together in families to make talent happen.

SHEILA: You want to stay in New Orleans, and you want to go to North Carolina.

ROOSTER: I knew at an early age I'd have trouble leaving. I'm a great deal like my mother. I've been fighting my emotions, sugar-coating our relationship. After a time, I'd spoil your life, too. You're so uncorrupted! Even the smallest creatures want to touch you. Oh, God, help me.

SHEILA: Nobody said it'd be easy.

ROOSTER: I can't involve you in this family. I don't want to worm my way through it. *(Jokes)* My mother's a study in cement, like she's mired in gray. After a day with her, you'd be so racked out. She can take the stuffing out of you.

SHEILA: I doubt it.

ROOSTER: You're like normal. You've got a chance. Mama'll be persistent in her abuse until she's destroyed you one piece at a time.

SHEILA: I can take it.

ROOSTER: Little bits of life. Little shreds of dreams. Acting like a happy four-year-old to ride over the difficult lines of persecution. Changing your personality to become mean to keep her at bay.

SHEILA: You must make the time to live.

ROOSTER: You know, Mama keeps a loaded shotgun by her bed. I never go in this house without screaming her name, because I'm afraid she might shoot me. My parents fought in front of everyone as if we were ghosts. Silent visitors. I couldn't protect you from her. I've scrutinized Mama, discovered what makes her click. I can tell her mood from the way she walks. But I have absolutely no effect on her.

SHEILA: You hate your mother.

ROOSTER: No, I love her.

SHEILA: You feel guilty about leaving--Especially now she's failing. Invent a life that's up to your talent. Embrace insecurity.

ROOSTER: I feel completely safe in New Orleans.

SHEILA: Pills won't make panic go away...

ROOSTER: It's the opposite of the fractured feeling I get elsewhere.

SHEILA: Distance might feel better than closeness. You could paint uninterrupted.

(SOUND: Phone rings.)

(ROO ignores it.)

ROOSTER: I chose painting to impose a direction on the pandemonium that was living with Mother... *(About the phone)* Leave it be.

SHEILA: It's all those little voices in your head. They're sucking you in. The reason I know is I've been sucked in.

ROOSTER: Nothing I ever did was right. Even if you've done nothing wrong--

SHEILA: To be an individual, you must set yourself free. Abandon relatives who can only tolerate practical things and live at the vortex of life. Ascend to a place where you see that "Life is a glorious series of nows!"

ROOSTER: Some people don't get good things.

SHEILA: God wants success for you.

ROOSTER Does he?

SHEILA: Artists are the few bright stars that flash in the sky. Some of them burn on and some of them—

ROOSTER: Burn out.

SHEILA: To get out of this bind, you must give something up? Materials goods. You can't hold God in one hand, and gold in the other.

ROOSTER: Clean slate, empty bank.

SHEILA: How many rich people do you know died happy?

ROOSTER: The pope. The archbishop! I can't think of one.

SHEILA: If you put your talent first, you'll get success.

ROOSTER: What if my body gives out, and I can't do the things you want?

SHEILA: When you get tired of psyching yourself up, a higher force can enter the mind and change it! You're my Southern treasure.

ROOSTER: Southern wimp.

SHEILA: No, treasure. The more I see you, the more certain I've become. When I'm sad I read the poets, to recall the glory of art. Poetry comforts so. The tenderness the hurt. I ride through feelings with Percy Bysshe Shelley:

> Art thou pale for weariness
> Of climbing heaven and gazing on the earth,
> Wandering companionless
> Among the stars that have a different birth,
> And ever changing, like a joyless eye
> That finds no object worth its constancy?

We could elope. Get married by a judge, and go to North Carolina. I'm starting to get an aching feeling for traveling tonight.

ROOSTER: My father was an alcoholic, but he'd a cat called Christmas. Its ears had been burnt in a fire. Every night that cat waited for Dad at the garage. And he'd walk the cat under his umbrella to his room. When Daddy died, Christmas got in Dad's room and tore it apart. Wadded up the sheets. Knocked everything on the floor. Howled. Tonight, I feel like Christmas.

SHEILA: You're leaving?

ROOSTER: Yes. But I have to go alone. . .It's a peculiar blend of starting over and using the scraps.

SHEILA: You really feel sad, don't you?

ROOSTER: Sure, I feel terrible.

SHEILA: That's not what I mean. *(Points to her heart)* You feel sad in here.

(SHEILA places her hand on his chest.)

ROOSTER: Home can only be appreciated, once home's irretrievable. ...I'm going to look good, but I'll be broke.

SHEILA: Take me with you. It will be fun rehabilitating your melancholy self into a house full of friends and joy.

ROOSTER: When I leave, I'll be devalued like a new car driven off the lot.

SHEILA: So? I once volunteered for the Little Sisters of the Poor, and it was my duty to stand on the sidewalk and pass the cup. I don't need much. I'll devote my life to you. Surely I am, beyond all others, your favorite agent.

ROOSTER: Are you losing your mind?

(SHEILA kisses ROO, and reluctantly HE pulls away.)

ROOSTER: *(cont.)* This makes no sense.

SHEILA: I don't want to lose you. Can I tell you a secret? Every evening when the locusts start to buzz, I fabricate a scene between us. I tell you that I love you. I'm so grateful for our sweet intimacy.

(SHEILA takes ROOSTER's hand. A feeling of bliss passes through ROO as if HE is free.)

ROOSTER: Marry me, Sheila... Tonight.

SHEILA: Yes, darling. Close your eyes and don't look back.

ROOSTER: It's so peaceful. I took one peak at the sky and everything turned peach and lilac, just like that!

SHEILA: A halcyon sunset.

ROOSTER: The wind's faint.

SHEILA: And there's a glimmer of the Morning Star.

ROOSTER: Shooting the moon.

(THEY kiss and exit.)

CURTAIN

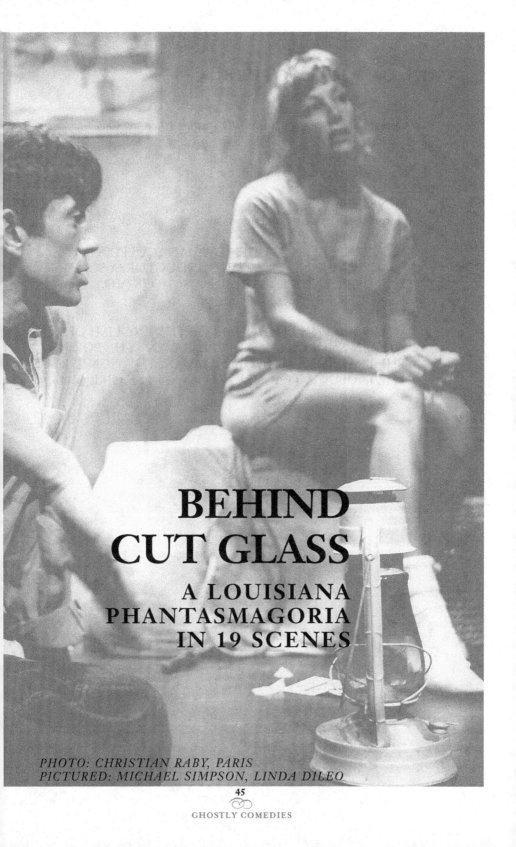

BEHIND
CUT GLASS

A LOUISIANA
PHANTASMAGORIA
IN 19 SCENES

PHOTO: CHRISTIAN RABY, PARIS
PICTURED: MICHAEL SIMPSON, LINDA DILEO

CAST OF CHARACTERS

KITTEN LEGER. 36
China doll gorgeous, occasionally stutters when nervous

BEAU ELLIS. 38
Her professor, athletic and intense

BUNKY, 14.
Her wild son, a writer and musician

ACTOR # 1 plays: A STUDENT, A MAN SCUFFLING, A
SOAKED ATTENDANT, THE CONDUCTOR, A SOLDIER,
THE WARDEN, THE CAPTAIN, ANCHORS (V.O.),
ANNOUNCERS (V.O.)

ACTRESS # 1 plays THE CHAIR OF THE ENGLISH DEPT, A
WOMAN SNORING, A FAT GIRL, RAVEN--THE PORTER,
THE BRAKEMAN, THE OLD WOMAN, THE HUNTER,
THE INDIAN, A TEACHER (V.O.), A LITTLE GIRL (V.O.)

ROSARY HARTEL O'NEILL

SETTING

A phantasmagoria* in exotic Louisiana.

August 2005, Louisiana, a sequence of real or imaginary places like that seen in a dream: an office, a rural train, and a depot in the swamps. Set is minimal and evocative; sounds and lights creating the optical illusions of place. Fraught weather gives the feeling that everything is a figment of the imagination; an illusion or apparition, each place simultaneously known and unknown, appalling, mystifying, and amusing.

Action takes place for the most part on a bare stage. Locations are defined by sound, lighting, and a few key props. Lights down and lights up. The physical actions of the characters create this comedy of life gone awry inside a magic lantern.

Phantasmagoria: A sequence of real or imaginary images like that seen in a dream: what happened next was a phantasmagoria of horror and mystery.

Origin early 19th cent. Originally the name of a London exhibition (1802) of optical illusions produced chiefly by magic lantern: probably from French fantasmagorie, from fantasme 'phantasm' + a fanciful suffix.

SCENE ONE: TULANE UNIVERSITY,
OFFICE OF DR. BEAU ELLIS

(Two posters, one of "Psyche in the Dark Woods", lights gleaning all around her. Another of the "Devil Scorned at the Gates of Heaven" dominate the room. BEAU ELLIS, 38 dressed in chinos slacks and a blue blazer, shows pictures of Greece to ONE STUDENT and the DEPARTMENT CHAIR. THEY are holding class in his office.)

BEAU: The romantic poets, Byron, Shelley, Keats, lighting bonfires on the beach...Surrounded by a wolf pack of friends. To quote Keats:

> *Heard melodies are sweet, but those unheard*
> *Are sweeter; therefore, ye soft pipes, play on!*

(The STUDENT applauds vigorously)

BEAU: If you liked my class, tell your friends. We need five students for it to go.

(The Department CHAIR, a brittle woman, comes over and gives BEAU his mail. The STUDENT exits.)

BEAU: How long will this go on? You're sitting in on all my classes?

CHAIR: Long as I, the chair, feel the students need...

BEAU: If you'd like to participate in the—

CHAIR: I'm not being reviewed for reappointment—

BEAU: What do you think I do?

CHAIR: Oversleep. Not prepare. Run off about your great American yet unpublished novel. The underbelly of any course in a private institution is recruitment. Students want to know how to make a living. That's why I urged you to do courses in business writing, technical analysis, remedial composition. If you must teach PO-ET-TRY, you've got to talk about job opportunities: working at a nonprofit, a poetry magazine (if one still exists), or in real estate: visiting the haunts of dead poets, leading a ghost tour in the French Quarter.

BEAU: Have you heard anything from the tenure committee?

CHAIR: Here's your schedule of classes.

BEAU: About my rehire...

CHAIR: Your student rosters—

BEAU: What's the deadline for notification?

CHAIR: The list of Department meetings.

BEAU: How am I supposed to plan, if I don't know if I'm fired?

CHAIR: You did get a graduate assistant. All faculty got one. Yours is Kitten Leger. New Ph.D. specializing in your Romantic Poets.

(CHAIR points to the hall, where KITTEN bumbles in with raincoat, hat, umbrella, purse, note pads, computer case, backpack. Her son, BUNKY, in ripped jeans and a T-shirt that reads "Don't Share," patrols nearby.)

CHAIR: Kitten graduated *summa cum laude*, with distinction on her honors thesis Feminism and the Iconic Hyperbolic Male— She'll sanitize your remarks for the Ole Miss—

BEAU: I'm not sure I'm going—It's a minority conference.

CHAIR: You have a problem with that?

BEAU: I write on weekends. I lose focus unless I work regularly—

CHAIR: Did you sign this department evaluation?

BEAU: Yes. Don't think I'm not grateful for this *rare* tenure appointment. When I first came to TU—lane, I thought I can't feel the sidewalk; I'm walking on air. It was a long time before I felt that as a writer. But I have to plan in spaces ...release myself from this ...hermetically sealed tautology all around. When I get motivated, I can get the students interested in a multi-level way.

CHAIR: I can't let you have the pulpit forever. You can charm Ole Miss on our behalf. It's *hubris* to think your first novel is going to be adored by the world.

(CHAIR leaves and BUNKY tries to enter. KITTEN closes the door in his face. Her phone rings. KITTEN rummages for it, dumping her purse, computer and backpack and scrambling for her cell)

KITTEN: *(Into the phone)* What do you mean? You can't take Bunky to fencing class. ...You said you'd drive... That was before... Quint?...Quint.

{KITTEN's phone has disconnected. SHE hangs up. Her beeper goes off. BUNKY yells outside the office.)

BUNKY: Ma! Come on! I told you I'm late!

KITTEN: My son. He's going to boarding school shortly.

BEAU: You've been appointed my graduate assistant.

(KITTEN'S watch alarm goes off. Her phone rings.)

KITTEN: Sorry. I'll get these— *(Answers the phone.)* Quint? *(To BEAU)* It's my husband. Should I talk outside?

(SHE turns away)

BEAU: No...turn off all gadgets. *(Pause.)* Are you one of the new students who is scared to look at me...

BUNKY: Mom. I'm waiting!

BEAU: You'll have to grade quizzes.

KITTEN: I've no time.

BEAU: You don't read them. You can tell in five pages what score they should get.

KITTEN: You judge them by their opening?

BEAU: That's what editors do. My feeling is if they can't interest me from the get go, why should the reader suffer?

BUNKY: We're late. Ma!

BEAU: I'll proof all your term papers *gratis.*

KITTEN: I don't think so, Dr. Ellis, because—

BEAU: Beau.

KITTEN: I've only been assigned to you fifteen hours a week, and your chair asked me to correct your lectures. *(KITTEN removes BEAU'S manuscript.)* We're to begin with your address to the Oxford Conference of the Book—

BUNKY: Mom. I'm waiting!

(KITTEN disregards BUNKY and speaks to BEAU.)

KITTEN: You've got to make some p.c. corrections... If you read this, the women at the conference will walk out. I'll coach you—

BEAU: You're not attending—

KITTEN: My son's off to boarding school, so *(Her voice breaks)* I could go. I never thought I'd be accepted at TU-lane, but your chair mentored me and—

BEAU: Well, this is y'alls decade. American women in popular fiction.

KITTEN: Black women. Asian women. Gay women. White women are passé.

BEAU: Let's not get confused, and say women writers are the best thing ever.

BUNKY: *(O.S.)* Mom! Come on—.

KITTEN: *(Calls out)* Hold on, Bunky. *(To BEAU)* You're such a...a...

GHOSTLY COMEDIES

BEAU: Misogynist? Should I ignore all opinions that came before?

KITTEN: Look I'm on probation. My background is feminism and history. If I've been assigned to you, you can't be high up. But if you win esteem, so will I. There are starter marriages and starter conferences. You are in denial that teaching is a business.

BEAU: Leave the notes. Go.

KITTEN: Let me help you. I love the old poetry books, too. I love to touch them. They're old friends, but—

(Outside, the rain falls in needles. BEAU touches his head, turns to the window.)

KITTEN: What's wrong?

BEAU: I'm allergic to rain.

KITTEN: You can have your own voice in your novel and still not insult people.

BEAU: How do I do that, with you bitches taking over academia and sending me the dumbest students?

BUNKY: *(O.S.)* Mom! Mom!

BEAU: Shouldn't you leave?

KITTEN: I'd like to – be a professor at this school of ambition—

BEAU: I'm not attending that fool conference. Faulkner was a misogynist and—

KITTEN: You'll go … and I'll assist you. You have a great novel in you, if you'll open your portals to truth.

SCENE TWO: A NEAR-EMPTY TRAIN

(Rainy morning a week later. BEAU is already seated in the Club Car. KITTEN, clutching an umbrella, a suitcase, and a ribboned basket enters. SHE passes a large covered dog cage and someone sleeping in a blanket. SHE skirts a MAN scuffling down the aisle, a WOMAN snoring on a seat. A TV bolted into the corner plays briefly.)

TV WEATHERMAN: *(V.O.)* Tropical Storm Katrina's wind speed is 46 mph. Her center is poorly organized.

(BEAU, impatient by a table, eyes KITTEN's huge basket.)

BEAU: Mmmn.

KITTEN: Date nut bread, cashews, Brie--spicy tomato juice. One should only travel light when one absolutely has to.

(Across the room, BUNKY peeks under a blanket, squats next to a dog. HE reads the tag on it.)

BUNKY: "Mathilda, Blind Sheepdog, Send to Death house in Hazelhurst, MS." *(The dog moans)* Shush. Dream the dream of the healing god. When you move out this cage, you'll get well.

(KITTEN AND BEAU sit, facing each other. KITTEN yanks out two books.)

ANNOUNCER: *(V.O.)* The 6:57 train to Batesville is running 25 minutes late. I repeat 25 minutes—

BEAU: Why must they repeat everything? *(Pause)* What you reading?

KITTEN: "Ph.D.'s for Housewives" and--your manuscript. "Four Funerals and a Wedding," By James Beauregard Ellis.

BEAU: Put that away.

KITTEN: You've got to quote from it at the conference... *(Reads scribbles on manuscript.)* "This manuscript has its insides blown out. What's the plot?"

BEAU: Critique from my editor. What does a Mississippi Press know about plots?

KITTEN: Before… you used to be--involved in the craft hypnotically.

BEAU: Well… when I'm teaching, I forget to write. When I'm writing, I forget to teach.

KITTEN: Won't your editor be at the conference?

BEAU: Not at my sessions.

KITTEN: You need to impress him…through rumor.…

BEAU: Writers write because we've got questions. I'm more interested in breaking through my writing glitch than lecturing.

KITTEN: Your writing is so sparse it gives me the feeling you have to put a sweater on to read it.

BEAU: I write because I love reading and I'm out of my mind. I'm not writing for the ones who think everything is fine.

KITTEN: I don't know you well enough to jump on you, but—

BEAU: Writing is going into a room alone, hoping the muse comes and my Chair doesn't.

KITTEN: Don't blame her.

BEAU: This whole department is about intellect, Descartes. When they gave me the slacker courses, my temperament let me down.

KITTEN: So leave and write your book and—

BEAU: I like to work in a group, in the buzz of other people thinking.

KITTEN: So stop the whining. Whan, whan, whan.

BEAU: I am Tulane when I am on the job. I have colleagues in other departments who are tenured and chasing their dream. It's just that my boss is Ms. Perfecto on roller skates.

KITTEN: You shouldn't apply for tenure now.

(SOUND of wind thrashing outside. Dog growls.)

(Lights change to BUNKY by the dog.)

BUNKY: Shush. I'll free you, soon as I save Mom -- *(Peeks at KITTEN)* She's different now, different from what... what's normal...

(Across the room, BEAU takes out a flask, offers KITTEN a swig, pours some in his coffee.)

BUNKY: Will you look at that. The guy she's with is a drinker.

(The TV pops on.)

OLD WEATHERMAN *(V.O.)*: The hurricane is still *(Static)* faraway *(Static)* hurricane.

(The screen freezes. BEAU reads a sign by the TV.)

BEAU: "30 minutes of TV for 10 quarters. Change machine broken." Typical.

(The porter, RAVEN, a huge woman, with an Afro and rhinestone necklace that peeks out from under her uniform, plows through the room. SHE ignores the dog, doesn't see BUNKY, and checks tickets.)

KITTEN: God. It's hot. Why didn't you book a plane?

BEAU: No planes to Oxford. You ever see a porter with a necklace? A porteress? Fabulous.

(BEAU points to a vent.)

BEAU: AC is blowing hot air.

RAVEN: Move. I ain't no mechanic.

(KITTEN spots a slug.)

KITTEN: Oh god. A slug. Kill it.

BEAU: You're hysterical.

KITTEN: When you're upset, you're concerned...But I'm—

BEAU: Hyper!

KITTEN: I'll check the weather.

(SHE reaches in her basket, pulls out a portable radio.)

ANNOUNCER (V.O.): *(In a thick Louisiana accent)* Billy Bob with your Pearl River Radio.

BEAU: Trashy accent.

RAVEN: Turn it up.

ANNOUNCER (V.O.): Don't do nothing yet but—

BEAU: Double negatives

ANNOUNCER (V.O.): The storm done turned-

(The radio fades off. SHE shakes it.)

KITTEN: Batteries are weak.

ANNOUNCER (V.O.): She be headed for—

BEAU: Verb disagreement

ANNOUNCER (V.O.): The Louisiana low lands.

KITTEN: Is that near us?

BEAU: Locals exaggerate to create a speck of excitement.

ROSARY HARTEL O'NEILL

(*BEAU unpacks his briefcase and KITTEN arranges her basket.*)

BEAU: It's cooler over here.

KITTEN: Why not start your speech with Lillian Hellman?

BEAU: I'm not quoting marginal writers.

(*ATTENDANT hurries through in a coat with missing buttons. BEAU goes after him.*)

BEAU: What's going on?

(*BEAU exits, following the ATTENDANT. KITTEN dials the cell phone.*)

KITTEN: Tammy? What are you doing on Quint's cell… Never mind. How's the weather? …What? … Where's Bunky? … Remind Quint to give our son his fifty dollars… Hello. Hello?

(*KITTEN shakes the phone. AN ARMY SOLDIER, a cigarette stuck in his mouth, barrels in followed by A FAT GIRL.*)

ANNOUNCER (*V.O.*): Batesville departure in 10 minutes. If you takes the train and we's got to stop, your money will be refunded back.

(*The FAT GIRL starts packing. The SOLDIER gathers up his supplies. BEAU, spattered with rain, re-enters and returns to KITTEN. BUNKY watches KITTEN, but SHE doesn't see him.*)

(*SOUND of wind.*)

BEAU: They're calling this storm, "Katrina." Another foreigner.

KITTEN: They s-s-s-ay it's headed to Louisiana.

BEAU: First stop is Hammond, then Hazelhurst.

KITTEN: Is that far?

BEAU: The rain should lighten as we move north. We'll outrun Katrina.

KITTEN: I've never worried about trains. Planes, yes. I board them, armed with religious medals and tranquilizers, delighted to see infants inside, thinking God won't destroy a plane with so much potential aboard.

(A loud train whistle.)

ANNOUNCER (V.O.): Batesville, Mississippi. Everybody on that's getting on.

BEAU: Why do they keep repeating prepositions?

KITTEN: Should we go?

BEAU: Sure. Why go back to real life if we can avoid it?

(RAVEN enters, goes to the counter. BEAU darts over to RAVEN)

BEAU: Coffee?

KITTEN: It's got 500 chemicals.

BEAU: Coffee increases sexual activity.

KITTEN: I prefer decaffeinated.

BEAU: It's probably got a thousand chemicals--five hundred more to deactivate those in the coffee. *(To RAVEN)* I'd like an iced coffee.

RAVEN: Ain't open.

(RAVEN counts bills, growls into the phone, "Club car now open." SHE pushes a Styrofoam cup over the counter.)

BEAU: I said iced coffee. It should come in a tall class with ice.

RAVEN: You got a glass.

BEAU: I meant a glass-glass.

RAVEN: You order anything, you drink from plastic.

(KITTEN goes and hands RAVEN a hundred dollars, returns to BEAU)

RAVEN: A hundred dollars!

BEAU: *(Under his breath)* Why'd you do that?

KITTEN: Raven's exposed the worst in you, your self-serving, privileged—

BEAU: Because I placed an order?

KITTEN: That's a male phrase–

BEAU: For iced coffee.

KITTEN: I don't call women writers "marginal."

BEAU: It's my fault "the canon" is male.

KITTEN: You degrade women--Order Blacks–

BEAU: I order everybody about.

KITTEN: The train's out of order.

BEAU: Louisiana's out of order. We ought to put a sign over the state: "Closed for repairs."

(Suddenly, THEY crash to a stop. The CONDUCTOR a paunchy man with a Cajun accent marches by, blaring through a speaker.)

CONDUCTOR: Your Conductor here. Engine's smokin' and we done found—

BEAU: *(Under his breath)* "Done found."

CONDUCTOR: We gots to stop—

BEAU: *(Under his breath)* "Gots to."

CONDUCTOR: In the Pearl River Swamp. Leave your things—

KITTEN: Is that safe?

CONDUCTOR: Ev'body off!"

BEAU: I must use the "F" word. Fabulous!

SCENE THREE:
OUTSIDE THE PEARL RIVER DEPOT AND SWAMP

(KITTEN and BEAU exit the train. THEY walk towards an empty shack that reads: "PEARL RIVER DEPOT")

BEAU: Looks like a ghost town that went under water. Bone gray marshes, skeletal shacks, a depot on stilts. To quote Wordsworth, "Shades of the prison-house begin to close/ Upon the growing boy."

(SOUNDS of cattails whipping about. Bullfrogs croak.)

(BEAU flings shells then grabs a stick and hits at slush.)

KITTEN: What you doing?

BEAU: Scaring off vermin. Did you see that nutria?

KITTEN: I knew I'd hate this trip and I have.

BEAU: Watch where you walk.

KITTEN: I should have rented a car, hired a driver, like my husband suggested.

BEAU: Careful, sugar.

KITTEN: Don't sugar me. Look at that sign. "Alligator Habitat?"

BEAU: Warm water coaxes all the animals out. Alligators float up. Crawfish tunnel over.

BEAU: Watch out, darlin'.

KITTEN: Don't call me, "darling".

BEAU: Ssh. A water moccasin.

KITTEN: That brown thing.

BEAU: It's opening its mouth. Hand me that board.

KITTEN: That filthy wood?

(BEAU grabs a board and smashes the snake.)

BEAU: Got it. It's dead... Step back.

(THEY enter an empty shack.)

(SOUND of a bird squealing above)

KITTEN: What's that?

BEAU: Any bird up there is a bat.

(BEAU grabs a broom, kills the shrieking bat, shoves it outside. HE looks out a window.)

BEAU: Ye gods. We're on stilts in the marshes. This depot seems to go back a ways.

(RAVEN hurries in with luggage. A wailing resounds from the train.)

RAVEN: Blind sheepdog named Mathilda, beating 'gainst her cage.

KITTEN: Bring her out here.

BEAU: I'm allergic. Give her a Valium. When will the train be fixed?

RAVEN: Ain't answering nothing, till the police get here.

BEAU: What?

RAVEN: Found a stowaway on the train. That's a Federal offense.

(RAVEN exits. KITTEN screams after her.)

KITTEN: When are we leaving? ... She can't answer me?

GHOSTLY COMEDIES

BEAU: That is her answer.

(BEAU tests the floor with a critical squint. KITTEN sets up the basket and brief-case. BEAU swigs from a flask.)

KITTEN: Guess we can work here as well as anywhere else.

(KITTEN opens the Oxford University Faulkner Conference brochure.)

KITTEN: When's your lecture's scheduled? Oh, here it is. "The Image of God as Woman in Faulkner." 8:30 PM.

BEAU: Awful time. Everyone will be off—

KITTEN: Bourbon for breakfast?

BEAU: I collect flasks from conferences across the South. Line them up alphabetically ...Alabama, Baylor, Chattanooga State, Duke, Emory, Fayetteville State ...I used to tack up the wings of birds I'd shot--I'd chop them off—

KITTEN: A butcher.

BEAU: A champion, birds' wings were trophies... I grew up on a sugar plantation, St. Ursula. I was hanging there like a bat with no place to go.

KITTEN: What else do angry boys do on-

BEAU: Besides shooting birds and chasing bored wives? You order the servants about. Become a drunkard like Faulkner. Strategize.

KITTEN: You don't want to impress your colleagues?

BEAU: No I want to write something important. I told you.

KITTEN: Your department chair says–

BEAU: That wench! She pops out her boob at commencement exercises and attaches this little suckling!

SCENE FOUR: THE TRAIN

(RAVEN and the CONDUCTOR frisk BUNKY.)

CONDUCTOR: He ain't got no ticket.

RAVEN: What's wrong with you?

BUNKY: Nothing.

CONDUCTOR: Okay nothin, you going to jail.

BUNKY: I'm a fugitive.

CONDUCTOR: What's that?

BUNKY: Word with 3 syllables.

RAVEN: You broke the law.

BUNKY: Are you going to get rid of me or are you going to bury me somewhere?

CONDUCTOR: Shut up!

RAVEN: *(To BUNKY)* How old are you?

BUNKY: Mentally or physically?

CONDUCTOR: Punk. You want to see your home?

BUNKY: No. They eat people there.

RAVEN: Where you running to?

BUNKY: Dad was sending me to boarding school –

RAVEN: Your dad's name ?

BUNKY: Putting your son in boarding school is as bad as murder.

CONDUCTOR: You going to reform school—

BUNKY: Yeah. Something like that.

RAVEN: Shut up. Where your dad work?

BUNKY: Dad is not a bad person ... all the time.

CONDUCTOR: You got a mom?

BUNKY: The only way I can soothe myself when Dad's home is to lie under water with my nose and mouth sticking out.

CONDUCTOR AND RAVEN: What's your address?

BUNKY: I've become a bit of a Bedouin. Here is where I live.

(BUNKY pops out a sword.)

BUNKY: Yahoo!

(The MEN wrestle.)

SCENE FIVE: THE DEPOT

(SOUND of birds beating against the panes.)

BEAU: A blackbird spun against the pane, conked out, and fell.

KITTEN: Birds sense a storm coming. I volunteer at the zoo.

(SOUND of Mathilda HOWLING from her cage. Rising wind.)

KITTEN: *(cont.)* Won't somebody help that dog! ... You scared?

BEAU: No programmed for disaster. My parents lost a beach house in '69.

KITTEN: Was it the surges?

BEAU: Never talk--about water...

(BEAU goes offstage, past a sign that says "Toilet.")

BEAU: *(V.O.)* There's a bat in the bathroom sink.

KITTEN: Flush it down the toilet. *(KITTEN wipes her brow, and reviews her notes.)* There's got to be something about your wife we can use in the opening—

BEAU: *(O.S.)* Why must you bring women into—

KITTEN: The title of the conference is "Feminism and Faulkner." About Elsa—

BEAU: *(V.O.)* I'm in one door. She's out the other. *(Returning from the bathroom)* My agent said, "Take Elsa on a date, clam up, and that's what it'll be like when you're married.

KITTEN: What happened?

BEAU: We didn't talk all night. But I married her anyway: she was good in bed, liked my daughter; had a fat bank account.

KITTEN: Sex, motherhood, and money.

BEAU: Reverse order. Elsa's got gold quarters in the back of her mouth. If she sold her property and her art, she could feed the city.

(THEY laugh. An awkward silence.)

KITTEN: I'd better phone my husband. *(Dials her cell)* Quint?

BEAU: You could live off your beauty, honey. It could feed you pure oxygen.

KITTEN: *(Into her phone)* Tammy! Let me speak to Q-q-quint... Is Bunky all packed to leave Monday? You'll have to take him to the airport. I wouldn't stop crying ...What! ... Bunky's off to a friend's. Who? WHICH ONE? ...You think! ...You don't know for sure. *(To BEAU)* God, Quint hung up.

BEAU: Sorry...Sugar.

KITTEN: Don't touch me. We're working on your speech, no matter what—

BEAU: Who are you saving yourself for?

KITTEN: An architect from Berkeley. No. He was gay. I don't want more men in my life. Once y'all marry, you become monsters. Quint disconnects. And you, you chop up birds. Y'all think we won't stop loving you, if you hack your way through life.

BEAU: How do I know Kitten is beautiful, 'cause when I'm with her, my bells start to ring.

KITTEN: I'm searching for a situation where I can feel s-s-safe without intimidation. I'm working on my fantasies, trying to be happy as I can be, by myself. *(Pause.)* I've been single ever since I've been married. For me to get this assistantship, it's like unthreaded territory. I'm comfortable in the knowledge that it doesn't get better than where I am. So I'm not going to get sidetracked from your speech. You could start off with something like "I like the physical feeling of writing. Just to be able to sit in a group interested in writing is a privilege."

(BUNKY rushes in, RAVEN on his tail. BUNKY waves his sword, RAVEN, a pole.)

BUNKY: Mama!

RAVEN: Your mama ain't here.

KITTEN: Y-y-yes I am.

RAVEN: You?

KITTEN: My--boss ...Bunky.

BEAU: That's your son?

BUNKY: Im-pos-ter.

KITTEN: You should be packing—

BEAU: This behavior is more esoteric than I'm ready for.

BUNKY: Don't you like my talent? Gonna blow out the stops. Pay back the wood. Break the skin to find the heart beneath. Pow! I'm setting the place straight. Ripping the tin. Breaking my bones against the wood.

RAVEN: Quiet punk!

(RAVEN knocks the sword out of BUNKY's hands. BUNKY pulls out a gun.)

RAVEN AND BEAU: OH! NO! WATCH OUT!

BUNKY: Gonna shoot myself and let the blood run.

KITTEN: B-B-Bunky doesn't know what he's doing.

BUNKY: Real pain's like a message from God. Ha. Ha. Maybe if I hit myself.

KITTEN: The gun's plastic...

BUNKY: Stop me. You can't.

KITTEN: Don't hurt him.

BUNKY: Hurt me. It makes me stronger...

SCENE SIX: THE SWAMP

(Outside the Depot, BUNKY taunts the OTHERS with stones and scoots off, dodging the CONDUCTOR, walking with a bull horn.)

CONDUCTOR: Passenger alert! All aboard!

BEAU: I'll catch Bunky. Y'all go on–

RAVEN: Hurry up.

KITTEN: I can't leave without Bunky.

CONDUCTOR: Final call!

(CONDUCTOR darts toward the train.)

RAVEN: Let's get this train moving.

(BUNKY runs back, taunting them.)

KITTEN: Look out! An alligator.

BUNKY: Eat me. Take me.

(BEAU tackles BUNKY. RAVEN ties BUNKY's wrists.)

PHOTOS: CHRISTIAN RABY, PARIS

PICTURED: BARRET O'BRIEN AND MICHAEL SIMPSON

RAVEN: He under arrest.

KITTEN: W-w-w-what for?

RAVEN: Carrying a weapon. Attacking the law. Nasty bastard. I should let you die.

BUNKY: I revive on the ground. Dust sticking to me.

RAVEN: Like the gutter!

KITTEN: Don't roll around. You'll hurt yourself.

BUNKY: *(Screams in her face)* Good!

RAVEN: "Rain's in February. Floods in May." Follow me, Bunky. One yard behind. No closer.

KITTEN: Least let him clean up.

BEAU: I'll speak to the Conductor after we take off.

RAVEN: We ain't going nowhere.

BEAU: They said all aboard.

RAVEN: Yes, but we got to wait for clearance ... And for the state police.

(BEAU exits for the depot.)

BUNKY: Where's my sword?

RAVEN: Amtrak don't allow no swords.

BUNKY: It was a joke.

RAVEN: Some jokes put you in jail.

(Coming out, BEAU drops some clothes by BUNKY.)

BEAU: Hope I don't regret lending you these. But, I always feel like shit when I look like shit. Feel like schlock when I look like schlock.

(BEAU and KITTEN head for the train.)

BUNKY: I'm not changing outside.

RAVEN: Stay wet.

(RAVEN unties BUNKY. HE changes. SHE scoops up a possum, curls its tail around her arm, swings it before him.)

RAVEN: *(cont.)* You mean like a possum. Anything this ugly bound to be mean. He faking sleep, playing possum. But if you throw water, he'll hiss. Why you so ugly?

BUNKY: Ask my therapist.

RAVEN: Mind doctoring's witches' work.

CONDUCTOR: *(O.S.)* All aboard. All aboard.

(RAVEN starts to leave and almost slips.)

BUNKY: Watch out.

RAVEN: Morton's neuroma. Nerve ends too tight from worry.

(BUNKY pops a knife from his calf strap.)

BUNKY: Ever cut yourself? See how much pain you could stand.

(RAVEN pushes the knife at BUNKY'S throat.)

RAVEN: Watch it, or I give you to them gators. They got eyes, ears, noses top their heads so they can see, hear, and smell you. Had a brother like you. Smart-stupid. Got shot robbing a bar. Zip. Zip. Zip. Dead on arrival at Charity Hospital at fourteen.

BUNKY: Congratulations.

RAVEN: Should've sent him to jail. He be alive.

BUNKY: Being alive's not so great.

RAVEN: You ain't dead. How you know?

(SHE binds his wrists.)

PHOTOS: CHRISTIAN RABY, PARIS

PICTURED: BARRET O'BRIEN

SCENE SEVEN: THE TRAIN

(Lights up on KITTEN, who pursues the CONDUCTOR.)

CONDUCTOR: Tracks broken.

KITTEN: You said, "All Aboard? "

CONDUCTOR: Inspectors are checking the tracks. All trains in central Louisiana is suspended.

KITTEN: For how long?

CONDUCTOR: 4 hours. Maybe more--State police coming. Engineer's turning Bunky in.

KITTEN: If there's a storm alert...why would they send boats from... some—

BEAU: You're like a wild bird with a dog on its tail.

KITTEN: How will I talk to the--bayou police?

BEAU: They'll want to speak to Bunky, not you.

KITTEN: God! I don't ask y'all to make it easy--just--bearable.

(KITTEN empties her bag on the ground as SHE scrambles for a vial. RAVEN and BUNKY walk up.)

BUNKY: Yeah, that's right. Ma, pump some chemicals from your fucking shrink.

(KITTEN downs a pill. BEAU wrestles the container away from her.)

BEAU: What'd you take?

KITTEN: Vitamin C. It's one of my fragile days. You touch me, I cry. I'm so brittle.

BEAU: Tranquilizers?

KITTEN: It's a prescription. Leave me.

BEAU: Where you want me to go?

KITTEN: To hell, mostly....Lord, I just want to be a good wife and mother. Now, I'm afraid my son ... *(SHE dials her cell.)* Is my husband there? ...T-T-T-Tammy! ...I don't care if he's busy... It's an emergency... What are you doing ...I thought I heard Quint... .What? You're sorry?

(SOUND of drizzle.)

(KITTEN opens an umbrella. SHE heads with RAVEN for the depot, redials her phone as SHE walks. BUNKY follows, yanking on the rope, singing an angry blues song and pretending HE is a rock star doing a wild dance. THEY enter the depot.)

SCENE EIGHT: THE DEPOT

(BUNKY wrestles, humming loudly as RAVEN binds him to a chair.)

RAVEN: *(To KITTEN)* I'll go wait for the state police. You guard him.

(RAVEN exits.)

(KITTEN regards BUNKY with profound melancholy, like one accustomed to enduring life's casualties. SHE clips a canvas neck brace under her scarf. BEAU plods in.)

(SOUND of thunder.)

(BEAU blots his brow.)

KITTEN: You think anyone will make it to Ole Miss?

BEAU: Sure. Conferences allow mediocre writers to mouth off about other's work. No one's missing that chance.

KITTEN: Well, let's fine-tune your introduction.

(BUNKY hums a rough blues song.)

KITTEN: You could quote from Virginia Wolfe. The woman was so brilliant and scared.

BEAU: That suicide? What kind of achievement was she?

KITTEN: A remarkably gorgeous writer. With a great heart and spirit to boot.

BEAU: No I'd like to begin with Keat's "Ode on a —"

KITTEN: It's a minority conference. Why not talk about your daughter? How is your relationship?

BEAU: A little chilly but not gratuitously... Last week she vanished from boarding school? It's two hours from New Orleans, if you drive ninety miles an hour, which is what they do. Fifty phone calls later, I tracked her down to "Chateau Estates." She'd badgered her friend's mother into renting them six porno movies. Relationships are like cars. I need a tune-up. Marcelle needs a brake job. Ha.

KITTEN: Why'd you have children if you don't like taking care of them?

BEAU: For posterity. Ransom to the gods–

(BUNKY hums a rough blues medley.)

BEAU: For Elsa.

KITTEN: Let's start with a reference to your lovely wife.

BEAU: Elsa's overeating again. Blowing up like a poisoned dog in the sun. She wears these moo-moos and massive jewelry. Hits the kitchen like a wild animal. Gobbles everything in sight.

KITTEN: Don't blame women.

BEAU: I don't blame the fire that my hand gets burned. With three mothers-in-law (one real and one step), a dog, three cats and a duck, you get upset.

(KITTEN's radio pops on. The DJ speaks with a strong southern accent.)

ROSARY HARTEL O'NEILL

DJ: *(O.S.)* A train derailment has taken place at St. Tammany Parish ...
(STATIC)

BUNKY: Louisiana?

BEAU: Turn it up.

DJ: *(O.S.)* Five cars have flipped—

(KITTEN shakes the radio so hard the batteries spray out.)

KITTEN: Can someone fix this?

BEAU: Is that an order?

(KITTEN struggles with the radio. Her scarf falls, exposing the neck brace.)

BEAU: *(cont.)* What's that?

KITTEN: Doctor said to wear it when I get these neck spasms.

BEAU: When did that start?

KITTEN: I ran a red light--Chasing Bunky.

BUNKY: Shut up.

BEAU: Nice.

BUNKY: Don't blame me.

KITTEN: I crashed into a police car.

BUNKY: Take it off.

(SHE unclamps the neck brace.)

BEAU: Why are you obeying him?

KITTEN: It itches.

(SHE scrabbles inside her basket, feeds BUNKY a bite of a sandwich, but HE spits it out. SHE stoops for it, when BEAU shouts.)

BEAU: Leave it. No, better yet, he should pick that up.

(BEAU unties BUNKY and gets him to pick up the morsel.)

KITTEN: Before, when I fed him, we talked.

(BEAU takes his papers across the room. BUNKY drags over and riffles through them.)

BUNKY: What are my papers doing with Beau's? You've contaminated them.

KITTEN: I didn't want Dad to see the F's. The psychiatrist said to work with you.

BUNKY: On vacation!

BUNKY: Were you going to get rid of my papers or were you going to bury them somewhere. I don't need reminders that I've failed.

(BUNKY beats against the sofa. Bugs soar out.)

KITTEN: What are those bugs!

BEAU: Termites. Ye Gods.

(BEAU and KITTEN chase the bugs out. Air out the room.)

(RAVEN comes in with suitcases, handcuffs BUNKY and takes him off. KITTEN gobbles cheese-nips and calls.)

KITTEN: Bring him back. He's got to eat!

(SOUND of rain falling with an otherworldly hardness.)

(BEAU unbuttons his shirt. KITTEN blushes, goes to a makeshift area to change. BEAU calls out:)

BEAU: Did you try military school?

KITTEN: They won't take him. When I tell Bunky to study, he screams, "F-u-c-k you, frigging bitch."

BEAU: He says "frigging"?

KITTEN: I'm not to react when Bunky tells me to fuck myself or when he farts in public.

BEAU: What does Quint say?

KITTEN: Quint treats me like you treat the porter. Always ordering her about. The counselor advises analysis for Quint's mother, biofeedback for Quint and group therapy for me.

BEAU: You going?

KITTEN: No. Quint doesn't want the firm to know we need psychiatric help. *(Returning)* Bunky leaves insane messages at the English department. Like-- "Bring a head of lettuce, a sharp knife, a dozen Carmello candy bars--"

BEAU: "And some quarters." I heard that.

KITTEN: Just because I didn't refuse him, he grew up thinking all was possible and wasn't contained by my negative opinions.

BEAU: I've been screwed by so many students I can tell you what they'll do to you. Women have been trained to nurture and give. And men have been trained to fight and bully and we better never forget that...

(BEAU finds a TV covered by newspapers and plugs it in.)

(STATIC SOUNDS of firefighters, and police rescuing a smoking Amtrak.)

ANCHOR: *(V.O.)* Steve Roberts, CNN anchor... Bogalusa, Louisiana, north of Pearl River... People are --trapped in train wreckage. 12 cars are overturned...

(SOUND of TV buzzing on and off.)

ANCHOR: *(V.O.)* A teacher from Chicago was traveling with her ten-year-old daughter.

TEACHER: *(V.O.)* We were in the second car--.

LITTLE GIRL: (V.O.) We 'd trouble getting out....

ANCHOR: Rescue crews in ... Louisiana are–

(STATIC hits and the screen goes off.)

KITTEN: Lord. I've got to find my s-s-s-son.

(KITTEN exits depot. BEAU follows her.)

BEAU: It's pouring down rain; you can't go out.

(SOUND of wind blowing violently.)

SCENE NINE: THE SWAMP

(KITTEN goes back in, gets them umbrellas, and THEY move slowly toward the swamp.)

BEAU: Nothing wrong with being upset like you are. You can't get it right.

KITTEN: *(Calls out)* Bunky!

BEAU: Bunky is capable. He's got this far as a stowaway.

KITTEN: *(Calls out)* Raven.

BEAU: You've got to force yourself to act from the place you've grown to.

KITTEN: *(Calls out)* Anybody!

BEAU: You can know about something and not be worried about it. Boys do grow up.

KITTEN: Raising adolescents is a nightmare, living from horror to horror.

BEAU: *(cont.)* God made teenagers obnoxious so it'd be easier to let them go…. How much time does Bunky spend with Quint?

KITTEN: They've these intense emails. The psychiatrist says I'm insufficiently affectionate. Lunatic males. They don't make sons do penance as priests did in confession. Shouldn't Bunky compensate me in some way? If you humiliate your mother, don't you have to pay?

BEAU: Bunky sees you lying to yourself. You're not attracted to your husband, but--you—

KITTEN: Sex doesn't mean anything.

BEAU: Course it does. Sex is important. Period.

(THEY pause breathless.)

(SOUND of rain battering down.)

BEAU: You feel guilty because your relationship is destroying your child?

KITTEN: Quint insults me in front of Bunky. Does he feel guilty?

BEAU: Your son's super-spoiled. When solving a problem, never overlook the obvious.

(THEY bump into a BRAKEMAN glued to headsets and the CONDUCTOR who slurps from an Orange pop bottle.)

CONDUCTOR: Some train went off the tracks and--

BRAKEMAN: We's behind it.

CONDUCTOR: Them ties that holds the rails down be breaking.

KITTEN: Where's my s-s-s–son?

CONDUCTOR: Raven went after him.

(CONDUCTOR points to the swamp.)

(SOUND of rain clanking down.)

(KITTEN and BEAU hold up their umbrellas and trudge off to the swamp.)

BEAU: We'll find Bunky. *(Sings)*"Wade in the water, wade in the water, children. Wade in the water. Jesus going to come to carry me home."

(SOUND of rain pouring.)

(The sky turns a brownish blue, tinged with yellow, like a bruise. THEY pause under a ledge.)

KITTEN: I'm no saint. Bunky's behavior is partly my fault.

BEAU: Your son probably won't acknowledge your virtues.

KITTEN: There's a f-f-f-fragility to his mind.

BEAU: It's something that has to be checked out.

KITTEN: I should have been f-f-f-firmer.

BEAU: It's not in the "Oh my God" category. It's—

KITTEN: Sometimes, when I hit bottom, I admit Bunky could be disturbed.

BEAU: Manic depression isn't a sin. You don't have self-control.

KITTEN: What influence have I over Bunky? That's a hard question to ask if you're a m-m-m-mother.

BEAU: Don't overfunction with people who are not grateful.

(SHE lunges out, skids, and falls.)

KITTEN: Oh no, an epitaph. "Bobby Bairns beloved son 1897-1938."… I never gave B--Bunky what he needed--. Lord, I've something in my contact. And I -I- I've hurt my leg.

BEAU: You're not going to quit. You're going to have a nervous breakdown.

KITTEN: I have to be a mother till I can't anymore.

BEAU: What good are you going to be with one leg and one eye?

(SOUND of wind howling.)

(KITTEN and BEAU dart back to the depot.)

KITTEN: We s-s-s-should work on your anger.

BEAU: *(Looks up).* Wonder of wonders--we're back at the depot.

SCENE TEN: THE CAMP (FORMERLY THE DEPOT)

(Inside the depot, a sign reads, "Camp Nun of Yo Bizness. Hang up your guns and skin your prey." A poster says "Swamp Tours," and has an open mouth of a crocodile.)

KITTEN: Where did these posters come from?

(BEAU reads the fine print on another.)

BEAU: "Pearl River Wildlife Area. 34,000 acres of swamp for crawfishing and hunting hogs, bears, and alligators. Black bears seldom attack. They get by, by puffing up, stomping feet, snapping jaws and grunting. Beware alligator nests where gators reach fourteen feet and one thousand pounds."

(A garish OLD WOMAN lumbers in. SHE is overly made-up, lipstick too big for her lips, eyes grossly lined in blue, too big bracelets. SHE is grumpy.)

BEAU: *(Whispering)* She's dressed like three actors, all different parts of her.

OLD WOMAN: You got to pay up front.

KITTEN: I thought this was a depot.

OLD WOMAN: It was... is. It's also a hunting camp, a motel. Depends on what sign is up.

KITTEN: We don't need a room.

OLD WOMAN: That will be $30 up front. Ya got to make your own bed.

BEAU: We're here for the depot.

OLD WOMAN: It's closed.

BEAU: Or... the camp?

KITTEN: Have you seen a b-b-b-boy—

OLD WOMAN: Free beans in that pot.

KITTEN: Or a porter?

OLD WOMAN: Toilet's shared.

BEAU: Do you rent vehicles?

OLD WOMAN: Shower's out back.

KITTEN: How do we g-g-g-get to the—

OLD WOMAN: You don't get nothing till you pays for a room.

KITTEN: How much, Ms.--?

OLD WOMAN: Ice. I period, C period, E period... .For all, services. Hundred.

BEAU: Dollars?

OLD WOMAN: You cheap!

BEAU: Money is immortality. If I have enough I won't die, Mrs...I period C period E period.

(BEAU parcels out the money.)

(WOMAN leads KITTEN, hobbling, and BEAU into a makeshift bedroom area.)

KITTEN: You call this a room?

OLD WOMAN: You can close them curtains if you needs privacy.

(SOUND of wind buckling the walls, rattling the pipes. A downpour.)

(KITTEN hobbles about, dials and redials her cell.)

BEAU: Let me wrap your leg.

KITTEN: Oh, shut up.

BEAU: When the rain lightens, I'll go get "trouble." Relax.

KITTEN: I can't wait.

BEAU: To quote Tennyson—

KITTEN: Don't.

(SHE glances out the window.)

KITTEN: Is that a skiff floating by the side?

BEAU: I know you're a driver. You like to be on the future arm of things.

KITTEN: I can't wait –

BEAU: *(cont.)* Why would Bunky calm down for you--when he's at the height of his prowess. It's not that he's a sycophant. He has this meta-reali-ty. And the train crew is lining up in a big way for it. To quote Byron, *"The little actor cons another part."*

KITTEN: What can I do?

BEAU: Stay away. Bunky's a performer. He doesn't like to watch someone else in the arena.

KITTEN: What about the state police?

BEAU: You think you're going to pole vault to full control. You've got to slow down and live through time. Let me handle things... If there is an episode of any kind, I can assure you, things will go back to the way they were, where I wear the gun and you cook.

(KITTEN hobbles about. Lights blink.)

BEAU: It's so Hemingway. You're all over the place.

KITTEN: My knee is always throbbing. It's a question of what level.

(HE leads her to a table, puts a cushion under her knee, gathers damp rag.)

(SOUND of wind getting stronger and the WAILING of a dog.)

KITTEN: I hope Bunky's with Mathilda. That sheepdog.

(BEAU hands KITTEN a flyer from his pocket.)

KITTEN: You think we'll still make this conference?

BEAU: Probably. Ole Miss has been in place for centuries despite every level of hurricane.

(BEAU tightens a towel around her knee.)

KITTEN: OUCH. *(Reads the flyer)* "This conference is near the Louisiana swamps. Where you can hunt hogs, bait alligators, fight wild dogs."

BEAU: How you feel?

KITTEN: Nurtured like a plant that's watered. OUCH.

BEAU: Scream.

KITTEN: Do something, Beau. It's not life as usual. I'm emotionally raw.

BEAU: I'll check on Bunky, when the rain stops.

(SOUND of pounding rain.)

BEAU: You think if you save Bunky, he will finally love you.

KITTEN: I didn't want him to go to boarding school but now he may die.

BEAU: You want me to dive into Noah's flood? Okay. Amuse yourself. *(HE puts money in a coffee can, reads:)* "Binoculars a dollar an hour. Panoramic View. 90% of this refuge floods. Access is mainly by boat."

KITTEN: Please go.

(BEAU grabs more binoculars, and exits outside.)

(The OLD WOMAN comes in with a first-aid kit marked $4.00. SHE examines KITTEN's leg on the stool. KITTEN nervously reapplies her makeup.)

OLD WOMAN: Let me fix that knee.

KITTEN: I'm so vain. I have to put on lip liner in a hurricane.

OLD WOMAN: Got a $4.00 special on this first aid treatment.

KITTEN: In my family, there were six cousins. The only thing I had was I was a little bit prettier than they were.

OLD WOMAN: I'm going to work at my own pace because I can't understand what you saying... .

KITTEN: I don't want you to be nice to me. I can't get into a relationship with ambiguity.

OLD WOMAN: You just want to talk.

KITTEN: I'm fine. Don't touch anything. I can't—

OLD WOMAN: You don't want me to--

(SHE whips off the leg wrap, slaps down a cold cloth)

KITTEN: Ouch! You were so... business like... before-

OLD WOMAN: That good?

KITTEN: I can't get inside your attitude.

OLD WOMAN: What cha doing with that cheapskate?

KITTEN: I was reading an unhealthy number of romantic poems and no doubt became deranged. I decided my life should be finalized with a degree.

OLD WOMAN: That man's a teacher?

KITTEN: I know, I know. He didn't go to Harvard. He's doesn't look gaunt and haunted looking. He's unspeakably confused, doesn't know how to sell himself except down the river. A lot of good work comes from people who can be strangely bad for a while. When he lectures, he musicalizes a poem, inhabits it as a person. I want to be able to teach like that, to snap my fingers and quote Virginia Wolfe. Or Emily Dickinson. I want to get my poetry degree so I've something to do when my son leaves. I want to mentor girls who write better than the men--Shelley, Keats, Byron, Tennyson-- and quote from women in my classes. But, "Success is counted/Sweetest by those who ne'er succeed." Emily Dickinson.

OLD WOMAN: Let me wipe your hands.

KITTEN: My hands are permanently wet. They're greasier than I remember. The defeat began with my son's estrangement. His presence gave me a way to recover from a-- If I had him with me I won, and if I didn't I lost.

OLD WOMAN: You'll get through it.

(SOUND of wheezing wind and rain.)

KITTEN: My son is out there somewhere MISSING. He's turned into a terribly sick dysfunctional beast. I should be good at this. Taking care of a psychopathic son is kind of like taking care of a husband.

OLD WOMAN: My name is Bernice; if you call me by my last name, I'll feel old.

KITTEN: I'm still heterosexual relatively.

OLD WOMAN: Just give me my $4.00.

(BEAU ducks inside drenched, finds KITTEN in the kitchen.)

BEAU: The weatherman said a little rain. I'm out there, and it looks like biblical proportions. There's three feet of water 'round the depot.

KITTEN: How's Bunky?

BEAU: He's been neutered and had fourteen teeth removed.

KITTEN: Everything in my body is s-s-s-s-shaking.

BEAU: Bunky's been put in custody. He's being held over night.

KITTEN: <u>Where</u>? I'm trying not to be obsessive.

BEAU: I found him having a Coke in the engine room, doing crossword puzzles with the crew. It's the final *coup de gras* to win over the Conductor. Bunky's gone from being Huck Finn to Alexander the Great.

KITTEN: What about the state police?

BEAU: Now that the train's failed, everyone wants to distance himself from any opinion. All the Conductor said was we'll leave eventually.

KITTEN: When? Even the idea of a departure time is better than none.

BEAU: Everything is complicated; it's Louisiana.

(BEAU spies beans, beers, moldy bread on a counter. HE discards six slices and butters four.)

KITTEN: What about Bunky?

BEAU: Raven will handle him. Someone I thought was horrific, I'm now appreciating. She is like a great ship anchored in uniform and diamonds. Under her control, Bunky has become even more charming. Before, he excoriated the train staff; now he loves them. He's like a Thomistic scholar, unusually arresting and prescient. But beware. In Egypt, soon as you become king, they start building your tomb.

KITTEN: You're so harsh.

BEAU: Hardened... Last time I went for my daughter at boarding school, she arrived late. She didn't feel like looking for me, so she took a $400 limousine home.

(BEAU serves beans and bread.)

BEAU: *(cont.)* Excuse the poor service, faux crystal, and hotel silver.

(KITTEN takes a pill.)

BEAU: *(cont.)* What you doing?

KITTEN: I take enzymes to help digest my food.

(OLD WOMAN stomps in, inspects egg carton.)

OLD WOMAN: You ain't paid for dat bread? Only beans be free.

BEAU: The muzzle is off!

OLD WOMAN: 10 slices?

BEAU: My wife doesn't feed me. I'm a hungry wolf all the time.

OLD WOMAN: Be six dollars for them beers you stole. Ten dollars for bread.

BEAU: Another leech hovering by.

OLD WOMAN: Men feel they don't need to pay 'cause—

BEAU: *(Slaps down bills)* I'm not King Midas. I understand money is key to everything in America.

(SOUND of wind and rain smacking debris against the panes. Meowing of cats.)

KITTEN: *(To OLD WOMAN)* <u>Can you take me to the train</u> in one of your boats out back? *(Pause.)* For $50.

OLD WOMAN: When I feeds me cats. They is carnivores. But each eats things his own way—

BEAU: *(At the window looking out)* That scabby one looks sick.

OLD WOMAN: Every animal has some cancer. It's like the measles. Practice not seeing; you'll be so happy.

BEAU: Storm's getting worse.

KITTEN: Can't you hurry?

OLD WOMAN: *(cont.)* I don't pay attention. Why would I? Each report has its own complaints and that confuses me.

(OLD WOMAN gathers her supplies. BEAU grabs a newspaper, opens it.)

OLD WOMAN: *(cont.)* What you doing?

BEAU: Checking the obituaries.

BEAU: *(cont.)* I want you to read the names of the dead out loud, because if anyone can bring them back, you can.

(BEAU pours sherry from a decanter marked three dollars and chugs.)

OLD WOMAN: Be $2.00.

(BEAU puts down $2.00. Looks at KITTEN)

BEAU: I'm not good with women. I thought my first wife was happy, till I discovered she was an alcoholic.

KITTEN: Like you.

BEAU: I'm not an alcoholic. Alcoholics go to meetings.

(BEAU hands KITTEN a deck of cards)

BEAU: When my first wife was laid up, she played "Wishing Aces." Maybe we can use that in my Ole Miss speech. Here. You flip every third card. If you turn an ace, you get your wish.

KITTEN: Cards saved her?

BEAU: No. She died at twenty-nine, the sunny side of thirty. Sunny is the young side. Shady is the old …I like things in a certain order. People should die in the order they are born.

(SOUND of a CRASH.)

(SOUND of huge THUNK of water.)

OLD WOMAN: Oh, gawd. The porch done fell.

KITTEN: Shouldn't we go while we can?

SCENE ELEVEN: THE SWAMP

(SOUND of rain pelting the roof and wind slapping through leaves.)

(SOUND of six wild geese waffling by.)

(OLD WOMAN lunges outside, rocking back. SHE whistles. BEAU and KITTEN come out.)

OLD WOMAN: Rescue geese. I can't leave 'em—

BEAU: You're not—

OLD WOMAN: Their parents got shot. They think I'm their mother. Got to feed them.

KITTEN: How long will that take?

OLD WOMAN: *(Coming back)* Hank is that beautiful goose, white with blue eyes. Because she was sitting on others' eggs, she didn't lay her own.

BEAU: Can you take us first?

OLD WOMAN: Hank's blind in one eye--she has an evil sister that wants to kill her. Eats all her food. *(OLD WOMAN whistles again.)*

OLD WOMAN: *(cont.)* "Finally here"--that's my wolf dog. "Finally here!" He don't come when he's called. That's how he got named.

(SOUND of displaced animals bungling about.)

OLD WOMAN: *(cont.)* Finally. Here! I don't move for the dog. The dog moves for me.

BEAU: *(To KITTEN)* Is her animal thing an addiction? I have to look it up. Is the bitch dangerous?

KITTEN: You're cursing.

BEAU: When I lose my grounding, I lose language in a weird way...How are you? Dislocation affects the immune system— Is your leg okay?

KITTEN: Everything is fine, except my calf muscles are throbbing...When I recover, I'll kick you.

BEAU: You're eccentric, the way people used to be.

KITTEN: Get me to the t-t-t-train.

BEAU: *(Checks his watch)* 3 p.m. I'll give Ice 20 minutes. Then I hijack her boat.

(HE reaches down and kisses KITTEN.)

KITTEN: Why you do that?

BEAU: I'm eccentric too.

SCENE TWELVE: THE TRAIN

(Lights up in the train where BUNKY, RAVEN, and the CONDUCTOR play a game of poker.)

(SOUND of rain falling.)

BUNKY: Let's go get Mama.

CONDUCTOR: Why. We ain't going nowhere. Give me one.
(Throws down a card. RAVEN redeals)

BUNKY: I need to see --

RAVEN: My ma passed last time we evacuated. The home put her in the chapel. Wouldn't take her.

(BUNKY stands by RAVEN, intent on cards.)

BUNKY: Let's barge through the swamp

CONDUCTOR: No one's going, less he wanna hunt, kill—

RAVEN: And quarter 'gators.

CONDUCTOR: I ain't moving less the eye come.

BUNKY: What's an ... eye?

RAVEN: The head of the storm, when all turn green.

CONDUCTOR: I watched Hurricane Andrew bear down on Lake Charles—

BUNKY: Katrina's 2 days away!

RAVEN: You best teach us all how to swim.

(BUNKY demonstrates arm strokes and leg paddles.)

(SOUND of tail flapping in water.)

BUNKY: Yikes! What did that--?

RAVEN: Is that a gator?

CONDUCTOR: Gators!!!

BUNKY: Thank god, they're endangered.

CONDUCTOR: No, they ain't. Them born here grows faster than them born wild.

RAVEN: Louisiana, got 1.5 million 'gators.

CONDUCTOR: More 'gators than people some places.

BUNKY: Let's play cards!

SCENE THIRTEEN. THE CAMP (formerly the Depot)

(BEAU flicks a switch in the makeshift bedroom.)

KITTEN: Are the lights broke?

BEAU: They're either broke, it's gotten romantic, or the wires are trashed.

(Lights blink on. BEAU peers out.)

BEAU: *(cont.)* That crazy hag is burning her garbage. We won't drown but we may catch on fire.

(BEAU wraps an arm about KITTEN. SHE grasps a phone, sits on the bed.)

KITTEN: A dial tone. I'm phoning my husband.

BEAU: Calling Quint is like a note in a bottle— Or words tied to a pigeon.

KITTEN: If Quint doesn't answer, he doesn't answer for God!

(SHE redials.)

(BEAU lifts her hand to his chest.)

BEAU: *(cont.)* Is it wet? The shirt?

KITTEN: *(Into the phone)* Hello.

(BEAU reads a sign)

BEAU: Dry clothes. $5.00.

(BEAU removes the shirt, exposing his strong shoulders.)

KITTEN: Don't take anything else off. *(Into phone)* Quint? …Tammy? …Put Quint on the cell. What do you mean he's not there…Wait. You're fading—

BEAU: You got Quint?

KITTEN: Some friend of his friend, a voice that won't let me through.

BEAU: One kiss.

KITTEN: Move! Over there! I don't want to die committing adultery.

BEAU: It's hurricane sex. You don't have to confess it.

(A lizard crawls up KITTEN'S shoulder.)

KITTEN: What's that bloody gray thing?

BEAU: A gecko, an albino lizard. Shall I kill it.

KITTEN: It's not part of my philosophy. I won't kill any insects because they're my guests.

(The gecko jumps down KITTEN's shirt.)

KITTEN: *(cont.)* Oh. Get it! Why can't I... I act brave—

(HE puts his hand down her shirt.)

KITTEN: *(cont.)* Like Genevieve — patron saint of France.

BEAU: It's gone round your back—

KITTEN: She stopped Attila--At the gates of Paris. Or Saint Joan?

BEAU: Take off your shirt.

KITTEN: *(Complying)* Did Joan cry at the stake?

BEAU: No.

KITTEN: She asked for "Water!" It's recorded.

BEAU: Got the gecko.

(BEAU touches her chest)

BEAU: *(cont.)* Your body is on fire. You've no skin.

KITTEN: I'm not doing what you think--this will lead to. Even if I wanted to... which I don't...I wouldn't. I c-c-can't. I'm too upset. Stop! Crazy. F-f-f-fool. I have to end this, because I don't have time to "repair" you.

BEAU: It's Katrina sex. Don't think.

(HE kisses her.)

(SOUND of torrential rain and of the floor creaking and stilling from below. A buzzing sound.)

KITTEN: My God! What's happening?

BEAU: We're falling or flying. God.

KITTEN: Oh. Jesus s-s-s-save me. We're being punished. I'm going to hell---

(The OLD WOMAN barges in.)

OLD WOMAN: We leavin'.

KITTEN: I'm too p-p-panicked! Can't m-m-m- move.

BEAU: There's a fine line between fear and procrastination.

(THEY exit the Camp, make their way outside.)

SCENE FOURTEEN: A BOAT

(BEAU and KITTEN get in a broken motor boat. The OLD WOMAN, a rifle at her side, swats ants.)

KITTEN: Is this your boat? God, it's so full of junk—

OLD WOMAN: Be quiet.

BEAU: F-f-f-f-fabulous!

OLD WOMAN: Ants all over the place, and some are bad.

BEAU: Hurry!

(OLD WOMAN gets out, goes and drags over some cages, piles them in back.)

KITTEN: God, what's that!

OLD WOMAN: Couldn't decide who to bring. I'm taking Hank. That's my daughter, and she can't be spayed, and the teenage geese. Baby ones will die in the wind. The old ones can fend for theyselves.

(OLD WOMAN gets back in the boat, passes BEAU Jack Daniels.)

OLD WOMAN: It's almost like a prayer. I drink the same thing every hurricane.

BEAU: Put your stirrer in and it'd stand up.

OLD WOMAN: Better hold on to your seat; it's broke.

(KITTEN clasps the seat. OLD WOMAN turns on the engine.)

OLD WOMAN: *(cont.)* People don't realize the power of water. Few hundred pounds ain't nothing for water.

(The boat jolts ahead. Actors mime the bumpy ride.)

KITTEN: Aren't we going to the train?

OLD WOMAN: <u>Need gas!</u>

(SOUND of a CRASH.)

(The OLD WOMAN slams off the engine. Honks.)

OLD WOMAN: 'Gator up ahead ...Chewing on something. Lord, he done flipped me cat in the air and sucked it down.

(OLD WOMAN tries to start up the boat.)

BEAU: What's wrong with--the ignition?

OLD WOMAN: After Hurricane Camille... gators was everywhere, what with surges, washing everything to the marsh...

(A snake crawls over the floor.)

BEAU: Gawd. A water moccasin.

OLD WOMAN: Get it!

BEAU: All right everybody, feet up

(BEAU tosses snake out, gets the OLD WOMAN's rifle, shoots the snake.)

(SOUND of loud barking.)

OLD WOMAN: You done scared off "Finally Here." Now I gots to go get him!

(OLD WOMAN jumps off, chasing the dog.)

KITTEN: Should we go after?

BEAU: No, let's wait... .

KITTEN: We're wasting time.

(KITTEN flops back in the boat, her hair tousled about her face.)

(SOUND of rain barely dripping.)

BEAU: You look like that poster of mournful Psyche in my office. Psyche means soul in Greek myth.

KITTEN: Shut up.

BEAU: Psyche climbed out of Hades by saying "No," to all the dying who screamed for help as she crossed the River Styx... I bet you had an imperial presence as a child.

KITTEN: Quint doesn't exist for me.

BEAU: Perhaps all isn't lost.

KITTEN: It could be beautiful, if I don't go back--a beautiful sadness like poetry.

BEAU: Penny for your thoughts.

KITTEN: I feel helpless like I did when I was pregnant. Big as an elephant. I thought I'd be happy, but I could barely walk. They'd put me to sleep and cut me open. The doctor said another... baby would be life theatening. Quint was sure I could have another boy.

BEAU: He wanted more sons?

KITTEN: Don't you all? I've such a headache.

(SOUND of rain dripping slowly.)

(BEAU opens a locket on KITTEN's neck.)

BEAU: *(cont.)* You must put your face in that locket. Now I open it, and it's blind. You set your face inside and keep admiring yourself; others will follow suit.
(HE kisses her suddenly, passionately. SHE pushes him off.)

BEAU: I'm a nymphomaniac. It's my only redeeming quality.

(SOUND of light rain, a steady breeze, and geese squawking.)

BEAU: That Old Woman isn't coming back. We'd better —

98

KITTEN: Borrow her boat?

(When the motor won't start, BEAU takes an oar and THEY plow off.)

SCENE FIFTEEN: THE TRAIN AND SWAMP

(Lights up on BUNKY punching some music into a computer. Blues music soars out, a recording with BUNKY singing soulfully a refrain about rain.)

RAVEN: That you?

BUNKY: I cut a record. That song's our anthem of independence. *(Dancing in step)* Come follow me to the swamp. I got to find my Mom.

(THEY slog in step out the train to the swamp.)

RAVEN: Which way your mom go?

BUNKY: Can't tell.

RAVEN: You see over there?… can't make out nothing.

BUNKY: I think there's a town.

(SOUND of hard wind. Cries of birds and steady drizzle.)

RAVEN: Sing something. Soldiers sing when they go into battle to lift themselves up. Go on.

(BUNKY sings a blues song about rain.)

(Moments later, KITTEN and BEAU plow through slime.)

BEAU: Keats might say: "I cannot see what flowers are at my feet."

KITTEN: I just read this book, Negativity and Death. It says when enough negative people gather together, they attract this evil force, the wrath of God. I regret not going to church on Sunday. If we die, I hope God takes us quick, in one great crash of sound. I want to d-d-die as if I'd fought for something.

BEAU: You've delirious!

KITTEN: It's raining 'cause the whole ecological earth is retaliating. We're being p-p-punished 'cause we've succumbed to the desire for power. If more women get involved, we can swing the world back.

(KITTEN punches in a number in her cell. BEAU tries his cell.)

BEAU: F-f-f-f-f-f----God, I may never see my daughter again. I just gave her hell for changing the message on my answering machine.

KITTEN: How old is she—

BEAU: 16. Marcelle had good grades before. Now she just recalls the next party.

KITTEN: You were the CEO of her life.

(BEAU'S phone rings suddenly.)

BEAU: Hello? Marcelle? Thank God I got you--

(NOISES through the receiver, BAR ROOM SOUNDS: Rap singing, shouts.)

BEAU: *(cont.)* Marcelle ...Where are you? ...A beer chugging what? ... Contest. You called the state police. Elsa says--what! What... *(The phone cuts off.)*

BEAU: *(Redials, talks to KITTEN)* Marcelle is trying to help us... Oh god... I used to take her to the library to study. Now we never talk.

KITTEN: You incarcerate her in Grand Coteau?

BEAU: *(Redials)* Last time I drove there, Elsa screamed, "Damaged goods from your first wife. Make sure that boarding school doesn't throw her out.

KITTEN: She said that?

BEAU: Elsa was always selfish, but with Marcelle she got to practice.

KITTEN: And Marcelle?

BEAU: *(Redials)* Rampant fury claimed her. She cursed nonstop, through the flat roads of Louisiana. At school, she charged past a ninety-year-old nun, upsetting her pusher and nearly killing her...

(Pockets the phone, hopelessly)

KITTEN: No one's all wrong.

BEAU: Marcelle's just a--There's a dark underbelly to all teenagers.

(BEAU AND KITTEN make it to another shack.)

BEAU: We're back at the depot again!

SCENE SIXTEEN:
LODGE NUN OF YO BIZNESS (Former Depot)

(A sign reads "Camp, Nun of Yo' Bizness-- Hunting Lodge")

(Inside the WARDEN, a 70ish man with a wiry beard and moustache stands with a goat. HE raises his arms in a victory pose.)

WARDEN: Rooms, guns, boats and hiking shoes.

KITTEN: I thought this was a depot or camp—

WARDEN: When the old woman is gone, it's a hunting lodge.

BEAU: You got any gas?

(The WARDEN leads the couple inside past a HUNTER with bags of ducks and alligator parts.)

HUNTER: Ducks and alligator tails!

(BEAU reads a sign.)

BEAU: "It is ricomminded you buy a 12-20 gauge shotgun, 2-3 steel shot loads."

BEAU: We need to—

KITTEN: *(Screams)* Get to the train—

WARDEN: Why is it when we're old, y'all yell at us. I hears fine. Room's $80. Gun's $60.

KITTEN: We already paid for a room.

WARDEN: Not from me.

BEAU: We just need gas.

WARDEN: Can't get nothin' less you buy a room from me.

KITTEN: But we bought one from the –

(The WARDEN turns.)

WARDEN: *(cont.)* Shush. Listening to you is too big a job.

KITTEN: We'll take … ah room 3. The gun and—

WARDEN: I'll get what you want, then you'll need something else.

BEAU: Do you take separate credit cards?

(The WARDEN studies BEAU.)

BEAU: *(cont.)* So she can pay half?

WARDEN: You some tight.

BEAU: You're not related to Mrs. Ice?

WARDEN: My worse half. *(Gestures to a window)* I seen her from afar… That's close enough.

BEAU: I know. She came over, introduced herself. It was like Mount Rushmore saying hello.

WARDEN: She don't grow on you. She should be less loud, less Cajun, and put on a wash accent.

BEAU: Wasp.

WARDEN: She's in the clutches of that wolf—dog. There's your room area.

(Strobe lights spin a heart-shape over satin pillows and a gaudy throw tossed on the floor.)

BEAU: The pure eroticism of the Garden of Eden without the spiritual content.

(KITTEN moves about nervously. Her anxious eyes take in BEAU by the window.)

KITTEN: What's that noise?

BEAU: More boats, straining at their ropes

KITTEN: Rent one. Get B-B-B-unky.

BEAU: Those boats have holes in them. It's a suicide mission…After this, I either go insane or become a priest.

(A despondent look seizes BEAU's face. HE grabs the shotgun and starts to charge out.)

(When RAVEN, and BUNKY, enter, KITTEN rushes to them.)

KITTEN: Thank God. You're okay …Where are the others?

RAVEN: Gone for help, maybe.

BUNKY: But they can't swim.

RAVEN: Shush. You believe that!!! They's strong.

(RAVEN nudges BUNKY to speak to KITTEN. BUNKY takes a photo out a plastic bag in his pocket, pulls KITTEN to the side.)

BUNKY: I know this is the wrong time and all, but …Raven says no secrets and I found this Christmas picture. There's Tammy.

BEAU: She's wearing the same fur as yours.

KITTEN: It wasn't like mine. Hers is mink. Mine is fox.

BUNKY: I said to Dad, "What you make of Tammy and Ma wearing the same coat?" "I don't read anything into it," he said.

KITTEN: He probably got them both on sale!

BUNKY: You even invited that woman to the family gatherings.

KITTEN: Quint asked me to…

(BUNKY slides KITTEN some rumpled office stationery, folded many times, lake a Japanese Origami toy.)

KITTEN: Ah. It's the Romeo and Juliet thing, the exhumed letter. (Opens the letter) Quint's gold family crest and an engraving Quint Leger, Inc., Suite 303, 2020 Causeway Blvd., New Orleans, LA… . Well, what does the man have to say? "I want to marry Tammy. For two years we've been seeing each other."

BUNKY: (cont.) I can't believe you didn't know.

KITTEN: Whenever Quint lies, he'll call you a sweet name first..

BUNKY: Didn't you sense Dad was bored?

KITTEN: No, I knew I was -- bored. Tammy's too cheap, too loud to be Quint's paramour. My God, she's only twenty-six!

BUNKY: No marriage is secretary-proof.

(BEAU looks at KITTEN. Her half-open mouth tries to emit some sound)

BUNKY: She's tacky, sleazy. Spits when she talks. "How wonderful. Spsh. Spectacular. Spsh." Dad takes her to Brennan's for breakfast. They discuss deals while touching knees under the table. I've never seen Dad so excited.

KITTEN: Your Dad wants a d-d-d-divorce…My skin is like paper. You touch me, I could rip.

BUNKY: Time to shed the skin. Get under the shower and wash it off—

KITTEN: For me, cooking is testing the cook's food. I can't empty a bag, wipe a dish. I'm p-p-p-part of the lost generation of wives. The marriage vow doesn't mean s-s-s-shit! War's over. Let's bandage our wounds, limp home, and pray for amnesia.

(SOUND of lightening striking)

KITTEN: *(cont.)* Jesus, forgive me. But I've got to live to tell Quint off. I'm not sending you to school in England. I'm evicting Quint from my home.

(KITTEN darts by the WARDEN and the HUNTER who pack supplies.)

BEAU: Can't you take us?

WARDEN: No room.

HUNTER: We'll send help.

(The WARDEN and HUNTER dive outside.)

SCENE SEVENTEEN:
THE BEDROOM AREA AT THE LODGE

(Lightning strikes. Darkness rushes about. BEAU plunges on a lantern. The walls turn eggplant colored, deepening to a seal brown.)

BEAU: I have only one regret: that we—

KITTEN: Don't.

BEAU: I wanted to—

KITTEN: *(Touches his shirt)* You've got a rip there. If only I'd the right needle.

BEAU: I heard from the Tenure Committee. They said (*Quotes from memory*) "Upon the recommendation of the Faculty of Letters, the Dean of Liberal Arts, and the Tenure Committee ... we regret to inform you ... you have been denied tenure at Tulane University. Your contract with the university will terminate this academic year."

KITTEN: Tulane fired you? W-w-w-why didn't you tell us?

BEAU: I got the notice Friday.

KITTEN: We're appealing this.

BEAU: Committee complained that none of my students have careers in writing but none of the faculty have careers in writing. There are *no* careers in writing.

KITTEN: You must call your Chair back.

BEAU: She's got cell range to Alaska, but I'm not responding.

KITTEN: (*cont.*) Why?

BEAU: I'm leaving academia. Doing it for all the 40-year-olds who didn't have the courage to break free, who shrank into mice, scurrying around, trying to make life work for their spoiled colleagues and chair.

KITTEN: But it'll go on your record permanently. You can't go back!

BEAU: Rejection doesn't mean a thing to me. Rejection means I'm going to dig in more. I'll tell everyone as I become famous how that bitch reviled literature and poetry. It's good to do things quickly rather than wrong.

(*A bolt spears the camp. KITTEN falls against BEAU. RAVEN and BUNKY enter*)

(*SOUND of something beneath them ramming the floor. Loud SQUEAKS*)

KITTEN: Are those rats!

BEAU: I should have brought O.C., My orange cat. I never got around to naming her.

KITTEN: I don't want to drown. What do the romantics say about death?

BEAU: Tennyson was hopeful:
    "Death closes all; but something ere the end,
    Some work of noble note, may yet be done—"

BUNKY: I'm scared.

RAVEN: Being scared ain't nothing'. Many scared souls save others. Pray.

BEAU: I've never been religious and I'm not going to start.

RAVEN: On the field, soldiers cries "God! Help me. Save me brother."
You've got to be willing to move on—

KITTEN: When time's up.

RAVEN: Say hello to Jesus.

BEAU: I want to apologize. To you, Raven...to Bunky, to ...I need some...

KITTEN: God to hold onto.

(The following lines are rushed and overlap. The characters look at the violent sky where the storm is brewing.)

SOUND of the building shifting and water rushing about.

KITTEN: The sky is coffin green.

RAVEN: Does that mean we in the eye of the storm.

BUNKY: Smells like wet leaves–

RAVEN: The insides of–

RAVEN: Of leaves.

(KITTEN scared turns to BUNKY. RAVEN raises hand in prayer.)

KITTEN: *(To BUNKY)* Say your act of contrition… "Oh my God, I'm heartily–

RAVEN: Quote. Go on.

(BEAU recites to himself.)

BEAU: Keats says, "She dwells with Beauty–Beauty that must die–
And Joy, whose hand is ever at his lips–"

BUNKY AND KITTEN: "Sorry for having...offended thee. And I detest
all my sins because–I dread the loss of heaven and the pains of hell"

BEAU: "Bidding adieu–And aching Pleasure nigh–"

RAVEN: Yes, Lord!

BUNKY AND KITTEN: "But most of all because I've offended thee, my
God––Who are all good and deserving of all my love–"

BEAU: "Ay, in the very temple of Delight– Veiled Melancholy has her
sovran shrine."

RAVEN: Amen.

BUNKY AND KITTEN: "I firmly resolve with the help of thy grace–
To sin no more– And to avoid the near occasions of sin "

(SILENCE. MOMENT OF PEACE.)

BEAU: *(At the window)* What's going on. The sky has lightened to yellow
blue … a verdant sky with its own prodigal gold. A blue moon has drifted
out. The swamp seems still.

SCENE EIGHTEEN: OUTSIDE THE LODGE

(NOISE of men approaching.)

LOUD SPEAKER: *(V.O.)* State police for Bunky Leger.

*(CAPTAIN GATEMOUTH enters. HE is a mottled giant in a ripped T-shirt,
shouts)*

CAPTAIN: Bunky Leger.

BUNKY: Yes.

CAPTAIN: You others from that train?

ALL: Yes.

CAPTAIN: Conductor waved our boat down outside. Got orders to take you to the Mississippi sheriff. Picked up a blind sheepdog a ways back.

BUNKY: The dog's mine.

BEAU: You the state police?

CAPTAIN: I'm an Iranian catastrophe specialist and—

(An INDIAN with rattlesnake boots, and a woman's sexual parts tattooed on his biceps bounds inside.)

CAPTAIN: This here is Cochise--a recovering heroin addict. He can find anything or anyone in the swamp. State police contacted your folks. Your daughter advanced us money to go out--Don't worry. We'll get through anything. More guns on this baby than a battleship.

INDIAN: *(Speaks into a phone)* Yeah, we got them.

(INDIAN EXITS. BEAU takes the phone.)

BEAU: Hello? *(Stammers)* Marcelle! God ...where are you? They found us ... Thank God. *(Holds phone out)* You did what!!! You charged ten thou-sand dollars to Elsa's Visa! *(Back into the phone)* Yes. I'm okay. *(BEAU flashes BUNKY a smile.)* You want to talk to my daughter?

(BUNKY sleeks back his disheveled mane and takes the phone. A noise blares out from the CAPTAIN's phone.)

CAPTAIN: Hold on; we got news--

(Presses a speaker on his cell phone)

SPEAKER: (V.O) This just in. Katrina's supposed to bypass the Pearl River Swamp and strike New Orleans tomorrow … We have the tip of Katrina on us now, but plenty of time to get out.

KITTEN: I think that entitles us to call ourselves–

BUNKY: Lucky.

RAVEN: No, blessed.

(BUNKY calls RAVEN over. THEY share the phone.)

BUNKY: (Into the phone) You hear anything about folks in Carencro? That's near Lafayette, where I've this friend, Raven… You're in Lafayette! Great… That's good to hear… We're all fine!

(BUNKY and RAVEN start belting a blues song.)

(THEY waft their arms and slap each other's palms. BEAU looks out.)

BEAU: The sky has lightened to deep opal blue, a restful color tinged with starlight.

CAPTAIN: (To BUNKY and RAVEN) Boat's out a ways. We'll take you two first.

(The CAPTAIN, BUNKY, AND RAVEN exit.)

SCENE NINETEEN: THE DOORWAY

(BEAU and KITTEN stand in the doorway, their faces luminous.)

BEAU: The Bayou seems a radiant place, glossy leaves, marsh phosphorescent like Mother-of-Pearl. No, a pale, purple gray of high brilliance…I don't want to act rhapsodic, but I thought this trip was our swan song. Yeats says, "The hour; when the swan must fix his eye, Upon a fading gleam—"

BEAU AND KITTEN: "Float out upon a long, Last reach of glittering stream, And there sing his last song."

BEAU: Going to write a poetic novel set in the Pearl River Swamp...
Marry a damsel in distress. *(Turns to KITTEN)*

KITTEN: I've no time for a new relationship.

BEAU: I don't date the woman I love. I marry them.

KITTEN: I don't have the energy to conquer you, to turn on my imagination.

BEAU: You could be mysterious at the beginning and at the end.

KITTEN: Let's keep things dangerous and wrong–

BEAU: How about a ceremony at Saint Alfonsus Church?

KITTEN: That awful area.

BEAU: We could be alone. With only those friends who dared to come.

KITTEN: I don't want to go back to being subjugated or become–

BEAU: "A being breathing thoughtful breath."

KITTEN: To keep a man—

BEAU: We'll party at the Country Club.

KITTEN: --Women have to be mean.

BEAU: We'll lead a cakewalk to the streetcar, have a six-foot Doberge cake?
Twelve layers chocolate, twelve Angel food–for all blended families. Let's
celebrate what's good at the start...

KITTEN: "O Wind, If Winter comes, can Spring be far behind." Shelley.

BEAU: Better yet:
    "The sun just touched the morning;
    The morning, happy thing,
    Supposed that he had come to dwell,
    And life would be all spring." By Emily Dickinson.

Now there's a quote to begin a life with.

(BEAU cradles KITTEN's face. Impatience creeps into his kiss.)

SOUND of BUNKY and RAVEN singing a Louisiana Blues refrain in the distance.

CURTAIN

PHOTOS: CHRISTIAN RABY, PARIS

PICTURED: MICHAEL SIMPSON, LINDA DILEO

GHOSTLY COMEDIES

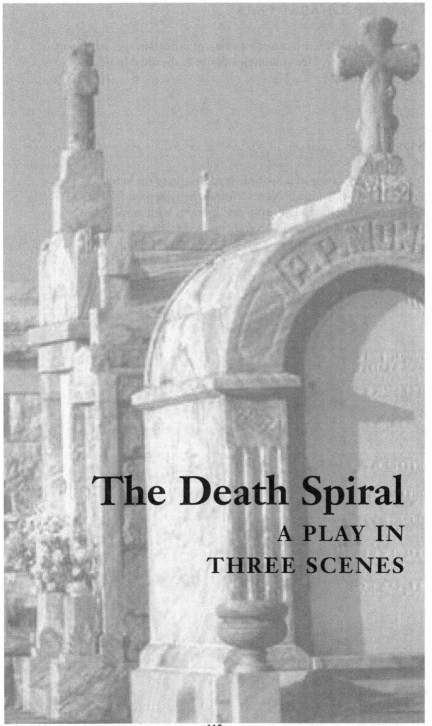

The Death Spiral

A PLAY IN
THREE SCENES

Cast of Characters

CLAUDIA, a beautiful woman of uncertain age, with long shiny hair. Her voluptuous figure is sheathed in moon-beam silk.

Setting

The interior of a Spanish-type mortuary on Veterans Highway outside New Orleans, the type with fake brick, too much wrought iron, and lanterns with amber glass or possibly glass in several colors. Tackiness is felt in the details: an overdone sign-in table, metal folding chairs, a pressed wood end table with Kleenex and plastic roses, and a coffin. (*The coffin may be placed in the audience.*)

SCENE 1

(A forbidding July night. It is raining; claps of thunder rumble the cheap building. Outside, the highway is full of sinister noises, gusts of wind, the slush of water, car brakes, muffled screams. The interior of the room is in complete darkness except for the vigil lights on the sign-in table. Candles flicker in their ruby glass cups. CLAUDIA appears, framed in the doorway. A wispy chiffon scarf floats free in the breeze, which blows from behind her. CLAUDIA points to her gown.)

CLAUDIA: What's this? The latest in shrouds. *(Turns around, shows her half-covered back and bare feet)* No back. No shoes. I don't worry how I dress because people don't look at you long inside a casket in New Orleans. This is the city that care forgot!

(LIGHTS: CLAUDIA flicks on a light.)

There's a young man laid out in parlor B, who won't say a thing. Those moody people from the Ninth Ward. I've to accept I've more education than he has. We're not going to speak. He'll never be from uptown. Why couldn't I have been buried from Bultman's—the mortuary on the avenue that's like a plantation? They know how to showcase a body. *(Somberly)* When I think of it pouring on my tombstone... my little patch of dirt.

(SOUND: A truck approaches, then passes.)

Trucks racing outside. A Taco Bell next door. I don't know anyone who uses a mortuary on Veterans Highway. *(Inspecting the parlor)* Tigerlily Kleenex boxes on every table, a blanket of plastic roses. *(Points to her casket)* And cheap lining, flamingo pink. *(Gingerly picks up the sign-in book)* Well, who do we have here? Death brings all the relatives out. *(Sadly)* Even in the rainy days of July.

(SOUND: Noises, hushed talking, and approaching footsteps.)

My family's at the door. They're sure enough late.

(SOUND: Muffled noises, talking, a harsh male laugh.)

My husband, Elliot. He smiled once or twice, and he was nice once or twice. If he gets any fatter, he'll lose his looks. They call him the walrus 'cause he flops about. Elliot was homeless once, for seven or eight months,

117

but it's okay now, he drives a Mercedes. He's got that jaundiced eye, from listening to the funeral director tally up the expenses. It was an extensive makeover. The man's got money, but he's not used to giving it to a mortician. *(To ELLIOT)* Come here, my hubby. Up close, you can see my eyelid wrinkle. My hair's still growing. Death's so messy. *(To MARGUERITE)* There's my little girl, Marguerite. Behind her daddy. That haircut looks awful. Marguerite. Never show those ears. *(Sadly)* Remember when I plaited your hair in ten thousand itty-itty braids, and I left it like that for the whole summer. Stay back. Better not see me up close. You've got my pictures. All those Christmases and Easters when I looked so pretty. Elliot, take her away.

(SOUND: The startled soft cry of a child, which intensifies as CLAUDIA speaks.)

Stop the sniveling, Marguerite. We need gentlemen and ladies, even at the mortuary. Pretend graciousness. You'll always be missing something, Marguerite. A mother who's weak is no role model for a daughter. I'm just a little stone in the river that you pass to move on. Look, I want you to stand over there by the wall. Think pleasant thoughts. I'm experienced in dealing with grief. That's my strongest point. Life's going to sling disappointments at you. So if you start out sad, you're already in trouble. Stay back. We mothers have got to go one by one. Perfectly normal procedure. God can't kill everybody at once. It's too expensive.

(SOUND: Whirl of cars passing. Heavy rain. A little girl shrieks.)

(CLAUDIA raises her hand as if admitting a secret to quiet the child.)

Your father said I fell off the roof of that six-floor building. But I didn't. *(Pause)* I was pushed. However, fair's fair. I provoked him first. Never touch a man in anger, sugar. They always hit back. Hard. It's not their fault, really. It's a testosterone thing. Can't have the little woman shoving them around. *(Pause)* I dove like a winged chariot. No back up. No props. Someone carted my remains over here. The soul is left to linger after a violent death. Spirits don't come and carry you aloft.

(SOUND: Bolt of lightning. Crash of thunder.)

(MARGUERITE howls.)

(LIGHTS: Lights rattle off and on.)

118

ROSARY HARTEL O'NEILL

Stop crying, Marguerite! I don't want to live again. Marriage is a curse. It both lifts you up, and gives men a vantage to shoot you down. Once you make marriage everything, you have the smell of desperation.

(SOUND: Mozart's Requiem *is played.)*

(CLAUDIA laughs hoarsely, running her fingers wildly through her hair, enjoying the music and moonlight.)

How lovely. I've such energy under the moon. Daddy told me he was faithful, again and again until I believed him. Before I go to Hell, I've one chance to avenge him. To have someone's name is to have some control over his soul. So, I'll roam around. Then, on an ugly night when Dad's got his hands on some pretty young thing, I'll violate his fantasies, clutch his throat with my cold, withered hands and scare the life from him. *(With a nervous chuckle)* That's something we ghosts can do. *(Pause)* Rain's stopped. Time to slip inside my mahogany box. Close the lid. Waiting's a tedious job, but I'll be back.

SCENE 2

It's ten years later, in the not too distant present.

CLAUDIA puts on a glamorous Louis XV silver wig, silken gloves and jacket walks up to the Orleans Club, a sumptuous 1868 mansion. It serves as headquarters to a ladies' social club and hosts many elegant teas and wedding receptions in New Orleans. SHE looks about fretfully, fearing to go inside and speaks to the audience.

CLAUDIA: Where am I? Can you throw the address at me again. I think I can remember but who needs the unknown right?

(Picks up a brochure)

Nice to go to a wedding in a 70115 zip code.

(Reads) Surrounded by lovely gardens and patios… you'll enjoy the finest silver, crystal, linens, and freshly-made gourmet delicacies at the …Orleans *(pronounced aw-lay-on)* Club.

The Orleans Club. Is Elliot still using my membership? In a women's club?

(Sees people coming, moves as if chatting ladies are coming past her. Screams out to ladies)

I'm dead y'all! I can't eat your smoked salmon. Your wild mushroom tarts.

(Ironic) No my husband wasn't being abusive. He tried to keep me on the roof. He's a praying man. HA.

(Pushing gossips off) Y'all get back now. Or, I'll send a wind before me.

I intend to come in. Though I'm not invited. Why am I here?? They need a new body to bury in the cemetery where I live. I'm coming to get one.

(SOUND: car breaks screeching)

(Calls offstage) Go away.

It took 10 years for that hearse to get here, it can wait a bit.

I'm not going back till I have to... That cemetery is a house of pain over there...All of that death around. So much unconsciousness... Death affirms death.

And the fluttering sweet peas and daffodils are of no help. Who says flowers are a little lifeline. ...Lifeline to what?

Still in the cemetery, I had this epiphany. My husband is a person. He has feelings, too.

(Takes out a recorder and plays it)

... I'll play Bach's *Fugue in G minor* written before he violated the chambermaid in Church. Toughen up before I have to--.

Oh. They let you keep one object from earth. And make 2 visits back.
(Looks about sadly) Nothing's changed. . .much.

I'll step inside.

(Delighted) My memory has come back. I'm me in a place of acquaintances.

— The pastor? Town gossips, wanna be's, would have and could never have beens!

Elliot's dull relatives.

(SOUND: gonging offstage.)

What's that bell?

(Looks at empty wrist) I've no sense of time. I'm still trying to start today.

(Looks up) Ah, the old grandfather's clock.

It's 6:30 on this lovely almost-autumn evening. God, I remember! I only have five minutes the first visit back.

(Feeling sad) I need different music, jazz... something in B flat minor--to energize me.

(Turns on celebratory music, like something from Wynton Marsalis)

(Peering in the hallway) The room is so big an eagle could fly around in it. I *forgot.*

There is a kind of *Crie du Coeur* inside now. . . . Despite the flowering vines, reception chairs with tulle, floral swags.

(Understanding) Everything for the wedding looks over the top gorgeous. If a bit too Chinese prairie.

(Spots ELLIOT)

Ah, Elliot, there you are. Oh, no. Are you still doing introductions? I didn't come in late enough?

(Nervous blustering) My. You're heading the reception line. . . Any further front you'd block the door...

It's been like a decade and a blip. Beautiful how we went off our separate spheres and crossed tracts back.

(Seeing ELLIOT) He's still socializing, prioritizing the money people in the room.

(Looks forlornly at an appetizer)

They've got my favorite *hors d'oeuvres.* . . .

Crab Cakes and *pate de fois gras* *(pronounced* pa-tay de foi-ah grah)

--Baked Brie in Puff Pastry...and Mint Juleps.

(Laughs adjusting her wig and gloves)

Ah, you've turned this way. Can you see my face? You're the husband I really count, because I was really married to you and had a child by you.

You're so adorable. But . . .you . . .don't recognize me. It's the *Louis Seize* *(pronounced loui says)* wig.

My hair keeps growing. It softens my face and frames my mouth. Long nails turning green. There's no cosmetics like death.

Don't let me scare you. The odds of us getting together on earth are messy; that being said, it's been my preoccupation.

(Pause. SHE laughs uncontrollably)

I'm here to make something beautiful, to support you before they destroy you. It's YOUR time.

(Looks at clock) Oh, no; four minutes.

I know how fragile breathing can be. No need to push and expect miracles.

(Screams) Elliot... speak to me.
I assume you've lost your hearing. Or have I mastered the art of talking to myself.

No, I don't miss earth. I miss knowing who I am... That part of being mom I'll always lack, having my daughter around.

(Sees her daughter MARGUERITE in her wedding dress)

Marguerite. I think about my daughter, and she shows up.

What a gorgeous wedding dress. Did you go wedding dress shopping with your Dad...

(Suddenly sad) I'm not sure how to... get to... what I intend to say... given now what I want to say...

Sometime I go into the land of *non sequitur*... and I can't find my way back.

...I look for connection... for what the images are telling me... I don't want to... speak bad about...

(To self) The lousy jerk—

(Loud to audience) BAD ABOUT HIM... because it'll only mean worse treatment for me.

(Puts on music; something like Rachmaninoff Vocalise Op 34 no 18)

(To MARGUERITE) I got to hear some music. Calm down. Allow myself to run you through my mind, so I talk to you in the calmest way.

(Struggling to make contact)

I like your Crab Cakes with Roasted Bell Pepper Sauce, the baked artichoke--

Don't turn away, Marguerite.

(To MARGUERITE) You look so young, so blissful.

(Looks about; breathes in flowers)

Nothing makes a cool, sophisticated statement quite like white blooms in the hand of a bride.

Oh, honey. I hoped you were the kind of person that if I did something, you'd do it next.

I took piano, you took piano. We'd make our genes go out to the stars.

–But you've forgotten me.

(Picks up MARGUERITE'S wedding book)

Ah, your guest book? Tied with a ribboned sash. Marrying a doctor . . .are you?

(Looking about) That tall one over there.

Nothing wrong with having your goals high...

If you can get one doctor... he cheats on you, you can get another one.

Remember, if he beats you, he's going to do it till the day he doesn't.

Why did I say that? ... *(Correcting self)* In the afterlife we can read certain things but - -

No... I would encourage you to keep repeating what you want. It's all about fooling men. Coming round the back door.

— Start being friendly and let some of the other doctors be interested. As a protection play hard to get.

Be a person, not a pleaser...

(Looks at clock) My goodness. Three minutes.

Actually I'll tell you. In death, I've been married seven times.
I never wed anybody unless I lie in the tomb with him for two or three hours.

Separation doesn't work for dead Southern girls cause we want to be loved. But-- It's forbidden to fight in the presence of grave diggers. So we mostly get along.

-----I'll go to heaven soon if I can contain my aggravation.

(Growing excited) I've got a s-s-s-star waiting for me there.

But I have pride to overcome. Maybe I *did* cause your father to push me.

Look, I didn't cheat. Depressed people don't have affairs.

Don't look away, Marguerite...

(Turns pages of the guest book)

Oh, no, what's on the back of your wedding book?... You kept my songs.

--Have you sung them? ...They represent my aspirations·

(Blurting) I was slightly diminished by earth. Shamed by the place.... And--

(Joyfully) Composing is my absolute guilty pleasure.

(SHE hums a song.)

Say you feel my presence. . . .

Ah, she's gone off to coo with her friends. *(Looking down)* But what a beautiful book... And what's this... her poetry? Wow. I see she writes too... There is a bond.

(Sees ELLIOT walk over)

(Gonging of bell)

The bell again.
(Screams) Elliot... Sorry, but I'm here to take you... to that other place.

They're busy till morning.
----Morning isn't that far.

I know you are a driver, Elliot. You like to be on the future arm of things. So part of my penance is to warn you.

(Looks at clock) Two minutes.

Your illness won't come immediately. It'll come late tonight . . .as if it . . had been there from the beginning.

You know that pain in your hip? Before it was just another thing. Now it's got teeth.

How long do you have? It'll be the perfect length when it's finished.

I'll see you a second time. Panic not; this is an updating, not a blitzing?

Oh, Elliot. Stop emoting. You do hear me; come outside with me!

--Don't turn yourself into a weeping man if that's not what you are.

--I hate doing this. It raises many questions about which I've no answers. How many talks do we have to not… face the end? Everything will be clear eventually or not.

What's my motivation coming here? Vanity.

(Picks up an hors d'oeuvre. *Laughs.)*

Seduction on a balmy day with spinach dip? Don't make me… laugh… Laughter's like popcorn. It just keeps bursting.

You're a reminder of who I used to be, and I need to close that door. I'm growing as a person in that cemetery. I may not have many friends there.

But I'm growing. The validity of what I'm doing just waiting comes as a surprise to me.

I'm trying to avoid self-deprecation

(Pause) There are times of grief. Sadness comes over me, but it passes.

(Looks at clock) One minute.
Sometimes I stage an exorcism so I can turn pain into something else.

I believe I've some feathers and Voodoo music here.

(Puts on feathers, plays taped music, and does a Voodoo Dance, moving about expressively with much theatrics.)

Voodoo dancing exorcises—

The knowledge of secret things.

You give up longing for the future,

finding lost people,

knowing complex things.

You ask the spirit for help

And it gives you power.

You speak in languages.

You've a strength,

beyond your sex and size.

Did you know—?

The dead can dance.

(SHE collapses, extravagantly breathing heavily, joyfully.)

Afterwards, being free in lovely weather, a gentle light carries me into darkness.

Takes my soul into Saturnalia so I weep for hours and then laugh twice as long… Good news, Elliot, is I've mostly forgiven you.

Enjoy your wrought-iron balcony, your oak-shaded courtyard, columned front porch and sit quietly, sazerac in hand till 6 am.
At this hour, when the moist air sits heavy on the streets, the hearse will come for your body.

The closer it gets, the less you'll recall.

You'll see images—smells, sounds, shapes of regrets, when you remember at all.

(*SHE turns up scary music, raises her arms, triumphant. Bell tolls and SHE disappears.*)

LIGHTS FADE

SCENE 3

Baptist Hospital, New Orleans. Another decade has passed.

(*CLAUDIA changes into a silken white robe. Ties her hair back with a satin ribbon. Speaks to the audience, distraught.*)

CLAUDIA: I hear the baby died. So what the heck. I called in my third visit.

I look like a bird with oil on my feathers.

If I don't freshen up, some screamer will see me! (*Confidentially*) People between life and death actually see ghosts.

(*Looks at a chart, nervous*)

Ah, the room records. They moved Marguerite to Critical Care… Oh no…

(*CLAUDIA raises her arms dramatically and calls out to the sky*)

Bah bah boo. Bam. (*To audience*) That's code for "Take me there."

(*SHE closes her eyes then looks up, delighted.*)

Marguerite's room. She's sleeping!
(*Horrified*) Lord! They should remove that bassinet. I'd do it but I'd have to create a wind blast.

(*Rings a bell. Waits by the bassinet. Rings again*)

(Intense whisper to heaven) Nurse!!

(Nurse screams O.S.)

--*(To audience)* She saw me!

CLAUDIA: *(Calling after Nurse)* Scream while you can.

(Picks up a baby blanket)

(To self) Lord, the blanket is still here—Such a pale blue.

(Whispers to heavens) From all of this, he is the only one who leaves.

I'll hum something. . . .Make sure his soul goes completely.

(SHE hums to self. Then turns on tape recorder with music to back her up. Sings something like "Who Will Buy this Wonderful Morning?")

(To MARGUERITE) Ah, you're awake? Marguerite? Can you see me. . . ·

(Spins around) It's always white long gowns, because an apparition is a dream.

Amazing how far your mother can go with a glamorous gown.

(Over enthusiastic) How're you doing? Rather poorly... News gets around.

(Awkwardly) ... Okay. We won't talk about you or *it* if you don't want to.

(Loudspeaker: "Visiting hours will end in 5 minutes".)

(To speaker, angry) They told me I had seven!

(To MARGUERITE) These past 10 years, I've been... busy, getting used to the mellow "after lifestyle." *(Awkwardly)* Life after life rejuvenates. Like plastic surgery. We don't age.

We eat and we don't get fat. Tomato aspic, oyster dressing, *dragees*—clumpy pralines.

I hang out with spirits who sit on a (*Avoiding word tomb*) who —sit on a tablature for one meal and talk about the next.

Weather is perfect there... Thunderstorms run across for five minutes, dump and move on. No claps desecrate the quiet of the--.

(*Looks at the bassinet. Rings a bell*)

Where are the nurses?

Let's see... I talk to your father, and the sadness of our marriage doesn't leave us blunted. On the contrary -- we get along.

In dea— (*Corrects*) life after life, it takes too much energy to be grouchy.

Then, too; I'm not forced to deal with bastards (*Corrects self*) living ex-husbands. I can hide in the cemetery. Only we're not going to talk mean about your father. Only if it's necessary.

(*Laughs*) Let's just say. It got so bad in the cemetery, he became the good guy.

(*Sarcastic*) When you're a ghost, you're forced to be elliptical and speak.

(*Picks up a baby rattle*)

(*To self*) A rattle... ? I'll just tuck it away.

...What else? We go shopping. At a place like Tiffany's we put on all the jewelry we want and take it off one at a time to see what works best.

Simplicity makes apparitions beautiful.

(*SHE steps on a bootie*)

(*To self*) A bootie?

(*To audience*) Don't they sweep in here?

(*To MARGUERITE, mad*) Junk all over. I'll toss this...

Where are the… aids?

Oh, yes… I've become a little purse whore. Here, I brought you one. We can buy them but we can't keep them.

My whole reason is to bring beauty to everyone.

Look… they've left you a tray of food. Cream of mushroom is quite pleasant on a warm night.

It helps you rest.

(Looks at the bassinet. Rings a bell)

You need to sleep as long as you can. …I could sing to you? I know the one you like--

(SHE puts on music something like "Hush little baby, don't say a word, Mama's going to buy you a mockingbird." When SHE gets to the word baby she changes it to "woman")"

(MARGUERITE sobs off stage.)

It's okay to cry. You had him for a week…

(To MARGUERITE) We are all hungry for hope.

(Loudspeaker: "Visiting hours end in 3 minutes".)

(To speaker) Shut up!!

(To Marguerite) Look, I know you don't want to listen to me-your *mother*…

It's counter intuitive, almost primal. I understand . . .

(Listens) The only affirmation you got from me was not being reprimanded?

(Pause) That's nice.

(Rueful) I don't want you to be like me.

But I yearn to connect with you... Show me a parent who never made a mistake, and I'll show you someone who did nothing. *(Calming herself)* Ah, there's crackers on your tray... Want one? ...One of the things that brought sweetness to my life and saved my marriage for a time... was appetizers.

(Loudspeaker: "All visitors prepare to leave..." Spsh. Static)

(To speaker) Somebody fix that.

(To MARGUERITE) I know you don't want to discuss *it*. But, I'm Taurus. I'm real stubborn.

You are a parent now, and you hurt! *(Sarcastic)* Surprise, surprise! --You hurt deep enough, you'll grow.

(Sadly) Your son was not meant for this world. His eyes moved but the rest of his body was paralyzed. He would never have had a normal life... Life has many little miracles. One of them is infant mortality. I don't mean to be harsh. Being a human being is more difficult than being a saint. Get crocodile skin. You raise children and give them to . . . their spouses or cruel fathers, who belittle you. I've been following your career. You are meant to be a great writer. To bring understanding to the world.

You can't be a poet with too many responsibilities and a lazy husband... Look, I'm sorry, but a child brings out conformity. You can't be a GREAT POET PART TIME. Soon as your writing perks, it's time for feeding. You can't say I'll get to it later.

You get tired enough in your day/night jobs, you'll take back any man. You forget he beat you, was an armchair general monster.

You become an accomplice to a... beast who is out to demean you every—

(Trips on something)

What's this?
(Reads a brochure) "Express Infant Caskets in blue or pink."

(To MARGUERITE) Your son is already in a state of bliss. His mission was to come to earth, smile, and leave.

God is happy with him. In heaven, the trees are happy too. The breeze…
He's enjoying the weather…

--I ran into him briefly in the cemetery… The only ghost I ever met who
cursed more than I did. I liked him right away.

(Finds another pamphlet)

(Reads) "Lined with soft fleece over pillow and mattress. Suitable for still
born--."

I'm putting this aside. *(Throws in trash can)* Order the first casket and be
done with it.

You have a great purpose: To bring healing through the songs you write.

Every bit of recovery is artists helping themselves and others… Shakespeare
buried his only son and wrote *Hamlet*. …Tennessee Williams institutional-
ized his only sister and wrote *Glass Menagerie*.

Write things that will help you and others grow.

(Loudspeaker: "Visiting hours end in 2 minutes.")

(To speaker) Heartless machine!

(CLAUDIA paces and steps on something)

(To self, looking down) A bib?

Oh, honey… Let everything that is cold and gone… leave… Inch your way
back to life. You wanted to be a mother. But you can't—… not possible…
Don't be felled by this.

Contradict the pain by writing… what you say you're not going to feel
while you're feeling it.

(CLAUDIA holds up the recorder and hums a song)

Sing with me:

"Amazing Grace. How Sweet the sound
That Saved a wretch like me.
I once was lost but now am found.
Was blind but now I see."

That's by an anonymous slave. People write songs because they embrace the feelings.

But the truth makes emotions almost irrelevant; it clears the air.

Will yourself—to sing your way back into life.
(To MARGUERITE, commanding) Release the boy and-- join the poets.
Loss is going to pull you to a bigger, bold thing.

(Loudspeaker: "Visiting hours end in 1 minute.")

(To speaker) Enough.

You may need to go deep into… this burial thing to see your way out the—

Afterwards will come words like. "Death once done there's no more dying now." You can alchemize pretty rough stuff into poetry.

I'd come to the funeral but this is my last visit to earth.

You want me to sing… Not… Greensleeves? You like the Lady Greensleeves!

(Sings upbeat version of 16th century ballad "Greensleeves.")

Alas, my dear you do me wrong,
To cast me off discourteously.
For I have loved you well and long,
Delighting in your company.

(Chorus)
Greensleeves was all my joy
Greensleeves was my delight,
Greensleeves was my heart of gold,
And who but my lady greensleeves.

(To MARGUERITE) You're one of the darlings of the earth.
You're eccentric in a nice delicious way-- very odd and lovely.

I suppose when I was alive you--were there. . . You were always there. . .
But I didn't know how to... *cherish* you.

Oh, darling... Touch your heart. It's beating and that's a wonderful thing.

Stay alive for me. And write.

You always gain something as you live. You gain a day.

Remember... Be the way you want to be — very dreamy

Don't worry... when you come to heaven, I'll track you down.

No other place blames and claims you... like the afterlife.

(Loudspeaker: "Visiting Hours are now over.")

(To speaker) Coming!

(To MARGUERITE)

You just write and you do it for a long time, sugar.

Leave behind something people can hold onto... after it's over.

Death is too easy. Stay on earth where you can live hard.

You never know where inspiration will come from.

You have to keep bicycling down the road, throwing flowers-

(CLAUDIA discovers a bouquet of roses)

My farewell bouquet. Rosebuds--so sweet.

Goodbye, earth and darling Marguerite... Don't cry!

The dead aren't sad. We sing and dance; performing takes the meanness out of people.

We make up happy tunes… we… can't hold on to ugliness… And we love lawns. And the rain and wind.

(CLAUDIA throws roses to audience. Then she opens an umbrella and dances.)

First thing I'm going to teach your son is the cakewalk and a few notes on the trumpet and how to dance with an umbrella in the rain!

(Puts on music and hums, something like Oh when the Saints Go Marching In.*)*

CURTAIN

GHOSTLY COMEDIES

MARILYN/GOD
A PLAY IN
ELEVEN SCENES

CHARACTERS

MARILYN MONROE - A movie star, 36. Dressed in a fluid cream colored silk gown slit to the thigh, sandal heels. She looks tattered.

VOICE and **AGENT** - Marilyn's Judges. Are offstage for the course of the play

SETTING

The action takes place in the mind of MARILYN on an empty stage with a chair.

TIME

Some time between 7:30 p.m. August 4 and 3:30 a.m. August 5, 1962, during MARILYN's final hours.

SCENE ONE

(SETTING: We're on an empty stage, in a space of limbo, during MARILYN's final hours. MARILYN responds to people SHE envisions. When voices answer, projected images appear on a scrim behind her.)

(AT RISE: MARILYN, age 36, in a creamy, silk gown is asleep on the floor. SHE awakes from a nightmare.)

(Fade-in sound of a phone ringing, incessantly blurring into a buzz...)

MARILYN: *(Terrified, calls out)* What's that? Who's here?
(Clanking of a metal door closing)
My eyes are swollen. I can't breathe.
(Snapping of a bolt lock)
Oh! *(Frustrated, humor)* Did I do myself in?
(Grating like a prisoner walking in ball and chains)
– Take too many pills? *(Jokingly:)* I tried suicide once; it didn't work.
(More heavy footsteps)
Hello! *(Baffled)* Where am I? New York? L.A.?
(SHE frets about this. Self-important.) My house is on a cul-de-sac! No one will find me.
(Swooshing sound of air shooting over the floor)
(Panicked) Who's that? *(Screams)* Somebody!

(We hear a labored breathing.)

(Forceful) I'm not finished. This isn't the end of me.
(Terrified) I'm shaking. Is it night sweats? Too many pills.
(Shrieks) Anybody here! Who's in my house.

(Behind her in the dimness we see Marilyn's house, 5 Helena Drive, on a small street, almost like an alley.)

SCENE TWO

(Lapse of time of only a few moments.)

OFFSTAGE VOICE: You're at the crossroads.

MARILYN: *(Reaching heavenward)* Someone's getting inside my body.

(Terrified) Who are you? Are you trapped too?

OFFSTAGE VOICE (AGENT): Your agent.

MARILYN: *(Angry)* You're not my – Johnny Hyde. I went to your funeral. An old man was in the casket.

OFFSTAGE VOICE: *(Voice echoes/fades)* I'm the voice he speaks through.

MARILYN: Johnny, come back! I'm barely breathing. Get a clinic to revive me. Private doctor. No publicity.

(Spreads her arms, rises)

Oh my god. *(Flabbergasted)* I'm floating over the scene, up 30 feet.

(Looks down, horrified)

I see myself lying on my side in a fetal position. It's quiet.

(A marquee appears projected on the scrim. Perhaps one with blinking lights.)

(Scared) There's a sign!

(SHE grabs her glasses, pushes them back on her nose. Reads the sign:)
"Heaven is a Hollywood set filmed by unseen cameras.
You must audition to get through those Golden Gates.
There will be signs along the way to instruct you."

(Removes her glasses, putting them aside)

What the – *(Throwing a tantrum)* Johnny! Where are you? I can't die now – and if I did, why would I audition for – ?

(Pushing on her glasses. Reads another sign)
"Complex lives need a final review.
You must bare your soul.
Not hide behind makeup, wigs, props."
(Rebellious) I'm not dying!
(Defiant) I'm studying Freud. Training with Lee. I'm still in shape!
I run, inspect my body for wrinkles, for age spots!

(Another marquee beams projected on the scrim.)

(SHE fumbles on her glasses. Reads the sign:)

"You can do a three minute scene from *The Misfits*. It's your last picture and you should know the lines."

(Disgusted, whipping off the glasses)

Do I have to? Where's my agent? Shouldn't he be the authority.

(Waits irritated. Shoves on the glasses. Reads:)

"He says *Misfits* was your best picture."

(Perturbed over the glasses) I've more to express than that role permitted. *(Reads)* "There was no porn in that picture and without a good clean audition, you'll go to hell."
(Self-important) What if I don't choose to die? *(Deathly pause)* Fine, I don't decide that. Okay. What are the rules?

(Reads annoyed) "You have 15 minutes to prepare while your agent finds a scene partner."

Look, I need a living audience to find me, to complete my form.
(Reads) "You may use the time to go over your scene or say goodbye to three people. Choose!"

(Throwing down the glasses) I don't know!

(Demanding) Why are you hiding behind all these signs?

(On the scrim, we see fleeting pictures of old actresses and movie stars.)

OFFSTAGE VOICE (AGENT): *(off)* Garbo retired at 36. Baby Jean Harlow, died at 26. You'll become a legend.

MARILYN: *(Imperious)* I can't die now. I know all about Baby Jean Harlow. She wouldn't leave home without looking at her "lucky mirror." Bill Powell – bought three crypts at Forest Lawn. For Harlow, her mom, and himself. *(Dismissive)* Harlow and Garbo were sex goddesses. *(Pause)* I'm more than that.

(Proud) I'm becoming a serious actress. I not only want to be good; I have to be. Acting is my way to grow and fix things.

I was an angry person before – the world around me was grim –

When acting, I can become my own mother. Make the world whole again. Speak like I'm not worried about anything. Sound like a real person talking. Characters are there. Always there. Permanently there. A script is my lifeline. If I wasn't an actress, I don't know what I'd call myself.
(Flabbergasted) Do you even know what I do onstage? I break down each scene into beats – that's Russian for "bits."

(Another marquee pops on.)

(Fumbles on her glasses. Reads:) "Choose what you'll do with your last 15 minutes."

(Throwing a tantrum) I'm thinking. Look, I don't like your proposal. *(Desperate)* Let me go back. I've got ten more good years – I'll weigh my actions with greater care. Keep my ways virtuous and simple.

OFFSTAGE VOICE (AGENT): You were never virtuous.

MARILYN: Right…You men made the conditions of my hire. I had to do awful things just to get an interview.
But I didn't marry you because I didn't love you. You were too old.
The real actress was me looking like I wanted YOU in bed.

OFFSTAGE VOICE (AGENT): Can the pity party. *(Pause)* I got them to put your lines on the wall.

MARILYN: *(Irritated)* I didn't say I'd use this fifteen minutes to work on my scene. I might want to go back.

OFFSTAGE VOICE (AGENT): Better fix up. Use a comb, rouge, lipstick.

MARILYN: *(Vicious)* You're an awful agent. Cold as a lizard and sly – .
Forced me to show off my girlhood!
Take pills and screw my head off and think I was a free spirit.
Put mirrors on my walls, and tables so I could scrutinize every angle.
(Pause) Be sure I had flawless skin, heavy lidded eyes, bright red lips.

(MARILYN pivots before full mirrors.)

Are all these mirrors part of the audition?
Look, I didn't say I wanted to use the time to prepare.
I'm thinking I want to go back.
(Mad) I don't believe one self lasts a lifetime.
I need to mature as an actor. I'm a businesswoman. I have my own company.
Still, standing by the mirror I greet "age:" tiny crow's feet, stretch marks,
(Lifts her hands) pale brown spots. My skin is pasty, my hair is fried.
(Clutches her chest) My breasts are flabby. Cut them off!
(Rips off her skirt to show her abdominal scar) I can't wear a bikini.
I'm like a bit of mercury. I press here and I squirt out there.
That gall bladder operation ruined my side.
I can't change my image!
(Riled) I know my hair's fried: my skin's pasty.
I was losing weight using amphetamines and cigarettes.

MARILYN: *(cont.)* *(Laughs, vexed)* I'd hoped to rally from this overdose and
wear sparkles to work!

(Collapses in frustration. Looks up slowly. SHE sees her deathbed.)

Oh no, down the hall, there's my housekeeper and the doctor. I know why
they're crying.

(Fade-in: a rushing SOUND like a tornado)

I'm a brain and eyes. I have no body. Here in space, I'm nothing but mind.

(Another marquee appears.)

(Pushes on her glasses. Reads:) THE MISFITS.
(Maddened) I didn't say I'd use these last minutes to prepare my scene.
I want to go back. Visit three people, while my scene partner is found.
(Exasperated) Am I definitely dying? Is there no hope?

OFFSTAGE Voice (TRAIN ANNOUNCER): There is always hope for
you, Marilyn, if people want you enough.

MARILYN: Who are you?? *(No one answers.)* All these voices! I'm so confused.

(Fade-in SOUND of siren and voices)

(Again SHE sees her deathbed.)

Oh no. I see the ambulance coming and people trying to get me out of bed. *(Urgent, provoked)* Can't they pump my stomach?

(Fade-in: SOUND of slow heartbeat)

OFFSTAGE Voice (TRAIN ANNOUNCER): During the last 15 minutes, the power of love could DRAW YOU BACK. If not, you'll have to audition cold. They'll be no rehearsals, no preparation.

(Fade-out SOUND of heartbeat)

MARILYN: *(A long cry)* Joe!

(Lights shift)

SCENE THREE

(Lapse of time of only a few moments.)

(Fade-in SOUND of a man breathing)

MARILYN: *(cont.)* Joe. Where are you? *(Blinks her eyes, anxious)* I blink. You appear there. *(Blinks again)* and there. *(Startled)* I can think you anywhere. *(Ecstatic)* You're my white knight. Stardust created many times over.

Every time I look at you – I see the sun, power, thrills.
My eyelashes go up and down and little stars come out of me.
Oh, Joe. You haven't heard from me for a few days…because
I'm here with all these ghosts!
I'm sure to end up dead if I do what they say.

(Fade-in SOUND of a ticking clock)

Call me back into my body. I went out through some opening.
(Demanding) Find a doctor. Pump my stomach.
I know life has to be savored. Enjoyed fully.

(Proudly) I want to return to play Chekhov, Ibsen, Somerset Maugham.

(We hear the SOUNDS of a couple shouting at each other and a man yelling.)

(Uptight) Don't you like that?
(Looks down, alarmed. Again SHE sees her deathbed.)
I see my body and the emergency crew.
They're shooting me with something, putting a paddle to my chest.
(Panicked) A stern doctor, nurse and strangers stand by.

(MARILYN is losing hold on reality. Her body is starting to disconnect.)

MARILYN: *(cont.)* Somehow I can't reach you. I'm underwater.
I talk, but you can't hear me...Joe!!
(SHE begins to shake.) Oh no, I'm going into your body.
I see and hear with your eyes and ears.
(Anguished) I can't cope with the–
I hurt you when I acted, but you wanted to love me.
I feel your warmth trying to help me be a GOOD WIFE.

(SHE comes out of his body.)

(Spooked) Your kindness scared me, so I couldn't accept it.
...My shrink says I'm too male in my ambition.
Forgive me.

(Guilt-stricken) In reality, I'm one window in your house. You've a lot of
other windows.

(Fade-in SOUND of lapping waves)

(Confused) Oops, I'm outside my body again.
Who am I if I can go in and out of Joe's mind? Then pop back inside
myself.

(Sees her deathbed)

(Keyed up) I know I'm in trouble.
The nurse looks scared. The doctor's left. I'm alone down there.

OFFSTAGE VOICE (CORONER): We can't get a pulse! We've lost her. She's gone.

MARILYN: I'm outside my head. I can't move it from side to side. I've slipped totally off my body, like a glove.

(Light changes)

SCENE FOUR

(Lapse of time of only a few seconds. MARILYN looks up transfixed. On the scrim appear beautiful clouds and sky.)

MARILYN: *(cont.)* Is that heaven? I took one peek at the sky, and everything sort of appeared. The golden gates look gracious. Having been raised near Paramount, I want to live amongst the buildings for a while.

(Fade-up of MUSIC)
Wonderful Music.

(A blinking marquee slides on.)
(SHE pushes on her glasses.)
(Reads) "You have had a glimpse of heaven.
– As we get closer to heaven, Music will increase."

OFFSTAGE VOICE (STAGE MANAGER): *(Off)* Ten minutes to your audition, Marilyn.

MARILYN: I want to see...Mama!

(MARILYN's arms lift like wings.)
Oops. I say something and I fly. I'm a fairy.
(Looks below, horrified) What are those dark buildings.
(Pause. Pushes down her fear) "Norwalk State Institution."
(Shocked) I fly through a door.
(Sniffs) What's this smell? Lysol?
(Gags) Don't they air the room? Change the sheets? *(To self)* Leave!
(Looks up, terrified) Mommie!
(Pause, grief-struck) It's Norma Je–, Je–, ane... Make a sound if you know I'm here.

ROSARY HARTEL O'NEILL

(Hears gasping SOUND. Moves closer to hug her mother, stops shocked.)

I can't kiss your face. My lips are only images.
(SOUND of a loudspeaker: "Visiting hours end in five minutes.")

MARILYN: *(cont.)* This is the last time I'll see you alive.

We can't live off my beauty, anymore. It can't feed us pure oxygen.

(SOUND of footsteps and door opening)

No. I can't change your bedpan or wash you!

(Buzzing sound)

Don't call the nurse. I repeat. Everything in my body is leaving. –
Without me there'll be no one to pay for –
Don't ring that bell. I'm going to have to put you to sleep and take you
with me.

(SOUNDS of distributing trays)

I can't feed you. Change your –

(Loudspeaker, "Visiting hours will end in three minutes.")

OFFSTAGE VOICE: *(AGENT)* Sell Mom on death.

MARILYN: You weren't the mom I wanted.
I wanted a mom who WONDERED me!
– who said sweet things and bought me pale pink underwear.
A mom whose reason for living was to bring beauty to ME.
Who touched my hand and felt my whole being.
Do you know what it is like to always be wanting your mother. MOM!
Give me back my SOMETHING *(Words slur)* I DON'T KNOW WHAT
YOU TOOK FROM ME BUT I WANT IT BACK.

(We move into Marilyn's fantasy.)

(MARILYN mixes a pill of poison in her mother's water.)

MARILYN: *(cont.) (To her mother:)* I'm going to put something in your drink to bring you along. Swallow it!

(Loudspeaker, "Visiting hours are over.")

OFFSTAGE Voice (MOM): MY BABY GIRL …

MARILYN: *(To her mother:)* DON'T SWALLOW THAT!

OFFSTAGE VOICE (MOM): *(Echo-like)* BA-BY …

MARILYN: *(To agent)* I can't kill her even though she DEFILED me.

(SOUND of a ticking clock)

(Panicked) MOM'S vanished…Am I saved?
I don't want to go back to dying!
(Fanning her cheeks, frustrated) I'm hot.
Am I in Hell? My thermostat is totally broken. I'm never at peace.

(Lghts shift)

(SOUND of a gurney clanking)

SCENE FIVE

(No lapse of time. SHE looks up, horrified, at a vision of her corpse.)

MARILYN: *(cont.)* Who's on that gurney? I can see through the sheet. That's me. Don't take me to the MORGUE. Some people DO come back from the dead!

OFFSTAGE VOICE (AGENT): Call Arthur.

MARILYN: *(Nervous)* I can't talk to him. It's not what I say it's WHO he is. He was the first artist/genius who RAISED ME UP!
I cheated and Arthur took me back every week for five years. Bobby and Jack Kennedy, Peter Lawford, Richard Burton, Elia Kazan, Marlon Brando, Yves Montand…
Can none of my lovers help me?

OFFSTAGE VOICE (AGENT): *(Echo-like)* A-r-t-h-u-r!

MARILYN: Glimmers of stability…

OFFSTAGE VOICE (AGENT): *(Echo-like)* A-r-t-h-u-r!

MARILYN: Even they went over time.

(SOUND of tolling bells)

What's that sound?

(Lights shift)

SCENE SIX

(Lapse of a few moments. MARILYN sees in front of her a study, a bedroom, but can't hold on to the image.)

(SHE is losing her grounding in reality.)

(A swooshing sound)

MARILYN: *(With dread)* Arthur's somewhere room –
(Perturbed, walks closer) My god. He's thinner than I recall. Life whittled him away.

(SOUND of a man snoring. It's Arthur.)

(To Arthur:) It's Marilyn. I'm dying, honey, but I can't let go of my yearning and attachment to you.
(SOUND of a man breathing)
You're fast asleep. I can't touch you.
I seem to be in some body, although it's not physical.
I have arms and a shape like a cloud of colors.
Wake up. Bring me back or help me die. I want to pass peacefully.
(SOUND of rain)
Another bad rain. *(Fearfully)* I'll decompose faster.
Oh, Arthur. You are the last one who can help me. I want to act again.
I'm greedy to make art!

(Jokes, self-important) I also want to be blown up on the big screen so I'll never be ignored.
It'll be dawn soon. Light vanishes me. I can't be judged now.
(Rain falls)
Awful rain! I didn't take the time to close off the angers.
I followed the mirror.
(Holds up a mirror) And now I can't see myself in it.
I wasn't afraid of death because I wasn't thinking of it.
Arthur! Don't get up. Light disappears me!

(Alarm keeps droning)

I've begun looking at the most important things in my life.
The biggest problem for us was me.

(Rain falls harder)

(To agent) I'm dissolving, Johnny.

Oh, Arthur. My life was filled with distractions, then I just became older, and there's nothing to show my real talent.

(Phone rings)

Don't get that. *(Angry)* Death was very much alive in you, Arthur. You lived the rising in the rising. Saw everything as it is.
I was like a peacock. So ashamed when someone pulled my feathers, I hid myself. Don't let me die tortured. Tell me what to do!
(Baffled) In case I have to pass.
Your lips are moving, but I can't hear you.
Maybe it's the rain. Maybe I'm deaf.
What's that you say? "Read poetry." Try harder. Talk louder.

OFFSTAGE Voice (ARTHUR): *(Echoes)* Poetry helps face the grave.

(Lights flash on a tiny golden poetry book. SHE grasps it but it falls.)

MARILYN: I can't hold the book.

(SOUND of a ticking clock)

Arthur, you're disappearing! Don't go!

(Picks up the poetry book)

Oh, now I can pick the book up.
(Astonished) Sometimes my hands work. Sometimes they don't.

(SHE skims through the book.)

(On the scrim we see the words in red.)

(SHE shoves on her glasses, reads.)

MARILYN: *(cont.)*
> "My Captain does not answer,
>   his lips are pale and still,
> My father does not feel my arm,
>   he has no pulse nor will."

I suppose Whitman is my favorite poet. But how can he help me?
(Scrutinizes a margin) What's this note in Arthur's hand?

(Projected on the scrim, we see a scribble.)

(Reads, flabbergasted) "Marilyn has no acting talent. How could she have fooled me?"

(Throws book down)

(SHE goes to a window.)

(Cowers) Is that street construction? I can't see through the rain gusts.

(SHE sees her corpse.)

(Horrified) No. That's me. I can see through the casket lid.
They're taking my body to the Hall of Memories! Crypt 24.
My god, I've died.

(SHE collapses on a chair. Looks up, staggered.)

(Baiting) Is there no sign now? I was a Christian Scientist then a good Jew.

(Imperious) Can't you get a rabbi to pray over--
Is there no assistance?

(MARILYN glances about. Spies the golden book, anxiously opens it.)

(Behind her, on the scrim, we see projected words as SHE bobbles on her glasses. Reads.)

MARILYN: *(cont.)* Emily Dickinson said:
> "Because I could not stop for Death,
> He kindly stopped for me;
> The carriage held but just ourselves
> And immortality."
> *(Pause, holding back tears)*

> "We slowly drove, he knew no haste,
> And I had put away
> My labor, and my leisure too,
> For his civility."

(Pause, forces herself on)

> "We passed the school, where children strove
> At recess, in the ring:
> We passed the fields of gazing grain,
> We passed the setting sun."

Light changes

SCENE SEVEN

(Lapse of a few moments. We see a gold-rimmed rising sun. We hear music of a soprano singing a cappella.)

MARILYN: *(cont.)* Lovely Music!
(Shoves on her glasses. Reads a sign:) "You are now officially dead.
– To get into Heaven, you must audition with a scene, a song, and an interview. If you pass the scene audition, you will proceed to the music audition and the interview."
(Yells) No more visits? Mercy!

(A streak of light.)

(Mystified) Whose arm is that shooting out the sky, grabbing me?
Tubes of light run up his hands. *(Astonished)* It's CLARK GABLE!
Clark, darling! Everything you do is strange and exciting –

OFFSTAGE VOICE (GABLE): I'm your scene partner. The lines are on
that wall.

OFFSTAGE VOICE (GHOSTS AND WIND): Marilyn. Is that…
Marilyn! Monroe. Act for us!!

MARILYN: *(To ghosts)* Leave!
(To Clark, aggravated) I can't do *The Misfits*!!
Oh, Clark. I cried every day the month you died.
– That was the first time I realized you weren't God.
(Disgusted) You didn't die from… me!
You were drinking and smoking three packs a day!
Arthur's script was weak. Scenes ranged from bad to tolerable.
The words were – . I couldn't do them.
(Cries out) You were bound to get tired of waiting for me.
Women weren't meant to be hunters. We're not good at it.
And men who treat us like equals get confused.

MARILYN: *(cont.)* I tried. Up at midnight running lines.
Gulping Nembutal, even pricking the capsules for faster effect.
(Laughs, miffed) Was I getting even for the years Dad never showed up?
Oh no! You're fading *(Cries)* Stay! We could read from these –
(Searches through her poetry book)
I do better with fresh material!
(Looks up, glum) Clark's gone.

(A marquee appears.)

(Struggles with her glasses. Reads) "Your scene partner's left.
– From now on, you must audition alone."
(To self, sarcastic) Surprise. Surprise.

(Another marquee appears.)

(Annoyed, reads) "Why not read a poem? Try Auden."

(Fade-up light on book. SHE scans the poem.)

(MUSIC: Echoes of Children's Music Box Sounds)

(A marquee appears with the words, "Audition Scene: Read this Elegy." SHE reads, disgusted:)
"But for her it was her
Last afternoon as herself.
An afternoon of nurses and rumours…
The current of her feeling failed
she became her admirers."
(Throwing aside her glasses) I don't want to act out a death poem.
When I'm not thinking of death, I'm not afraid.
Can any poem express how sorry I feel. Ashamed that I've nothing to say!

SCENE EIGHT

(There is no lapse of time. Just the sound of wild applause.)

OFFSTAGE Voice (STANISLAVSKI): *(Russian accent)* I approve. You have passed the scene audition. You may proceed to your interview, Norma Jeane.

MARILYN: But I was – Who are you?

OFFSTAGE Voice (STANISLAVSKI): Stanislavski.

MARILYN: *(Breathless)* You're not…the great Russian master!!!
(Falls on her knees) Then I'll respectfully correct you.
I'm Marilyn Monroe. I use my mom's maiden name.
(Looks about) Appear, please! I need to stare into your soul.
(Spots him, gasps) Mr. Stanislavski! Waive my audition.
I followed your rules. Kept a Russian coach. Used emotional recall.
God knows how many times I killed Maf, my dog.
I was always your devotee. Hiding with my script to score my lines.
Studying your books because all the dumb models died tragically and unknown.

Maybe if I hadn't read them, I wouldn't feel so…so stupid.
Actors rehearsed for years in Moscow – They didn't do interviews!

OFFSTAGE VOICE (AGENT): Ordinary English baffles Stanislavski.
He's gone.

MARILYN: No. *(Calls out, anxious)* Mr. Stanislavski!
(SHE paces as a metronome clicks.)
Where are the dead poets? Appear, cowards!
I'm losing everything, my house, my relationships, my body, my mind.
(A marquee lights up on the screen.)

(SHE puts on her glasses uncertainly.)

MARILYN: *(cont.)* *(Reads)* "We don't have to show up; we're God. You are
officially dead."
(Revolted, SHE reads on.) "And, death once dead, there's no more dying
then."
(Fed up) How can I feel so alive and be so dead?

(Another marquee appears.)

An obituary? "August 4, 1962: Marilyn Monroe found dead with an empty
bottle of barbiturates.
– Her fame as a sex goddess outshone her acting talent."
I can't be remembered like –

OFFSTAGE VOICE (AGENT): Pass into a higher plane –

MARILYN: I can scarcely think of my career without weeping.

OFFSTAGE VOICE (AGENT): And you'll be rediscovered on earth.
(Sound of street noise fades into dreamy violin Music, Ravel, Daphnis et Chloe.)

SCENE NINE

(Lapse of a few seconds. SHE looks up fumbles on her glasses, frustrated.)

MARILYN: *(cont.)* "Part two: the music audition. You have fifteen minutes."

(SOUND of heavy piano Music intrudes)

"You will be given 2 songs and one dance piece. We are looking for actors

that move. – First song is 'Happy Birthday!'"
(To self) Oh yes, they do that at Lee's Studio.

(SHE hums a Happy Birthday song. A siren goes off.)

Oh no! What's that screeching –
(SHE pushes glasses back on her nose. Reads sign:)
"You have insulted our President. You could go to hell. Pick another song."
But I knew him before. *(Hollers)* Turn that up!
I don't want to audition anymore.
(Lights flash on and off.)
I don't want to go further.
I'm moving toward some sort of audition at the end of the tunnel.

(Stage lights grow larger and larger.)

Turn down the lights. I can't see where my accompanist is.

(SOUND: Music explodes about her.)

MARILYN: *(cont.)* Look let me sing from something I know.

(Another alarm goes off.)

What the…is – that?

(Shoves on her glasses, exasperated.)

"You may pick your own song."
Thank God!

MARILYN: *(cont.) (Reads on)* "But you must do an interpretive dance with
your song, and the movement can have no relationship to the song."
You're tough! Fine. I'll move faster or slower than the Music.
You think I haven't hoop jumped before?

(SHE sings a few bars of a familiar tune. SOUND of heinous laughter.)

Don't laugh at me, jerks.
You judges hiding out in the black out there.
That number made me an icon in the U.S. of A.

OFFSTAGE VOICE (AGENT): That a girl. You tell them, baby!

(There is the SOUND of circles clicking black to white.)

MARILYN: Oh no. A small group of circles are ahead of me…
– making snapping sounds as they click white then black.
I can't see who is inside, but their voices are harsh.

(SOUND. jeers fade in and out)

What did you say? My talent never existed?
I was allowed to imagine it? It was all a joke.

(SOUND: Mocking laughter rising and falling)

How could I have made that up? This can't be eternity. Let me do my sig-
nature song.

(Lights dim)

Don't dim those lights and tell me damnation is waiting. Who the hell are
you! *(Peers out)* It's dark and immense all around, but I can do it. Give me
my song!

*(MARILYN sings again with more passion. This time there is huge applause!
Fireworks! Graffiti flowing down. Another marquee appears. SHE searches about
for her glasses and reads, exasperated.)*

MARILYN: *(cont.)* "The second part of your interview has been approved."
How could that be? I was panned. Insulted! By some …cowards…
(Pause) No. I didn't give up on myself. That's right.

(A blinking gold marquee appears.)

"A higher power intervened."
Who judged me?

(Flashing red, blue, gold, marquee)

"William Shakespeare!"
I didn't know he knew music.

He's even greater than Stanislavski!
– All these "S" men Stanislavski, Strasberg, Shakespeare believe in me!

(Bach's Keyboard Concerto No 3 in D major, *plays.)*

SCENE TEN

(Lapse of a few seconds. SHE looks up swan-like as a marquee flashes on.)

MARILYN: *(Slips on her glasses:)* "Part three: the interview. You have fifteen minutes for three questions."
"First Question! Why do you want to act? Prove you searched for love and knowledge."
The why question. Makes me want to crawl under the table!
(Scared, but strong) I act because I love beauty.
I want to give back. I come from love.
I view myself with each role a god with a small wand, inventing a universe.

OFFSTAGE VOICE (AGENT): 14 minutes!

MARILYN: A play is a wonderful little island for me.
The character comes with a story. I embrace her lines.
She takes hold and, I float, like a balloon…set free.
Acting is dreaming. It's my window to creation. It's everything I call god.

(A marquee blinks on.)
(SHE fumbles on her glasses.)

"Shouldn't you quote someone?"

(Over the glasses) I don't want to hide behind somebody.
That's dishonest. But, when I talk, cracks appear.

(Another marquee pops on.)

"Use Emily Dickinson. She felt like nobody, too."

(Lights up on the book. She opens it quickly.)

(Recites uneasily:)
"It's all I have to bring today –

This, and my heart beside –"

OFFSTAGE VOICE (AGENT): 13 minutes!

MARILYN: "This, and my heart,
and all the fields – "

(SOUND of fanfare: balloons popping, trumpets blaring, ribbons flapping.)

(A marquee flashes.)
"You've passed the first question. Meet your judges."
My, I'm rising like a silk scarf. Isn't it dreamy!
(Fade-in Music: Ravel's Daphnis et Chloé)
(Lights shift)

SCENE ELEVEN

(No lapse of time. Silver forms float through a mist.)

MARILYN: Who's there? Emily? Thirteen little angels. *(Plays peek a boo)* I see you. You can't be my judges.

OFFSTAGE VOICE (AGENT): 12 minutes left.

MARILYN: Come closer, angels. Your faces shine like diamonds.
(Rubs her stomach) I've lost 20 pounds!

(The SOUND of fluttering wings fills the stage.)

You want me to climb that spiral staircase?
I can't lift my feet.

(The room darkens. SHE turns about, freezing.)

(Shivers) Monsoon season! Where are the little angels?

OFFSTAGE VOICE (AGENT): 11 minutes.

(SOUND of squealing rats)

MARILYN: I never realized how alive death is.
(Shouts) You poets! Tell me what to do when the angels leave!
Some artists must – Are you trying to trick me?

OFFSTAGE VOICE (AGENT): You have 10 minutes.

MARILYN: *(Screams)* Come back, angels!

(SOUND of trolls hissing.)

There you are. Tell me, darlings.
What's that? You're my dead babies?
(More tattling sounds)

What?! You're the godhead. My judges.

(A marquee lights up.)

"Second question: "How many abortions did you have?"
You're tough…I had five procedures in seven years. I couldn't go to the
gym and punch the shit out of something.

MARILYN: *(cont.) (Loudly)* All this back and forth with the studio, and…
crude birth control. Primitive rubbers. Blood clots from IUD's. Pills that got
you bald, fat, or dead.

OFFSTAGE VOICE (AGENT): You have 9 minutes.
(Image of a doctor's office)

MARILYN: *(Sniffs)* Oh, no. I smell blood!
I'm back in time, watching studio doctors work on me. It's awful but…
I feel the way the baby and I felt when –
– I'm a ball of light screaming, no sound.
The studio sent roses, a silver platter with lunch, and a card.
"You only have the pressure of being beautiful, which you are."

OFFSTAGE VOICE (AGENT): 8 minutes to explain.

MARILYN: *(Angry)* The most advertised girl in the world can't be pregnant. When I got better the studio wrote, "Wear a hat at the beach or you'll
get freckles and look like a goose egg."

OFFSTAGE VOICE (AGENT): *(off)* 7 minutes.

MARILYN: *(Angry)* First time I did it, I'd a little dalliance with pills.
It wasn't a full-fledged affair.

Next time, I took a pill regularly and felt more human.
After the third…Norma Jeane wanted to kill Marilyn Monroe.

(Sees an ugly slew of baby photos. SHE pouts as pictures flash.)

Norma loved babies but – Marilyn forced herself to act from the place she'd
grown to. She knew that tiny spec wasn't real life.
She had to ride life. Let it ride her. Let go of the steering wheel.

MARILYN: *(cont.)* Marilyn saw when not fed, these movie moguls would
perch and wait for fresh meat. *(Screams)* "After the first death, there is no
other!" Who said that?

OFFSTAGE VOICE (AGENT): 6 minutes.

MARILYN: I lied. I had thirteen mistakes –
– I still ride on the horns of the death wish which says, "Kill it so you can act."

(A luminescence permeates everything.)
Explaining feels wonderful.
I'm racing toward a golden halo. A baby is inside it!

(MUSIC: Schubert's Ave Maria)

OFFSTAGE VOICE (AGENT): 5 minutes.

MARILYN: *(Waves)* Beauty boy. You're my best baby?

(A marquee shines on. SHE flounders on her glasses.)

"Third question. "Did you kill Arthur's baby?"
No. I was pregnant with Arthur three times and I carried one long enough
to know I had a son.
(To baby) I was ready for you, wonder boy.
My husband was a millionaire and a genius.
Your enormous spirit stirred inside me, gluing Arthur to me.

(Paces) But back-room abortions had busted my insides.
My blood pressure got higher, and the swelling went up here, through the behind. The more I tried to hold on, the more I finally lost.
Maybe I took too many pills. But I...didn't throw myself down the basement steps.
I slipped...on...And – after...the fall – they took your life to save mine.

AGENT: *(off)* 4 minutes.

MARILYN: Fans sent condolences. Arthur's baby.
Your death cut the threads between me and Arthur.

He divorced me and turned me into a drug addict in his next play. *(Looks up distraught)* My baby boy's gone.

(A marquee slides on.)

"The interview's over."

OFFSTAGE VOICE (AGENT): 3 minutes to curtain.

MARILYN: But I haven't JUSTIFIED MY ACTIONS. Validated my – Did I pass –

(A rainstorm of yellow light.)

I'm rising. Forgetting everything I aimed for or wished for or thought –

(SOUND of bell ringing.)

Golden gates look like Paramount! Don't close them!

OFFSTAGE VOICE (AGENT): 2 minutes to curtain.

MARILYN: Let me in – So many have come before – Beings, brighter and –

(SOUND of specters approaching)

GHOSTS: *(Whispering)* "We are the dead/short days ago/We lived, felt dawn, saw – " [John McCrae]

(MARILYN looks out at the sea of ghosts.)

MARILYN: *(Shouts to the ghosts)* Who's from California? Two or three million. We die young.

OFFSTAGE VOICE (AGENT): 1 minute to –

MARILYN: Let me stay! *(Kneels, begs)* I know I did all these bad things.

OFFSTAGE VOICE (AGENT): 30 seconds to –

MARILYN: I was in a delicious whirlwind of – Stardom!! We all have these dark ambitions!

OFFSTAGE VOICE (AGENT): *(Loud)* Places!

MARILYN: FORGIVE ME! *(Freezes in a beam of light)* DON'T IGNORE ME.

(As spotlight closes in on MARILYN's face)

(We hear an aria from Purcell's Dido and Aeneas, *Dido's Lament (*"When I am Laid in Earth...Remember me!"*)*

(As stage lights go out, MARILYN's image takes over the scrim.)

END OF PLAY

James Dean & The Devil

A PLAY IN FIVE SCENES

CAST OF CHARACTERS

JAMES DEAN. A movie star. HE looks 34, not 24. The T-shirt, red jacket, jeans on his muscular body are torn and distressed.

SETTING

"The Highway of Death", Cholame. CA. Sundown, chilly.
A shoulder along the road. September 30, 1955. We are in the mind of James Dean during his last moments on earth. Visuals and sounds or the lack thereof saturate the stage like a stark dream.

SCENE 1
HELP ON THE HIGHWAY OF DEATH OR
MEETING MOTHER

At Rise: JAMES DEAN bursts in, comet like, from an unsuspected place. HE is terribly battered, his red jacket torn, his jeans ripped. HE hallucinates, talks to himself and to imaginary images HE sees.

(Thrum of exhaust of passing cars. Fades in a few moments)

(Horrified, to self) It's got to be here. One minute I'm hugging the wheel--. Next I'm--...How can you lose a Porsche?

(Cries) Where am I? *(Jokes, looks about)* On the corner of Pain and Pain and Stab Me and Run?--Did someone take my car?...Who was I with? ... Where are my glasses?

(Flash of headlights. HE rushes about)

Stop!!!!!! *(Panicky)* Didn't that guy see me? *(Shouting after cars)* Stop! Stop! *(Blinking)* Oh, my eyes are so sharp. I see clearly without glasses. . .

(Gasping) I'm short of breath. *(Jokes)* Stick an I.V. in me and shoot in caffeine.

(HE trips on broken glass.)

(Screams) Oooh. What's that? Ooooh. A piece of windshield? *(Peers in, shocked)* I look so old and sick.

I'll do an acting exercise. *(Pause)* Do an overall sensation-like being in the shower-something that makes me feel good.

...Where am I?

(Eerie music like Vivaldi, Nisi Dominus.*)*

What's that giant red scroll doing floating straight ahead. It's got words on it. *(Reads, fearfully)* "You've one hour to pass a series of tests and be saved.

Saved from what? *(Defiant)* I don't believe--Says who?

(Reads more words) "Tibetan Book of Living and Dying. If you pass the tests you will be healed in this life or the next."

(Keels over, laughing) Is this some weird death spiral--Signs can't just come in and out like that. I think someone drugged me and stole my car.

(Reads) "In Tibet. Gurus keep a chart of dying souls to be purified. How you'll be reborn depends on karmic forces at the time of--"

(Calls out) I'm not a Buddhist--I was briefly a Quaker. I won't apologize--

SOULS IN TORMENT: *(V.O.)* *(Breathing heavily)* Stella--Errano--Sans toi--terre aride-

JIMMY: *(Scared)* Who's that? Look I'm a big star, a public commodity. People are trying to consume me

(Defiant) I can't die. I'm greedy for life. I sleep an hour a night. *(Discovering, reads)* There are new words on that scroll.

(Reads) "First test: Get your Mother's forgiveness for choosing fame over family."

(Annoyed) Idiot! My ma's' dead.

SOULS IN TORMENT: *(V.O.)* *(Cries in strange languages)* Au bout d'une-- Un tiengo Y Dulce Chau-

JIMMY: *(Screams)* Speak English I got to find my car 'fore it's hurt. *(Looks up)*
More words! *(Reads the scroll)* "Your mom will visit from the other side." Wha the--Says who? *(Terrified)* Am I sick or crazy?

What's that behind the highway?

(Sound of clanking chains. Ghosts drift in the distance. They are the Souls in Torment, hellish figures who prod JIMMY to his death. HE fumbles in his pocket)

SOULS IN TORMENT: *(V.O.)* *(Whisper nastily)* Cross over.

JIMMY: *(Peering out)* Something's moving? *(Listens, scared)* Is that the state patrol?

Where's my combat scotch? My switchblade? *(Slipping out a knife, Suspicious)* Come closer--

You move but I can't read you?

Are you an animal? A... a poltergeist?

SOULS IN TORMENT: *(V.O.) (Viciously)* Cross over.

JIMMY: I'm not afraid of visitors from outer space, talking animals, flowers.

(Sharp raps)

(Contemptuous) Are you a human being? Make one sound. *(Silence)* Are you a spirit? Make 2 sounds.

(Two loud knocks)

Are you my mother? Make three sounds.

(Three rapping sounds <u>rush in</u>)

(Horrified) Oh no.--My Ma ... would... never—

(Looks up) The Red Scroll again. *(Reads, fearful)* "Note from Mom: Ghosts can't say much because we frighten people. That's why we whisper. We just get a few words per visit. We make sounds thru the trees, water, wind--"

(Sound of horrid wind)

(Excited) Fine! If you're my Mom, show me... my age when you died.

(Ghost knocks 9 times)

Nine years.

JIMMY: *(Distraught)* Right. What was the last thing I gave you?

(Lights up on a rose strangely blooming by the road.)

(Looks aside) Oh, no, a... a rose. *(To self)* A rose bloomed on the home asteroid of the--

(To ghost) What was my favorite book?

(Lights up on The Little Prince*)*

Oh! *The Little Prince.* My book must have spun from my car--

(Nostalgic music like Saint-Saens, The Swan. *)*

(HE picks up the book and opens it.) The rose was the one that the Little Prince loved.

JIMMY: *(Breaks down crying)* Oh Ma... It is... you.

(Rustle of wind. Ghost appears veiled in distance.)

Oh God *(Breath quickens)* It's like you're there and not there. *(Thrilled)* Luminous and see through. How I've missed you.

MA: *(V.O.)* *(Speaking breathy with great difficulty)* Read from that book...when you feel sleepy. It'll... prompt you *(Fading)* to keep focus... hold on to earth.

(JIMMY sits lost, opens book, reads)

Oh no. *(Calls)* Ma! Don't go! It's true. Like the pilot in *The Little Prince*, I'm marooned in the desert in a damaged vehicle. *(Hollers)* Ma! Help me find my car!

MA: *(V.O.)* *(Painful breathing)* Ah... ah... uh—

JIMMY: *(Squints)* Oh God, there you are. Your lips move, but I can't hear-- *(Looks up)* What? Are you suffering?

SOULS IN TORMENT: *(V.O.)* Help... o ...ou... stop—

(Vision of the Red Scroll. HE reads)

(Reads) "Son, I represent all the hurting ones. I'll be doomed--If you die unpurified. Because I left you."

SOULS IN TORMENT: *(V.O.)* *(Hyena-like)* No . . .don't . . go soft—

JIMMY: *(Confused)* Who is that--What?

MA: *(V.O.)* The lost ones. Pay no attention. I'm here to guide you.

JIMMY: *(Reads)* "You must apologize for wounding others in your search for FAME!"

--What, Ma--? I did it for you. *(Waving book)* You told me to be like that pilot flying from Paris to Saigon faster than anyone-

MA: *(V.O.)* *(Ghost vanishing)* No . . . oh no—

JIMMY: Don't back off. When I was little I thought we were one person... Now my... skull feels like it'll fly off. And images from *The Little Prince* keep appearing in my mind.

(Vision of the Red Scroll. HE reads)

"*The Little Prince* offers clues to your salvation. After years of denial, you are becoming mindful."

Okay Fine! If I apologize--will Ma take me to my car!?

(Waits for a sign. Sweating, nervous) Help me focus. Set my course like radar and I'm the plane!

(Lights blink. Ghost reappears)

There you are again! *(Triumphant)* I'll take that light as a yes!!!

(Engine sounds. HE pantomimes driving.)

Oh, Ma. Wait till you see me race that car. It was featured in the Beverly Hills showroom and contoured for my body--the seat raised, the pedals pushed forward. Can't you find it?

(Spinning the wheel) Br-r-r-h! That car was part of my family. The thing I could trust! Yahoo!!!!!!!!

MA: *(V.O.)* *(Low breathy)* "Repent! Leaving –".

JIMMY: You got a lot of nerve. I did what the family wanted! Rode the train with your casket to Indiana--Jumped out when they mistakenly moved your coffin. I screamed "Oh, my mother. That's my mother."

--It was wrong of them to make me watch your casket, as it started me fantasizing--

I kept reading that dern *Little Prince* book, telling myself, that while it looked like you'd died, you had not. Your body was too heavy to take with you to another planet.

SOULS IN TORMENT: *(V.O.) (Squeaks) Eke... Ou... ah*

JIMMY: *Shoosh! (Sinister, to Ma)* I was glad you died. Did you read the curse I put in your casket. "I don't need anybody clinging to me because I'm going up too fast--to be a star, and you'd be extra weight."

Still I forced myself to touch your eyelid before they closed that casket to make sure you weren't asleep.

SOULS IN TORMENT: *(V.O.) (Cawing) Cro... ark... ak... croak!*

JIMMY: What's that? *(Looks down)* A dead bird. *(Skirting the bird)* Blood and squashed--

(Defiant) I gotta get to this race. My Porsche has my clothes in it, my wallet, water. *(Staggers slightly)* I'm so thirsty.

My arms hurt, my legs... are-- Haven't I repented enough, Ma! Didn't I visit the cemetery each week--reciting on your tomb-- sleeping on it...

SOULS IN TORMENT: *(V.O.)* You defiled her tomb?

JIMMY: No, I acted there--perfected my elocution. Didn't you hear?

(SOUND of rain)

(Uneasy, checks his shirt) It's pouring but I'm not getting wet.

(To Ma, lying) You bet I felt strong. When I finished hitchhiking those 10 miles to your grave. *(Sneers)* I knew I had to find my own planet. I had to get free of--, to break loose from... to find some bright asteroid where more perfected beings would teach me what was right, wrong, real, unreal. ...One with roses that didn't die and volcanoes that weren't extinct.

Haven't I apologized sufficiently? Knock twice for, repent more. But I'm warning you. I'm getting fed up.

(SOUND of two thunder bolts, rain)

Two claps!

(Vision of the Red Scroll. JIMMY reads)

(Reads, nervously) "You abandoned your aunt and uncle."

(Vision of the Red Scroll. HE reads)

(Reads, annoyed) "You should have helped them take care of the farm--."

--*(Defiant)* Fairmount--No actor should live in cornfields with pigs!

(To Ma)--There's no alone like being in the Midwest.

(Reads) "Son, I begged my in-laws to raise you--If you don't repent I won't be able to... to cleanse myself... I'll be condemned... too"

SOULS IN TORMENT: *(V.O.)* *(Painful breathing)* O ...salu--tare--hos--ti-a—

JIMMY: Quiet! *(Nastily)* I should never have listened to Mom Ortense or you. That's right, I called Aunt--mom--too. And I read *The Little Prince* to her.

(To Ma) She knew I needed speed. To hurdle across the ground. To go to other stars, visit unknown worlds and conquer them.

I stayed til Aunt had a real son. Marcus the smuck Jr. And I left.

MA: *(V.O.)* *(Hoarsely)* "Are you sorry -"

JIMMY: *(Reads)* Are you sorry you screwed Dad and birthed a bastard? *(Enraged)* I actually liked it at Uncle's, better than at your house. But being a farmer or an auctioneer isn't me. I'm better than that.

MA: *(V.O.)* Repent, son.

JIMMY: *(Trying not to cry, angrily)* Why should I?

 I begged you not to die. To go to the doctor when--No one ever did a thing I wanted. I did it myself. I don't owe Mom Ortense, you, or anybody, anything. Not one god damn thing. *(Starts to cough)* I've had enough! *(Doubles over suddenly)* My chest feels like it's stuck on something. I can't breathe! *(Shouts)* I'm not repenting till you find my Porsche! My photographer was following me...

SOULS IN TORMENT: *(V.O.)* *(Sly in strange languages)* Fuerte... Morto... perdito—

JIMMY: *(Looks about)* Look. That car has my book of patrons, the scripts I'm supposed to consider—

MA: *(V.O.)* *(To souls)* Evil ones.

JIMMY *(Calloused)* Men move ahead because women quit--I decided to be and was fucking great without any of you.

SOULS IN TORMENT: *(V.O.)* *(Sneering, hisses)* You were a--God.

JIMMY: Yes. I'm a superstar. All over television. Did you jokers see my TV shows? I have Marlon Brando's number.

(Imitates Brando in Streetcar Named Desire*)* *(Laughs)* Brando in *Streetcar*.

(JIMMY rips off his jacket and yells)

Hey, Stel-la. Stel-la. *(Irritated)* Do you know who Brando is. *(Demanding)* Or Montgomery Clift?

(Imitating Montgomery) "The closer we come to the negative, to death, the more we blossom."

(Picks up a glass shard) God I look worse. My eyes sag. My fingers look yellow. I may have broken my nose.

(Vision of the Red Scroll. HE reads)

(Reads, obstinately) "Why did you put being a star before family and friends?"

(To Ma) What--!! I pursued the seed of glory you planted in me, for you . . .for Us. I denied myself.--Broke 3 fingers in *Rebel* to get the right feeling. Screamed myself hoarse in *Giant*. Climbing up the oil rigs. Going too far, flirting with the edge, doing what most actors never dream of doing. . . .To create a mythic world.

One with roses that didn't die and volcanoes that weren't extinct like in *The Little Prince.*

SOULS IN TORMENT: *(V.O.)* *(Heinous)* Let go excuses!

JIMMY: *(Looking off with contempt)* You cowards who never . . .walked on burning ice . . . . I dare you to get me. I'm not apologizing--

(SOUNDS of drumming dead pilots marching towards him.)

SOULS IN TORMENT: *(V.O.)* Come, JIMMY.

JIMMY: Who are you? I know I'm not alone. I ride in on the shoulders of all you dead pilots.

(Anxious) If you're here to escort me out, it won't work. All I'm looking for could be found in . . . *(Delirious, searching for items in* The Little Prince*)*--a single rose, or a little water...'

SOULS IN TORMENT: *(V.O.)* *(Urgent)* Cross through the doorway.

JIMMY: *(Confused, recalling* The Little Prince*)* a few grapes . . .an orange . . .some wine.

(JIMMY pushes through a fog of people, finds a flashlight, points it.)

Leave!! Or, I'll disappear you.

(JIMMY doubles over suddenly.)
It's hard to inhale-- *(Cries)* Ma! Oh, sweet... Do something, somebody. Call someone. Get transportation.

(The Red Scroll looms up and HE reads)

(Reads, horrified) "Names of Dying to be Prayed For and Purified: Jimmy Dean." *(Yells out)* James Dean doesn't die!

(Desperately, Reads) "Only the body dies."

JIMMY: But I love the body and the earth. I love the road--
--the sky, my friends, music, my Porsche—

SOULS IN TORMENT: *(O.S.) (Screaming, fiendish delight)* That car was YOURS.

JIMMY: *(Obstinate)* I've got to find it! I've so much more to do.

(SOUND of racing wheels, which fade when HE begins speaking)

(Suddenly recalling, shocked) Oh no.. . . I . .I'm recalling. This huge Ford-
-was crossing my lane. I floored my car-But my foot got stuck--I slammed into this tank and I careened off--

(Terrified) We landed-- By a telephone pole--Something exploded in flames.--Car filled with smoke and I was moving and coughing--as if through a tunnel. People were screaming, groaning, and crying--

(Vision of squashed Porsche)

MA: *(O.S.) (Pointing)* Come <u>claim</u> your spyder!

JIMMY: You knew! *(Horrified)* That mangled heap.--Oh no--Is that me--Slung onto the passenger seat. How can I be here . . . and there at--?---
(Obstinately) I've got to get to . . .some hospital. . . .I'm not dead yet!

(Vision of the Red Scroll. HE reads)

(Reads) "You are out of time. Nothing you can do about it."

(Yells) How long have I got? *(Reads)* "It feels like an hour earth time but, it's actually the blink of an eye." *(Angrily grabbing a stick and waving it)* Whoever makes this Red Scroll would you come out? Face me!!!

(Reads, scared) "Your mom says, "You haven't sufficiently repented" *(Accusatory)* How do I do that... if I'm innocent?" *(His arms bolt up like wings)*

JIMMY: Oh God I'm lifting off. Is that me below? I see some... Is--?

(Recoiling)--The man's face is sliced. His neck broken *(Horrified)*--His seat flung out the car. *(Fluttering of lights)*

Ma, you're back! Why can't you forgive me? Don't you care—

(Vision of the Red Scroll)

(Reads) Now you and your mother are both banished to--

To what!! *(Accusatory to the Red Scroll)* Another asteroid? Look, have you ever had the feeling it's not in your hands. You've got something to do and you have no control over it?

When they talk of success, they talk about reaching the top. Well, there's no top. You've got to go on and on, never stop at any point.

To me the only success, the only greatness for a man is in immortality, to have your work remembered in history, to leave something in the world that will last for centuries. That's greatness. That's why I want fame.

(SOUND of black wind. Fades as HE reads)

(Vision of the Red Scroll. HE reads)

(Reads) "Your mom withholds judgment. But she does pass you to the next test. "Get your father's forgiveness for seeking fame."

(To self) Why? He's a devious opportunist who gets away—

SOULS IN TORMENT: *(V.O.)* *(Demonic laughter)* Hold on to the anger!

SCENE 2: FACING FATHER

(*SOUND: footsteps.*)

(*JIMMY sees image of his father reading a newspaper*)

(*Calls out*) Dad! How did you get here? Dad! (*Pause*) Oh you don't answer... Surprise. Surprise--Look, I need your pardon . . .(*Apologetically*) It's not life as usual. I'm possibly dying—

(*SOUND of a grave being shoveled*)

They are digging some tomb—

Dad. Put that newspaper down.

Oh, no! I just popped inside it. I can read the paper, too!

"James Dean killed Today In Highway Crash."

(*To Dad, mad*) There's some mistake.

Dad, pay attention. I'v got to get your pardon for my--ruthless--ambition . . There's no in between for an actor. You're either famous or forgotten. . . .Look, you were aware of my sense of being different, of my need to be perfect.

Don't flap air under the paper; listen. It's true I wanted fame. I was reaching for praise whenever it was available.

After you left me on the farm, I wouldn't accept isolation or defeat. I liked crossing off each day I succeeded without you.

(*Lying, affectionate*) I suppose you--were there. You were always there. But I didn't know how to reach you.

(*Lying*) I love you?
(*Recoils*) Why is it so hot!

(*Vision of the Red Scroll. HE reads.*)

(Shaken, reads) "It gets hot when you lie."

SOULS IN TORMENT: *(O.S.) (Sinister laughter) Jardin Chinois. Jardin Chin--*

(To Dad) What ... Dad?

Your lips move. But I can't hear. ...Don't leave! Forgive me, you bastard!

(Accusatory) I was nice to your new bitch wife. I didn't take it personally when she locked me out--surrounded me with her gaseous loathing. I took those retarded courses in business and law--

But when I heard Jack Benny on the radio—*(Imitates Jack Benny)* "There`s only five real people in Hollywood. Everyone else is me."

Or saw Monty Clift at the movies, *(Imitates Monty)* "Look, I'm not odd. I'm just trying to be an actor; not a movie star, an actor," I had to go for the glory!

(SOUND of flies buzzing and footsteps)

Why are all these flies after me?

Dad, do I have your pardon or-- *(Screams)* It's getting so all the excuses are going away. . . the only thing you ever gave me was a used vehicle!

Acting was a great balm to me because I saw your flaws--You bloody narcissist. You bet I wanted stardom. Fame gave me the chance to get respect and love, to replace the sadness, to walk, no vault past the jeers... to celebrate being a bastard in a silver Porsche convertible.

(Vision of the Red Scroll. JIMMY reads)

(Reads) "Your Dad pardons you! He admires your guts."

What! *(To Scroll)* I don't want that fool to pardon me. Well, then...there...now.

(HE sings/dances, triumphant, punching at the sky pretending HE is Popeye, the sailor man.)

JIMMY: *(Cringes in pain)* What's wrong with my neck? Oh, no, I'm inside the accident scene.

(SOUND of cars screeching to a halt.)

Oh, good! Cars arrive at the wreck. One I nearly hit seconds ago. Drivers get out-

When the first man sees me, he gasps, clutches his face, and dashes to find a phone... More cars stop.

(SOUND of distant sirens)

An ambulance! Hurry... can't breathe. My body shakes.

SOULS IN TORMENT: *(O.S.) (Sneering)* Keep grasping.

JIMMY: Two drivers get out! I'm going to . . .oh, no, I'm weak, falling asleep.

(Hallucinates looking up) The sky is black, popping with light!

(Vision of the Red Scroll. HE reads:)

(Reads) "Your mom fears your rebirth is coming. Time is running out?"*(Reads)* "Your return to earth is just for a brief pit stop."

(Defiant) But they are rushing me to the hospital. I want to get fixed and live...

JIMMY: Ma you're supposed to guide me. *(Screams)* Let me heal on earth. Don't fail me again.

(Looks in shard of glass, shocked)

I look yellow . . .no grey. Like when you're made up for a death scene. How far is the hospital?

SCENE 3: DUMPING DIVAS

(Vision of the Red Scroll. HE reads)

(Reads) "Next test: Get forgiveness for climbing over women to fame."

MA: *(O.S.)* Confess—tell me about your girlfriends.

JIMMY: Shouldn't you know all this. Ma?

Okay! You had a synapse. Fine *(Nervously)* I was having sex with everything
I could get my hands on. *(Pause)* My best girl was someone with--
(Pause) with a high sexual drive. I met her at a rehearsal club. She was...
She did what she wanted... I didn't epitomize good, Ma. I was on the
criminal side of things.

SOULS IN TORMENT: *(V.O.)* *(Ugly)* Embrace your masculinity!

(MUSIC: Ravel, Daphnis Et Chloé)

(To Ma) The girl and I shared this hotel room... She became my lover...
She didn't get pregnant like you. She was careful-- I was in NYC to escape-
(Pause) Someone. *(Pause)* No one.

(Pause) I wanted a female like a <u>male</u>. One hard enough to walk with me
through challenges--But soft enough to give me... animalistic love.

(SOUND of cold wind baying. Snow falls.)

(Looks up) Is it snowing? Wha--t?

MA: *(V.O.)* At level three, weather varies.

JIMMY: *(Shivers)* Look, I had to dump the girl.

MA: *(V.O.)* You're unstable, son.

JIMMY: No, I'm wild. Unstable people shoot themselves and others. I'm an
explorer.

SOULS IN TORMENT: *(O.S.)* Fuel your anger!

JIMMY: All men think about different relationships. *(Pause)* Most drop them. *(Pause)* But I said, fuck it, I'll try this and that--*(Pause)* See what I like. *(To Ma)* You don't understand--I couldn't get tied down by being a "boy-friend" or a husband. *(Anxiously)* I had to couple with the beautiful—I told my girl to be careful, watch me and have the courage to cut me.

I couldn't get engaged. She let the thing go on too long. She wanted to exchange rings. She should have left. Gone off with that dance troupe—I couldn't set a date.

MA: *(O.S.)* You put her heart on a table and sliced it.

JIMMY: I couldn't marry her *(Wailing)* I just realized I was old. I wasn't 18. She wanted sex. Begged for it!

(To Ma, shivering) I did everything I could to--to break it to-her--I was holding on to the cliff edge-

(Guiltily) Marriage is for the middle part of life thirty to fifty. . .I'm sure we'll get together. When I have the ability to dream!

MA: *(O.S.)* You should have married her.

JIMMY: Okay. You wanna know! *(Pause, awkward)* There was someone--

SOULS IN TORMENT: *(O.S.)* Your rich patrons: Mr. Rich. Mr. Richer. Mr. Richest.

JIMMY: *(To Souls)* Shut up! It's nobody you know--

SOULS IN TORMENT: *(O.S.)* And Mr. Obscenely Rich.

JIMMY: Ma you're shocked, and I'm sorry. But I gotta live hard. I gotta live true. And in the end, I gotta have *(Pause)* something *(Pause)* else.

(SOUND of girl sobbing)

(Cries out, suddenly) I need to get behind the wheel of something. When I'm under this dysfunction I need my car!!!!. Pardon me!

MA: *(V.O.)* *(Wailing)* No. I don't forgive you!!

JIMMY: ...I said I was sorry, Ma. What was I supposed to do leave soot marks on her wrists as a sign, that there was no way out thru me.
(*A hot breeze. HE scrunches over*)
--I'm going to die and go to hell if--you don't have mercy!! It's so hot but--I've stopped sweating- These tests are-- My chest is exploding. (*Looks in a shard*) My senses are dulled. I'm in the body of an old man.

(*Screams*) I'm sorry, Ma!

(*To Ma*) How much time have I got!!

(*Wrathful*) What has my old girlfriend been doing that she wants me to die? Is this . . .some kind . . . of revenge? I didn't mean to--

(*Vision of the Red Scroll. HE reads*)

(*Reads*) "Good intentions are not enough, son. You must try to feel what the loved one is feeling. Heal her pain."

(*MUSIC from a broken car radio continues subtly under Souls in Torment moaning. HE sees his body!*)

JIMMY: Oh no, there's the accident site. Oh great! They unwrap me from the mass of aluminum and lift me onto the gurney. Good!

(*A gurney appears on the scrim*)

(*SOUNDS of cameras flashing*)

(*Horrified*) Oh no. Air is coming from my nostrils. But my forehead and my chest... uh no... are caved in!

God! Somebody is taking pictures of me. I'm struggling to breathe, and someone is--doing a photo shoot!

SOULS IN TORMENT: (*O.S.*) (*Gleeful*) You reap what you sow.

(*Vision of War Memorial Hospital*)

JIMMY: (*Thrilled*) We've made it to the hospital. Whoa! What a sudden stop.

Stop! Don't slide that other man out and treat him first

Hey, I'm in trouble--man. I've got this blood... Red... everywhere, splattered on my... my----and a bright pool flowing in my chest.
(*His arm pops in the air and he can't pull it down*)

But no! I'm outside my body. A hundred feet up and south of the accident. The intense neck pain has turned to pleasure. Oh, no. Help! I'm leaving the planet, going beyond the stars, the galaxy, beyond anything physical. This world gone and grass and hills. Everyone I loved is gone!

(*Vision of the Red Scroll. HE reads*)

(*Reads*) "Next: Get forgiveness from your Ma for the way you treated your agent."

(*To Scroll*) That feline made money off me.

(*Suddenly light-headed*) Look, I'm not playing-- Going through ... more hoops.

(*Impatient*) Ma! Come here... Correct all this.

(*Vision of the Red Scroll. HE reads*)

"Embracing truth could heal you."

(*Accusatory*). Does that mean I'll be resuscitated? What would make the difference?

(*Vision of the Red Scroll. HE reads*)

(*Reads*) "Prepare for death, or for that matter, for life."

JIMMY: Appear, Mama Jane. I need your pardon. (*Vexed*) Mama Jane!

MA: (*O.S.*) Who was Mama Jane?

JIMMY: My theatrical agent. I called her, "Mama."

(Guiltily to Ma) I called lots of women Mama."... *(Breathing hard)* Get me to ... to the emergency room... fast.

(Lights get hotter. HE wipes his face.)

(Commanding, to Ma) I ... I know I ... .defied the contracts. I needed to perfect the script . . .to be true to my talent, to follow a higher standard than those producers were using.
Yes, I rewrote my lines and hit the director. It was war. I knew the part better than he did. And he wasn't used to an actor being smart. *(Penitent)* I can't be part of a group of dopes. Let them take the guts out of me. What's an actor without guts? So I raced cars, to power myself to fight the fury of those in charge--

(Starts to get faint, grabs The Little Prince, *reads)*

(Reads, confused) "You never know where to find them. The wind blows them away, They have no roots."

(SOUND: TOCCATA IN F MAJOR. *FADES when voice starts)*

(Accusatory to Ma) You should come to my dressing room and take your turn on the gallows. Sleep sitting up, six pillows behind your back, a gun in your pocket. Always ready for their bushwhack. I don't care about their profits or paperwork. I won't be remembered as a *minor talent.*

(Vision of the Red Scroll. HE reads)

(Reads horrified) "You have failed to get pardoned. Prepare your state for - -"

Don't fade away!

When I lost you, Ma, I lost myself. You were the person who told me what was right, wrong, real, unreal. Then Aunt Ortense became mom but she... only understood...

I thought I'd found my other self in my agent, so when she didn't side with me... when she arrived on the set like the wandering Picasso. Sometimes with me but most times not... I attacked her!

SOULS IN TORMENT: *(O.S.)* Use that anger—

JIMMY: *(Delirious, dying, groans)* Ma where are you? Can no one bring me back to the emergency room? Oh my god! Some-bo-dy!!! He-lp!!

(Dazzling light around JIMMY.)

Are those headlights? A dissecting table? I've got to keep from falling asleep.

(Opens The Little Prince)

(Forcing speech) "Where are the people?" resumed The Little Prince. "It's a little lonely in the desert..."

MA *(O.S.)* Answer one question, and get pardon. And you can die without regret.

JIMMY: *(Angry)* But I'm on some table! I think they are saving me!

MA *(O.S.) (Sobbing)* What were you really looking for?

(Burning lights)

(Looking around,) It's suffocating. Is this a hospital? Yes! *(Rebellious)* Look, Ma, I'm obsessed. I broke 3 fingers hitting that desk in *Rebel—*

SOULS IN TORMENT: *(V.O.) (Jubilant)* Blood spurting everywhere!

JIMMY: I was exhausted. I had to do movies back to back. And race in between... I needed to "not think" to bust open my memories- I should have stopped making movies when I got depressed. Helped other actors make movies so they could get depressed. Do you know what it's like to finish a movie! *(Anxiously)* It is like--Being on a bus that crashes into a stonewall.*(Delirious, fighting off sleep)* and yes I'm haunted by--nightmares and... waking mares... when I do movies... because ... because--

(Forcing himself awake. Grabs The Little Prince. *Reads)*

When I do movies--*(Reads)* "It seems to me that I'm carrying a very fragile treasure."

JIMMY: Didn't you read my letter? "A fish that is in the water has no choice than he is. Genius would have it that he swim in sand. We are fish and we drown."

(Vision of the Red Scroll. HE reads)

(Reads) "Temporary pardon granted."

JIMMY: *(Energetically, pulling himself together)* Hooray!! I passed!

(Exuberant, HE rips his shirt off, puts a cracker in his eye, pretending to be Pop-eye. HE dances and sings a sea chantey.)

(A rush of wind. JIMMY lifts up)

Oh god, no. I'm soaring again. Over my--Where am I?

(Reads a sign: War Memorial Hospital)

(Recoiling) There's a hospital gurney *(To staff)*

(To staff) We made it to the operating room.

(SOUND of monitor flatlining.)

Oh no, vital signs are plummeting.

MEDIC: *(O.S.)* We've lost him.

JIMMY: Is it me?

(Airy lights)

God. I can't stop bobbing on the ceiling. I'm like a balloon. *(Squinting)* I don't recognize that body down there. *(Light)* Hey, you guys. Come get me. I'm up here.

(Shouts) Can no one hear?

(Panicked) *(Angry)* I can't lower myself. I can't --see through to . . .get back to living. Can't they correct whatever . . .did this!!

(Vision of the Red Scroll. HE reads)

"Next test: "Get forgiveness for exploiting starlets." *(Cries)* I've had enough.

(Reads) "Otherwise you and your mother will be damned--"

JIMMY: No. Stop! *(Frustrated screams)* I think I've got amnesia or something. I can't remember who the starlet was --

(Feeling off-balance, HE reads The Little Prince*)*

(Reads) "She was useful because she was so beautiful."
(Overcome with grief) Oh yes. She was an Italian icon… It was the studio's plan to fix us up for… a fake love affair--because--I *(Blots forehead, ashamed to Ma)*--I hadn't dated girls … since… you know who.

MA: *(O.S.)* Tell the truth! Did you destroy another woman?

Okay! I led her on! Yes, I did put my hand down her shirt and other things--

(Nervous) The only way I could say no to that Italian was to not be around. It was goddess love. For blocks of time she didn't know me.

(Breathing quickly, screams a retaliation) Yes. …I got her pregnant--! She said she wasn't … at first… but-… She got rid of it.

MA: *(O.S.)* You got rid of your baby!

JIMMY: Sorry! *(To Heavens)* Put me back into the pit of darkness, let me become a beast.

(SOUND of something like Vivaldi, Nisi Dominus, *followed by woman sobbing)*

(Hallucinates, pointing her out, To Ma) Oh no. There she is, doelike green eyes, light brown hair. Anna Maria Pierangeli. Part goddess. Part cat. I think of her and an image appears before me, the way I left her.

(Awkwardly, quickly) No baby!. Don't… don't cry.

Forgive me and tempt me back. I want to hold you all night… touch hands and feet.

Let something come through me that's bigger than my career.
(Urgently) You're not still angry? There's this thing about you Italians. You think you're completely normal.

(High strung) Look I'm screwed up. I live on highways. *(Hot, breathes quickly)* I can't have a wife. I'm too close to suicide. I love you, … isn't that enough? Pardon—

SOULS IN TORMENT: *(O.S.)* Others yearn for you—

JIMMY: *(Accusing)* Sugar. To be an actor in America is not to expect lasting affection. I cried and cried, too. I was . . . feeling things I'd never felt before. In trying to partake of emotion to the fullest, I allowed myself--to love complete---and then when I lost--I suffered completely. When I heard you married, a singer, you barely knew-- The only way I could face it was to play Bach on the HiFi. Hang a noose from my ceiling with a sign, "We also remove bodies." Fall asleep, looking at that noose.

(We hear something like Bach's Toccata in F major *subtly under until HE speaks)*

JIMMY: Oh Sugar--I'm in limbo. Permanently parked. They'll bury me in a racing helmet, a steering wheel beside me, if *(Struck with guilt, yells)* I beg you-- re-lea-se me.

(Vision of the Red Scroll. HE reads)

(Reads) "Son, I forgive you even though that starlet will die of an overdose and a broken heart."

(Relieved but anxious) Well . . . then, there now! *(Falsely happy)* Whoopee!

(Uneasy, HE rips off his shirt, slouches on a cap and dances)

(Whirling sounds. Great light)

Oh no! Stop! I don't want to . . .Stop. I'm spinning through this tunnel. Gosh! I can't look up because I . . .I . . .

(Pointing forward) Out there the light burns like the sun.

(From this point on snippets of music and sound create a cacophony effect building to the end.)

(A Vision of the Red Scroll.)

(A bell gongs.)

(Reads) "A mindful bell will mark 3 times till you're pronounced d-e-a-d."

Who's ringing the bonger? *(Screams)* Anybody? Ma! Ma, aren't you supposed to alleviate something. Don't exile me from earth to pay for my . . . I tried to satisfy women but the only time they were happy was in bed and . . . They was jealous . . . jealous of my ambition. Let me go back and correct the pain I caused.

SCENE 4: SQUASHING THE SOULS IN TORMENT

(Vision of the Red Scroll. HE reads)

(Reads, warily) "Proceed to the next test. Get forgiveness from the Souls in Torment." *(Horrified)* Who are they?

(MUSIC: Raunchy music fades in and out)

(Cries) Look if I find out what I did wrong and apologize, can you revive ... me somehow... administer a native rehydration treatment like they did in *Little Prince?*

(Yells) People do come back from the dead.

(Vision of the Red Scroll. HE reads)

(Reads) "Restoration doubtful but possible. An orgy of truth telling may replenish the neural pathways. In any case, you have 10 minutes to shut down."

(LIGHTS fade. SOUND of clanking metal door)

Oh god. What's that stark metal and-- Don't tag that toe. I am NOT dead! Don't put me in a bag. It's so black. Let me out-

(Vision of a Death Certificate. HE reads)

(Reads, terrified) "5:45 PM, condition directly leading to the death of James Dean: broken neck."

(SOUND of airplane landing.)

JIMMY: Where am I? *(Looks about, confused)* Sign says, "Indianapolis air-port"? What's going on over there? People with so many roses. Why the roses?

(Pause) Oh no, I can't focus. I don't want to fade off... drift from earth com-pletely. Where's that--that—

(SOUND of car exhaust)

(Squints) A hearse from Hunt's Funeral Home is meeting a--? Casket com-ing off a plane? I have a weird feeling that's <u>me</u> in that coffin.

Who are those people waiting for that plane. Their lips move but I can't—

SOULS IN TORMENT: (O.S.) We're the lovers you used.

JIMMY: Tell me what I did to--so I can get your forgiveness?

SOULS IN TORMENT: (O.S.) Nine minutes!

JIMMY: *(To Souls)* Quiet!

SOULS IN TORMENT: (O.S.) You acted like an animal with no feel-ings—

(Anxious) It's true, I did . . .certain things to . . .get hired . . .in movies. Less than 3% of American actors are employed-- *(Intensely)* Under the sur-face contracts control casting . . .. Each time, I believed they were in place and this once only I'd do "the thing."

I used people--*(A bit manic)* And they knew it--Sex got gradually worse and it got worse quickly!

--I planned to stop and enter the priesthood of the great classic artists. Survive ship wreck by floating on a wooden coffin like Ishmael. Leave my body on earth to go home to my planet like the Little Prince.

(A bell gongs louder. Another sign reads:)

JIMMY: (*Reads*) A mindful bell!

(*Attacking*) I thought later I'd find my special flower. Later love could be a sacred experience.

(*MUSIC: Debussy,* Prelude to a Faun)

(*Vision of the Red Scroll. JIMMY reads*)

(*Reads*) "Have you forgotten *The Little Prince*? You're responsible for whom you've tamed! For the people you made love you. (*Rebelliously*) I was nice to those babes! I made each "date" be as much as it could be for as long as it could be. After they left--you could have wiped the floor with me.

(*Maliciously*) (*Screams*) Look, people! Wherever you are. I'm sorry!

(*Vision of an Indiana Funeral Home*)

JIMMY: Oh no, we're at Hunt's Funeral Home. (*Cries*) Return me to the hospital. Can't we make some new deal?

MA: (*O.S.*) You're terrified, but that's normal.

JIMMY: Who is in that casket. There's some notice and, gosh, I can read it

(*Reads*) "A native son . . .with a brilliant flash of genius was brought back home this week for last rites . ."

Ma! (*Anxious*) Don't let that be me.

(*MUSIC: Somber music fades in*)

(*Vision of the Reverend DeWeird*)

Oh, God no. A reverend is blessing that casket. Oh, I know this preacher.-

SOULS IN TORMENT: (*O.S.*) Seven minutes.

JIMMY: We recited poetry by Ma's grave. He comforted me. Introduced me to Shakespeare, bull fights, the Indie 500.

(Vision of the Red Scroll. HE reads)

(Reads) "Did you *rendez-vous* with him too. Were you 'One of them!'"

JIMMY: Wha-I can't believe you'd--
(Picking a fight) I've a trifurcate life! My identity is based on what I do. It's hard to say who I am. --I'm insulting one of my other selves!!
(Cries out, suddenly aware) Hey, all you people, my lovers. Forgive me. I know some day soon--I'd merge with another, connect so completely that our lives became inseparable.

--I want that. I do. Forgive me.--I know I used you. I was out of touch. Didn't come from gentleness.

(Joyous sounds like Bach's Sleepers Awake.*)*

MA: (O.S.) You are forgiven!

(JIMMY does a dance of celebration and sings a Second Line Medley, his anguish leaks through)

SCENE 5: KILLING ONESELF

(Vision of the Red Scroll. HE stops short, swallows hard, reads)

(Reads) "You have reached the final test." *(Thrilled)* Then, there, now!

(Belligerently, reads) "Here . . .you must prove you didn't commit suicide" Why would I do that?

(Reads) "To secure everlasting fame." *(Mutinous)* So I'm definitely dead!!
(Losing temper) No answer.

Look, I didn't kill myself!

I had everything to live for. Nonstop work between pictures. Roles that demanded depth . . .gravitas. *(Laughs, unsure)* --My personal life was improving.

(MUSIC: Something sleazy. Stops when commanded)

(*Impatient*) Can that music!--When people moved in close, I . . .I was . . .keeping my . . . direction.

---(*Anguished*) Oh God. Will I never see my friends again?!

(*Picks up windshield shard*)

My eye's bothering me. Oh. It's all yellow. There's a broken chip . . .of-- How long has my eye been like-- I'm not careless! I wasn't afraid of losing the race. Salinas was my lucky town. Where I'd shot *East of Eden*. --I'd even had a physical to make sure all my reflexes were normal. Would I do that if--

(*Vision of his Porsche with "Little Bastard" written on the side.*)

That morning I'd showed Father my car the Little Bastard--no top, no bumpers, toy windshield. I tried to get him to come along--

SOULS IN TORMENT: (*O.S.*) (*Vicious*) Five minutes! Let go ignorance.

JIMMY: (*To Souls*) Stop! Look I was traveling with the best mechanic in Germany! He had built the dern car.

(*A bell gongs louder than the first. The Red Scroll reads:*)

"Second mindful bell!"

(*Cries out*) Revive me somewhere. . .Somehow! Reverse the—

(*Baroque Adagio. Something like* Oboe Concerto in D minor.)

(*JIMMY fights off sleep*)

True! I knew the roads in LA were terrible.--But I was going to grab that wheel--race, till something released me. Watching the sunset while doing 120--I touched god. I slipped out my body, flew into the breathing! Like that outlaw in Crime and Punishment--"destroying the present for the sake of the better." And I loved the desert.

(*Tense MUSIC. Saint-Saens*, Danse Macabre.)

JIMMY: Awful truth is--(*Looks out, desperately*) I didn't turn on the head-lights or take an inventory of the road. I was used to doing 120! Just west of Choland, I almost hit this Pontiac—

(*Vision of the Red Scroll. HE reads*)

(*Reads*) "A family of 4 were in that car. 2 children!" (*Anguished sobs with guilt*) Oh no! I almost killed these kids. (*Reads*) "Do you know how many little ones have been slaughtered on highways"

(*Pictures on the Red Scroll of children killed on highways*)

MA: (*O.S.*) Resolve relationships!

JIMMY: Stop! (*Remorseful*) I didn't know--who was in the cars. They weren't people . . .they were--

I . . . I felt lightheaded as we sped out of Polonia Pass--where 466 would turn into 41--

(*SOUND of revving engines! Wind*)

It was warmer. (*To Ma*) I could see further. Hear better, feel connected. I relaxed.

SOULS IN TORMENT: (*O.S.*) (*Suspicious*) You were making a peaceful environment for--

JIMMY: No! Then . . .Then there was this speck! This car came right up to me. I remember screaming. "He's got to see us."

I didn't slam on the brake. I pushed that pedal. I'd crowd that car. Jam in front.

(*SOUND of crash*)

God! (*Remembering*) Oh god . . .no what . . .what happened to the others?

(*Vision of the Red Scroll. HE reads*)

(Reads) "The other driver is fine. Your friend was flung 12 feet, has massive injuries and is struggling for his life."

(Horrified) Oh god. . . What have I done? I didn't want to hurt anybody. *(Distraught, collapses sobbing)* How could I have done that to--He was my best . . .friend--

(Reads) "Transform your affliction. Prepare to leave this compound body of--Your state of mind now will determine your new life!"

SOULS IN TORMENT: *(O.S.)* *(Quieter)* Three minutes.

JIMMY *(To Souls)* Shut up!

Punish me! But help those poor men. I did torture many people on my way to . . .fame! Pardon me!

(A bell gongs loudly. A sign reads:)

(Reads) "The third mindful bell!"

(Vision of the Red Scroll. HE reads)

(Reads, recoiling) "You are partially forgiven. But you are totally dead. You're being admitted to weigh station to serve time."

(A placard reads, "Donald Gene Turnupseed, 23, a Cal poly student Kills James Dean.")

(SOUND: Baroque Adagio fades with rain)

(Stunned) What's that ball of golden light--growing until-- *(Scared)* Within it, there is a cemetery near a cornfield shaded by evergreens. *(Disturbed)* Paths are pretty, nice tombs. All those collections of leaves look like mysterious creatures.

MA: *(O.S.)* We've both made it to--I'm forgiven too. You'd buried by me.

JIMMY: Can't I go back? Christ and Lazarus were in the tomb 3 days.

MA: *(O.S.)* Even if we live old, life is a short ride.

(*Vision of the Red Scroll. HE reads*)

(*Reads*) "The cemetery bridges life. A lot of sadness comes thru here. You see things only God should see."

SOULS IN TORMENT: (*O.S.*) (*Voices straining, getting fainter*) Two minutes.

JIMMY: (*Overlapping Souls*) Stop the countdown. I'm not staying here.

(*Ponderous MUSIC: like Vivaldi*, Nisi Dominus)

(*JIMMY sees his funeral procession.*)

God, there's my funeral procession. And there's fresh dirt and the hole they'll—

MA: (*O.S.*) It's about balance. Ask for pardon

SOULS IN TORMENT: (*O.S.*) (*Nasty*) Let go ego and confusion.

JIMMY: (*Angry*) I made no will! I can't let my father get it all.

(*Sees his casket being carried out*)

Oh no, my varsity team is carrying my casket to the tomb. They look so young. Have so much life ahead.

(*Funeral bells*)

(*Reads from a Vision of the Red Scroll*)

"You'll linger above your tomb helping kids to learn caution."

(*Calls out*) Can't someone help me? I know my mind wasn't--I cut God out, but—

(*SOUNDS of people walking by*)

(*Repulsed*) There's Uncle and Aunt, sobbing . . .my agent, Father. . .I wish I could go back to earth. I had love all along but I threw it away. Help, Ma!

(*Wails uncontrollably*) I'll never be able to tell these people I loved them.

(*Sound of cranking. JIMMY's corpse is lowered in the grave*)

JIMMY: Don't put me in the grave.

SOULS IN TORMENT: (*O.S.*) (*Gasping quietly*) Say goodbye. Forty-five seconds.

JIMMY: (*Anguished*) I was brought up thinking love should be first. . . But I decided to prefer fame and to love people sometimes but most times not… Forgive me! Ma! I was out of touch. I didn't come from grace.

(*Bold organ MUSIC like* Albinoni Adagio *Continues under and fades at bells*)

JIMMY: (*Panicky, begging on death bed*) OH LET ME BE PARDONED. DON'T LET ME DIE IN THIS FALLEN STATE. Only love exists-- (*Desperately, falling on his knees*) I lived in hallucination.

(*Triumphant funeral bells*)

MA: (*O.S.*) All is forgiven.

JIMMY: Hooray! Thanks!

(*HE reads from a vision of the Red Scroll*)

JIMMY (*Reads, scared*) "Your assignment is to hover at your grave and warn kids of your fate. So they'll grow to be more peaceful humans, and you'll learn love. "

(*Maliciously*) That may take centuries.

(*Reads*) "The process involves a deep softening of your personality. A release into eternal connecting. . . .Because you die young, you'll be immortalized beyond your wildest dreams."

(*To self, delighted*) That's something at least.

SOULS IN TORMENT: (*O.S.*) (*Barely a whisper*) Fifteen seconds.

JIMMY: (*To Souls*) No more!

(*JIMMY finds his glasses, looks out shocked at the other tombs*)

(*MUSIC: Something like, Pachebal's* Canon)

JIMMY: My glasses! (*Shocked*) I see better without them! Look at the tomb-stones. So many people are watching me! (*Bows, waves*) I hope they aren't too friendly. What the heck, bring on the tourists, the signs, the shrine.

(*Cameras flashing. Photo of grave site becoming bigger.*)
(*To spirits, triumphant*) Actors are strange people. We're used to going to strange places, meeting strange people.

(*Raising hands in air, fiercely brave*) And we are used to surrendering into the hands of god!

(*MUSIC: Something loud and funky*)

(*Mug shot of JIMMY with cowboy hat*)

(*Black out*)

CURTAIN

DECICATED TO KEN DINGLEDINE WHO SUGGESTED
AND INSPIRED THIS PLAY.

MONTGOMERY CLIFT AND THE ALL-GIRL FAN CLUB

A PLAY IN TWO ACTS

CAST OF CHARACTERS

EXPANDABLE CAST OF 6 - 30+

MONTGOMERY CLIFT. 37.
A movie star: sallow cheeks, wayward hair. MONTY has
pushed himself beyond reasonable limits in his pursuit
of acting and family approval. HE is critically ill from an
automobile accident, which has disfigured his upper lip
and nose. HE has severe back pain and is often in a state of
altered consciousness.

MRS. ETHEL "SUNNY." FOGG CLIFT 67.
His mother. SHE is one of those striking women, nerves
of steel, who adores organizing her children's lives.

DR. BILLY. 32.
Montgomery's doctor, attractive. Could be played by a
man or very strong woman.

APPARITION. 37.
An unreal character. The ghostly vision of Montgomery's
twin sister. Plainer than Monty. (Could also play Marilyn
Monroe)

BARONESS IRMGARD GASSLER. 28.
Austrian heiress with mysterious wealth. SHE has loved
Montgomery for ten years, and has roamed the world to
marry him. SHE heads the all-girl fan club. (Could also
play Liz Taylor)

ROSOVSKAYA (or ROSTOVA). 47.
Montgomery's hard-nosed Russian acting coach.

LIZ TAYLOR. 25.
The famous lavender-eyed, brunette star.

MARILYN MONROE 31.
The famous blue-eye blonde star.

ALL GIRL FAN CLUB.
Ruby, Virginie, Ellie, et al.-- Hysterical teen girls who
believe in Montgomery and chase him.

THE PLACE

The MIND of MONTGOMERY CLIFT as HE hallucinates.
Most times we are in his mansion in New York, but sometimes we
are simply on the roof.

SETTING

The house on East 61st Street has a bare surreal quality
with mirrors draped in black

November 1957. Six months after his near-fatal car crash.
Somber music something like Tchaikovsky, *Romeo and
Juliet Fantasy* drifts up.

ACT ONE

*AT RISE: Midday rain light casts shadows on MONTGOMERY CLIFT,
37 in silk pajamas. One side of his face is bandaged. HE walks along the roof ledge.*

Below in the waiting area, DR. BILLY: 32, boyish confronts the glamorous
SUNNY CLIFT, 67.

DR. BILLY: Does Mr. Clift know we're removing the bandage?

(DR. BILLY waits nervously, looks about.)

DR. BILLY: Your son could be violent--

SUNNY: *(Flirtatious)* I can handle Southern depressives, my in-laws being
from Chattanooga--Don't worry, Doctor, I'm here to help if you need anything. *(Shrieks)* Mont-gom-ery! Maybe he's in the "toilette". *(Teasing)* If I
pressure him, he thinks I'm a bad mother. *(Calls)* MONT-GOM-ERY.

DR. BILLY: *(Inspecting about)* Books on… rewired jaws--?

SUNNY: I take them from his room so he can sleep. *(Secretive)* You wouldn't
believe the medical tomes he read… after--the disfiguration. *(Her smile cracking)* That's how I refer to his face since *(Faltering)*…the car crash. Even after
six months I can't stop thinking about how buttoned up elegant he was before.

ALL GIRL FAN CLUB: *(O.S.) (Faintly from the distance)* Montgomery! We lo-ve you!

SUNNY: Fans still surround the house--despite the rain. Sherry?

DR. BILLY: I HAVE TO REMOVE THE BANDAGE.

SUNNY: Shouldn't his surgeon do that?

DR. BILLY: Your son keeps postponing him.

SUNNY: What's the hurry?

DR. BILLY: It's unhealthy to keep that gauze on. The surgeon thought his psychiatrist--.

SUNNY: You? *(Laughs)* I hate any word that begins with a PSY--*(Pause)* Monty can't do another film.

DR. BILLY: I don't agree. He worked with a wired jaw and completed *Raintree*.

SUNNY: With Amphetamines, Barbiturates, Intravenous Morphine!

(Lights up on MONTGOMERY on roof ledge with a bottle of pills)

MONTGOMERY: I wonder how many of these babies it takes to never wake up. They say this capsule gives you a cold for a day, like a virus, and presto you die in your sleep. Your heart explodes! Ha! ... But can you believe those bastards who say that?

(MONTGOMERY leans dangerously over the roof edge.)

(FANS and the Austrian BARONESS, 28 extravagantly dressed, rush over with binoculars from a connecting roof.)

ALL GIRL FAN CLUB: STOP! ...Mont-gom-ery!

BARONESS: *(Austrian accent)* I reesk my life coming from my roof to save you-You valking disaster, bourbon on your shirt, bandage on your cheek.

ALL GIRL FAN CLUB: Montgomery! We LOVE you!

MONTGOMERY: Quiet, girls!

BARONESS: But I'm your Baroness. I run fan club. Darlink! I got binocu-lars. For you and zee girls. Zey can stand back ven zey study you, and you loook at us ven you vant.

MONTGOMERY: Just--Tell me if I'm conscious. Am I hallucinating? Mad?

BARONESS: Your mind ees unstable. You go een and out of consciousness—

MONTGOMERY: So this bandage is REAL.

BARONESS: Yes. Your jaw vas rewired for second time since car crash. I tink you vill loooook better. Play mu-sic, a sym-phony. Relax your face into vat you vere before! Vith right music, your face could reshape itself into features you had in *Red River*.

(Thunder. Rain falls. MONTGOMERY goes to his bedroom, plays a record, some-thing like Tragic Overture Opus 81.)

(DR. BILLY and SUNNY enter.)

SUNNY: Lower that! Ah, son! You weren't in the rain!!

MONTGOMERY: I need fresh air.

SUNNY: *(Lighthearted)* I keep towels ready--I can't keep him off the roof. Put away those binoculars! *(To DOCTOR, flirtatious)* My husband wouldn't allow binoculars in the house. Said they were for the beach.

MONTGOMERY: *(Slurred speech)* Bi-no-culars express a tr--uth about the para--meters of f-f-reedom.

SUNNY: How drugged are you? Won't you let me get closer?

DR. BILLY: Sit! It's time to remove that bandage.

ALL GIRL FAN CLUB: *(O.S.)* We LO-VE you!

BARONESS: *(O.S.)* PLAY A SYMPHONY!

SUNNY: I've brought a tiny mirror.

MONTGOMERY: Did you know *(Pacing)* powerful music releases endorphins—

SUNNY: You can look at a little part of your face—

MONTGOMERY: --like heroin of the mind. The right song triggers a gateway--

SUNNY: *(To DOCTOR)* He's mad!

ALL GIRL FAN CLUB: *(O.S.)* Put on a cowboy song. Put on your hat and holster. Come to the window!

MONTGOMERY: Let's play the sound track from *Red River*. Listen to sounds of suffocation .... heat. Let Matt live again!

(Acts out a cowboy scene)

DR. BILLY: Stop emoting!

MONTGOMERY: I'm connecting with this ENERGY SOURCE to create a surge of strength--

SUNNY: Let us help you.

MONTGOMERY: Chopin fought tuberculosis, fueling up with music, till 39-- Brahms kept powered up with one *Overture* for ten years.

DR. BILLY: I understand you're upset. Those butchers botched the first surgery. There was nothing to do but break your jaw again and rewire it. But if we have to rectify a problem, it'll be harder to do if your face gets infected--

MONTGOMERY: You said I could take another knife.

DR. BILLY: Take off that old bandage and let your cheek breathe-- A shot could relax you—

MONTGOMERY: *(To DOC, violent)* No closer with that needle.

ALL GIRL FAN CLUB: *(Shouting O.S.)* Come to the window! We LO-VE you.

DR. BILLY: If you prefer--you can remove the bandage. Give yourself the injection... Call me and your mother when you're ready. We'll be just outside.

(DR. BILLY and SUNNY exit. MONTGOMERY puts on music, injects himself, raises his arms to heavens.)

(Looking to the heavens) Kindly sounds! Relax my muscles into the way they were before.

(Lights tremble. Theatrical music plays something like Chopin, Scherzo No 1 in B Minor Opus. 20. An APPARITION dressed like a mourning monk with cowl pulled down, walks through the mirror.)

APPARITION *(FRIAR)*: *(Echo-like loud)* It's a long way across... but you can't quit now. I'm here to guide you.

MONTGOMERY: *(Freaked)* Who are...? I'm not Catholic-- Oh my!!--Did that shot do--

APPARITION *(FRIAR)*: Even half paralyzed you can't quit.

MONTGOMERY: --me in? Am I hallucinating? I'm trying to find the guts to take off this gauze. *(Chuckles)* Guts/gauze, kinda poetic.

APPARITION: Review your journals.

MONTGOMERY: --Are you serious--What pills have I—

APPARITION: You kept notes to give yourself courage. READ! *(The FRIAR hands him a book. HE reads:)*

MONTGOMERY: My first journal. Oh--no! *(Reads nervously)* "Melancholy I is the most famous enigmatic print in history. Her dejected demeanor reveals imbalance. Melancholy knows science can't create art. A plane, ruler, stone--lay abandoned as she gazes upward." *(Recalls triumphant)* Dürer wanted to achieve the highest artistry in every work! But how can Melancholy I help me now?

(The FRIAR disrobes and becomes a little girl with a boyish haircut. SHE speaks in a baby voice. Another record drops on, something like Vangelis, La Petite Fille do la Mer *which sounds like a music box.)*

MONTGOMERY: My god! Are you--. . .Sister? <u>But you're dead!</u>

APPARITION: No, I'm in Omaha, Nebraska.

MONTGOMERY: This has got to be a nightmare! . . No--

APPARITION: Our communication can still be strong. It's like living in a double house, we share the same door--So I can guide you.

MONTGOMERY: *(Scared)* But you're a dre-am?

APPARITION: No, I'm you. We've linked through the mind. Let me take off your bandage. I'll direct what you do. I was always the uglier twin.

MONTGOMERY: When I look in the mirror I don't want to see you!

APPARITION: Fine! You want to define yourself with surgery, like you did with a bow tie.

MONTGOMERY: I can't take your ... your provocations--Where you accuse me of self-pity! *(Fights sleep)* Before I acted like... as something that came--into my own mind--like drawing a bucket from a well. Onstage, I'd come out dressed a certain way and I didn't think about it, I'd be wearing the same insides. On screen, I'd tap the same pulse. I was in a circle of giving before; now I'm in a cocoon of selfishness and it feels great.
(Angry, gets confused)
I hate being an actor. It feels so simultaneously noble and trivial. I gave all to the theatre. Did everything. Learned everything. But sometimes I fear I'm just a grown man, playing dress up. In another family, I might have marched beside a King or led a combat patrol--

(SOUND of a distant wind chime)

APPARITION: I can't stay. The longest dream lasts 7 minutes. Listen. The rain cries for you! You've dealt with agony before.

MONTGOMERY: Before...I didn't have to... rely on words that took me nowhere. *(Sleepy)* I could always find--the hallow log--for the feeling! In *From Here to Eternity*, I rehearsed—

APPARITION: You've got to be the actor who loves you.

MONTGOMERY: What's that mean?

APPARITION: Take off the bandage. You'll come back from this a better artist--with more feeling.

MONTGOMERY: I don't want more feeling. I want a face. I want to stay inside the hope ... before. OKAY pull it off. You were born first. You're the brave one. I didn't want to come out. Oh God please give me a face I can control and move in front of the camera, a face that'll keep me working... worthy for a... lead. A face people recognize so I don't have to apologize and say first, "I'm Monty Clift." But what music should I play?

APPARITION: Whatever record falls.

(Gloomy MUSIC resonates on the Hi Fi, something like Schubert, Symphony no 8 in B minor. SHE pulls off the bandage and disappears. HE collapses on the bed.)

(Next door, DR. BILLY and SUNNY confer in a waiting area.)

SUNNY: He's playing calming music. ...We can go in soon.

DR. BILLY: Why is he obsessed with art, with music--You schooled him?

SUNNY: In everything. Tutoring and European travel were part of the grand scheme... My children were beautifully educated, associating only with each other... and with... their own kind.

DR. BILLY: Your son rarely sees his father. Were the Clifts angry about your being an orphan?

SUNNY: *(Shocked)* You've done your homework... I'm a descendent of the Anderson/Blairs. When I was 18, Dr. Montgomery who delivered me told me who I was.

DR. BILLY: Your family never accepted you.

SUNNY: They promised if I raised my children as aristocrats to--

DR. BILLY: But they changed their mind, as the rich do. Your son is a cyclops. Half of his past is missing. Help me push him forward. Under my watchful eye, he achieved perfection in *Raintree County*--

SUNNY: While drinking up a storm on the set. He defends his crazy behavior, saying it was approved by "Victor," code for you.

DR. BILLY: We're close. I believe in him.

SUNNY: I do too. Montgomery was the darling of Broadway. Once he chose a career in theatre, I channeled my energy into that--taking him to singing and voice lessons, ballet classes. I should have confronted his... his... obsession with that leather satchel, with 200 types of painkillers. If he hadn't gone back so sick and finished *Raintree,* perhaps his face might have slowly mended, but now that's finished. "An opulent circus" is what the critics called it.

DR. BILLY: Montgomery needs the carefree childhood he never had. Dressed in white suits for grandparents who slammed the door in his face?

SUNNY: You're not blaming his condition on me.

DR. BILLY: But I am--If he lives differently, *freely*, his strength will return. I've advised him to lock his door so he can choose whether to let you in *or not*.

(Fade to bedroom where MONTGOMERY approaches the mirror, HE exercises his face)

MONTGOMERY: *(To self)* I had a shot I'm feeling more human. True artists keep growing themselves. *(Commanding himself)* Don't be a coward-- Will yourself to stand before the looking glass.

(Removing the veil on the mirror)

Lord, it can't be… When I smile, I can't pull my lip up. My jaw's frozen. My eyes are moving but the rest of my face is paralyzed… wooden. *(Turning)* My profile is ok… but ok isn't good enough for a screen star! You have to be the all American male 100%. *(Recalling)* Oh God! I can't remember my face. I'm not the same. I peer in the glass and the man I knew is gone. Where are those journals? If only something I wrote could - -help me adapt to the unlivable!

(Opens a book, puts his finger on something)

Lets see what the poet Auden says: "Far from his illness/The wolves ran on through the evergreen forests. The death of the poet was kept from his poems."

(Phone rings. MONTGOMERY answers, dazed, sits, clutches his head. We see LIZ TAYLOR on her hotel room phone.)

(As HE talks on the phone with LIZ, HE roots about looking for his journal almost tripping over the long phone cord.)

MONTGOMERY: *(Into phone, despairing)* Liz… Yes… off it… is… Improved?… No! My face has too much *gravitas*! *(Laughs)* The sides of the face don't match.

LIZ TAYLOR: Maybe it's the mirror. Or the light.

MONTGOMERY: To think I used to enjoy catching glimpses of us together.

LIZ TAYLOR: Look again while I'm on the phone. Another plastic surgeon might—

MONTGOMERY: No. They said this was the last time I could go under oxygen. It would kill me. *(Sudden discovery)* Montgomery Clift died the day I came back from the crash… It's like a century and a blip. *(Jokes)* I'm going to have to wear all black to work because I'm in mourning or wait for people to die so they'll forget who I was. Better yet I'll live with a mask over my face. Every time I take it off, I'll allow myself to cry. I haven't cried since I was eight and this bully tried to drown me in a ship's pool. I burst a gland in my neck trying to breathe.

LIZ TAYLOR: I'd like to visit you.

MONTGOMERY: Not now! I shouldn't have had that surgery. There's a fine line between feeling surprised and feeling manipulated. I didn't believe my looks were going because they'd never left me before.

LIZ TAYLOR: *(Hearing him, distracted)* What are you doing! Talk to me.

MONTGOMERY: I'm looking for for my... other journals. For Things... Things I learned that could help—

LIZ TAYLOR: I've got good news—

MONTGOMERY: For instance... In this journal there's... pictures of—

LIZ TAYLOR: Wait. I did something that...

MONTGOMERY: Ah Ha. Philip the Bold and John the Fearless--.

LIZ TAYLOR: I invested in a role for you-

MONTGOMERY: These alabaster statues... of monks--the mourners of the Dukes of Burgundy--surround their caskets—

LIZ TAYLOR: A role in my film *Suddenly Last Summer*—

MONTGOMERY: Hey... What?... Repeat that.

LIZ TAYLOR: I financed a role for you in--

MONTGOMERY: You PUT UP MONEY? BOUGHT ME A PART?

LIZ TAYLOR: I made a donation to the company so you could--

MONTGOMERY: I can't take a bought role--.To do it I'd have to give up being me. --I'd love to read for the part. *(Joking)* TELL COLUMBIA MONTGOMERY CLIFT WILL AUDITION FOR THE ROLE.

(HE hangs up.)

(SOUND: ocean waves.)

(We see MARILYN MONROE on a distant phone in California. She wears white silk and blows on her nails, which SHE is painting.)

(MONTGOMERY'S phone rings. HE answers, confused.)

MARILYN: *(Into phone)* Montgomery? ...Montgomery?

MONTGOMERY: *(Scared, to phone)* I hear a double sound. Are you <u>the</u> Marilyn? Dreams come and go. I may be in one now. I don't know.

MARILYN: No, baby. I'm real *(Squeals)* Whee! I'm in California. Did you take off the bandage?

MONTGOMERY: I'm busy honey... Looking through some books. Could you call later?

MARILYN: Tell me about the surgery. *Do you like your face?*

MONTGOMERY: Don't ask me that question. *(Giggling)* I'm too neurotic. Hey did I leave my last journal with you. I three-hole punched my script used extra paper for research, script, dreams, crises etc. It got me through *Raintree.*

MARILYN: How, baby?

MONTGOMERY When I saw my... face in the rushes, I'd journal something.

MARILYN: I'll check. But I don't think I've got your book here. ...Why not go to the Actor's Studio?

MONTGOMERY: That dingy room--

MARILYN: Turn psychology into behavior! Choose *courage.* Protest for the future! --Or come here. *(Breathy)* We'll get between white satin sheets with Jungle Gardenia perfume and seconal. Bye.

(MARILYN hangs up and so does MONTGOMERY. APPARITION enters, blows on an hourglass; it illuminates. Eerie music like Ravel, "Prelude a la Nuit.")

APPARITION: I'm here to help you. Use our secret twin language. *Bavel boo boop*

MONTGOMERY: Bee baa, bop… Go! …You're not real.

APPARITION: We can talk extra-sen-sor-ily. In our private code. *Keep, karp, cape…* You don't need a book!

MONTGOMERY: But I… I do! Writing kept me… from exploding. While waiting for a shoot, I'd sit apart with my journal. My jaw was freshly wired and made terrible snapping sounds but… I kept a picture of my crashed car in that book, to remind myself it was a miracle I was alive. When I couldn't sleep or had to talk to press people, I'd find a way to…

APPARITION: I never thought I was attractive when I was younger.

MONTGOMERY: You weren't *(Stops himself)* Go! *Farp, mark, fap…* I'm got to shave. Then my face will look better for sure.

(Arranges supplies, starts to shave)

APPARITION: *Zeep, zap, zarp!* Don't busy yourself out!… Before when you leaned into the glass, you knew how beautiful you were; the mirror would find you. Now you must find the glass.

(Wind chimes. SHE blows on the hour glass; it goes black. SHE vanishes.

(DR. BILLY enters, goes close to MONTGOMERY.)

DR. BILLY: *(Aggressive)* Come closer. Lets talk doctor talk. You've removed the gauze. *(Cautious)* The nose and lip are mending. The chin is—

MONTGOMERY: Battered. Immobile. Back. . . Mephistopheles.

DR. BILLY: Can you move your upper lip? Yes the shape is—

MONTGOMERY: Barely *(To mirror, angry)* Baa Baa Baa. Baa--baa--I'm a billy goat. Don't you know. *(HE cackles a child's nursery rhyme)*

DR. BILLY: Let me look at that scar. Here in the light.

MONTGOMERY: No, Judas. I'm shaving! The inner journey was what that *Raintree* book was—

DR. BILLY: Oh don't move away. How can I help you if you give me your back? When we were together on the set, you coped—

MONTGOMERY: *(Rage)* I could hardly move. Sometimes you had to lead me by the elbow. I was in a trance.

DR. BILLY: But it was I who supported you—

MONTGOMERY: Out! Lucifer.

DR. BILLY: I made you write in that book. Contain your feelings… Your face isn't that bad, now.

MONTGOMERY: It's worse than before.

DR. BILLY: Don't wave the razor. You want to cut your--

MONTGOMERY: Should I slit my throat or yours. *Freeek*--

DR. BILLY: You got so much attention when you completed *Raintree*. You had all these actors radiating around you. Sort of like a frat party at the genius level. That'll happen again.

MONTGOMERY: It was the gold coins--PRINCE OF DARKNESS. By the end, people resented me because I'd gotten so many privileges--. I couldn't tell--If they weren't supporting me because I couldn't act anymore or if they were just sick of me. …

DR. BILLY: You were disappointed when you looked at your face? Help yourself not to be reactive. Your skin will relax into it's own tension.

MONTGOMERY: When? Tomorrow? Next week?

DR. BILLY: Let me worry for us both. There's increasing research that anxiety will destabilize you.

MONTGOMERY: I'm hungry for hope!

(SOUND of rain. Knocking on the door.)

SUNNY: *(O.S.) (Pushy)* Open up! This is your mother!

DR. BILLY: Action follows being. *(Quietly)* If someone bullies you habitually, they're a torturer.

(SUNNY bursts in. MONTGOMERY puts gauze back on his cheek. Hides inside a journal. Sound of intense rain)

SUNNY: Awful rain. I wanted to see if you'd closed your windows--You need anything?

MONTGOMERY: Come close. Stare. Why don't you. I just opened this boyhood journal and it lands on the statue I like best. The marble *Demidorf Table* by Lorenzo Bartelini. I kept this image to teach me something.

SUNNY: May I see your face son? Why are you acting foolish?

MONTGOMERY: Inspired! *(Pause)* Florence 1812. The subject is Cupid-God of Generations--

SUNNY: *(Shocked by his face)* Now.... Some people aren't—

MONTGOMERY: Stretched out upon the plan of the world--

SUNNY: --classically beautiful-- But you can't take your eyes off--

MONTGOMERY: Cupid--Watching over the genius of debauchery who snores in his sleep--

SUNNY: The French call it Ugly/pretty.

MONTGOMERY: --his head extending beyond the rim of the world. *(Pause)* Here look at my face, bitch! Before it was just another thing. *(Turns, growls)* Now it's got *teeth*.

SUNNY: Why are you mean? To me, you're still a star.

MONTGOMERY: No, whore. *(Hostile)* There's a certain confidence leading men have that says I deserve to be watched.

SUNNY: I think *Raintree* will be your defining role.

MONTGOMERY: How can you say that. The reviews say I struck out.

SUNNY: That director bullied you.

MONTGOMERY: I stood up for myself many times-- …I don't know where I belong in this bloody structure-- I'm not going to be in projects I don't believe in or *kowtow* to men I don't admire.

(HE runs up to the roof. The BARONESS waits nearby. HE looks around.)

MONTGOMERY: *(Defiant)* I'm looking for this big black notebook. Marked 1957. Did you see it?

BARONESS: *(Crazed)* I've been vaiting for you. I vant to lo-ve you. I don't care vat you look like. Vhy you need zese book?

MONTGOMERY: In *Raintree*, I explored… Dostoyevsky's idea of darkness. On set, I scourged myself to create a new reality. To overcome… feeling so weak, I plumbed certain things… I can't remember… the swamp, the fiendish rainstorms—

BARONESS: *(Thrilled)* You're vonderful. More perfect zan your roles.

MONTGOMERY: *(Nasty, Laughs)* NO! When I play these men, these magnanimous characters, I say "Am I magnanimous or am I just good at playing it?" Sometimes, I feel noble. I'm showing humanity themselves so we can evolve. Mostly, I just want the applause. I want to be loved, and I don't care by whom. Now could you help… locate my book.

BARONESS: Don't vorry, my darlink! *(Theatrical)* I find eet. Love only zose who l-o--o-ve you.

(SOUND of light rain. Below SUNNY and DR. BILLY straighten the bedroom)

SUNNY: *(Grief struck)* I'll just put away some of these awards while Montgomery's away. That's him on that pedestal-I want you to discourage him from further acting--

DR. BILLY: He needs our support.

SUNNY: His Oscar nominations? *(Nervous)* Why remind him.

DR. BILLY: Because he's going back.

SUNNY: His face is like Stonehenge. *(To self)* You never know the sacrifices that are required. It's sad you never encouraged him to return to the theatre. He could have been a director. He was such a lover of theatre and a non-lover of movies.

DR. BILLY: Monty needs to believe there's *hope*. He knows he'll probably fail, but in case he won't he should audition.

SUNNY: *(Moving some pictures)* I'll put my relatives photos in front. Monty collects them. He bears an amazing resemblance to both sides--Fine boned like the Blairs, dark expressive brows like the--Andersons.

DR. BILLY: I'm ordering you to put his acting pictures back!

SUNNY: Have some soothing sherry, doctor. ... *(Reminiscing)* You can't let the theatre go. It's boot camp for artists. Neither you nor Monty understands the connection between a movie career and sex appeal.

DR. BILLY: He can work if he's not typecast as a—

SUNNY: A romantic hero. But he has a natural proclivity to that! The public doesn't care about those invasive techniques the Actor's Studio encourages--Falling into icy rivers, fighting till the point of collapse--

DR. BILLY: He can go to the edge with a small role. I won't let it all come crashing down on--

SUNNY: You want him to cry when he returns to his dressing room--Let out wails of purging. Become so drained, he can't walk!

DR. BILLY: He needs to fulfill his ambition! He can eat raw eggs and milk to keep himself energized. I'll limit the shots of codeine in his dressing room. Take away the—

SUNNY: Will you catch him when he hangs off the roof ledge? *(Pause)* How am I supposed to encourage this. I who... cancelled his early auditions when it rained. Not allowing him to get wet. I, who encouraged proficiency in the expensive sports--fencing, riding, tennis. Made him conjugate in Latin, dissect the Concertos of Bach, discuss Marcel Proust in 5 languages.-- Now he can gracefully retire.

DR. BILLY: I admire you *(Pause)* because I know you won't listen to me. You're from the generation of tough old broads. Crocodile skin. You got in front because you were tougher than the men. I always feel like you should be looking around for a spittoon.

(ROSTOVA, the acting coach, beautiful in a scattered way, enters with roses. SHE has a slight Russian accent — rolled r's and monotone.)

(MONTGOMERY walks in from the roof. Outside wind and thunder mount.)

ROSTOVA: *(Hyper)* Allo peoples! *(Shocked at his face. Rolls her r)* Dearest Monty! I've come to dirrrect your career!

MONTGOMERY: *(To DOC)* My acting coach. Come closer, pet and give me advice on this journal entry.

ROSTOVA: I bring flowers. A little lifeline to stage.

(SHE gives him flowers, but is horrified. HE hides in his journal.)

MONTGOMERY: Thanks. Dürer thought artists like flowers shouldn't strive for one standard of beauty--He said, *(Dramatic, reads)* "If you wish to make a beautiful human figure it is necessary you probe nature and the proportions of many people, a head from one, a breast, arm, leg from another." So, who's hiring me, pet?

ROSTOVA: Sweetheart, no good news, but *(Looks around, jealous)* I wait.

DR. BILLY: *(Jealous)* Excuse me. I need to go feed my dogs.

(SUNNY and DR. BILLY exit.)

ROSTOVA: Patience, love. Starrrs have bodyguards around them--So we must wait.

MONTGOMERY: I'm itchy to work. Did I leave my *Raintree* journal with you?

ROSTOVA: Listen to me! Nobody want you now as leading man. They all talk...Brando--

MONTGOMERY: That book brought... sweetness to my life.

ROSTOVA: People look at your rrrushes and say, "If you don't star-

MONTGOMERY: I know what I do well and I know what I don't do well. I'm a leading man. *Hamlet, Henry V,* Tom in *Glass Menagerie.* It's not that that's surprising. I don't think about it for periods of time.

SUNNY: *(O.S.)* MONT-GOM-ERY!

ROSTOVA: *(High pitched)* Get rid of crrrazy mother!

MONTGOMERY: *(To MOM, vicious)* Leave! *(To ROSTOVA, obsessed)* Where's that journal! I put enough work in my roles that it's hard to cast me as a secondary part unless the lead is great because it unbalances the show.

ROSTOVA: You can't compete with youngerrrr smarrrter actors.

MONTGOMERY: *(Finds gloves)* Ah boxing gloves. *(Pantomimes boxing)* I'm fractured in my experience of--I need a part where I can violate somebody-

SUNNY: *(O.S.) (Shrieking)* Mont-gomery!

MONTGOMERY: Where I connect with a power source—

ROSTOVA: People don't want arrrm waving--

MONTGOMERY: Go someplace that isn't crafted or controlled.

ROSTOVA: Thrrowing energy---

MONTGOMERY: Fight the character's last fight--as they say at the Studio--. I hate being self-focused. I'm a man now I'm not a boy and -- *(HE goofs off boxing the air)* Robert E. Lee "Prew' Prewitt here: Find my journal and let's move forward--It's good to do things slowly rather than wrong.

ROSTOVA: I don't want tell you--About Liz's film. Liz called me.

MONTGOMERY: I made it through Monday. I've got to ease into Tuesday.

ROSTOVA: Columbia want you audition. I say you won't. But such rrrre-versal... Why trrry out when they would offer it. I decide-

MONTGOMERY: Why?? *(Theatrical)* Auditioning is my absolute guilty pleasure.

ROSTOVA: You're auditioning?! They say you call them. Word spread like brrrushfire. Montgomery Clift is auditioning?...Liz was paralyzed. I was paralyzed. While it's hard for her, your doing genemral audition, it's impossible for me. Here's script. Columbia says you too frrragile for lead. You should work yourself back into something. --You're up for brrrother--nice cameo.

MONTGOMERY: I'M AUDITIONING FOR A CAMEO?

ROSTOVA: I can't talk morrrre... brrreak into tears. I leave scrrript from Liz. Look at it. Let me know.

(ROSTOVA exits. MONTGOMERY turns on a record. Gentle music like Ravel, Prelude a la Nuit *drifts up. HE picks up, scans the script.)*

MONTGOMERY: "To audition or not to audition. That's the question. Whether tis nobler in the mind to suffer the slings and arrows of outra-geous *(Riffs on the poetry)* rejection or by retreating, flee them--To quit, to perform no more and by stopping, end the battery of public assaults the actor is prey to."

(HE tosses the script. APPARITION walks through mirror wearing shorts, a white shirt, and a bob haircut. Talks in strange language.)

APPARITION: *(Intrusive, unrelenting) Bovel beard boo bai babie--Yeep Yup!* I need to know. You've accepted a role?

MONTGOMERY: Shush! I'm reviewing a script. *(Scared) Ikwo leez a roo noo.* Am I dreaming?

APPARITION: Yes.

MONTGOMERY: *(Angry) Fip Kip* What drugs did I take? Let me see... Nembutal, Doriden, Luminal, Seconal, Phenobarbital?

(SHE reads over his shoulder.)

APPARITION: The film of *Suddenly Last Summer* By Tennessee Williams. We read the play together! …They don't know who the male star of the show is?

MONTGOMERY: Where did I put my pencil? My good pen. *Fip Fook!*

APPARITION: The screenplay is by Gore Vidal. Fantastic.

MONTGOMERY: I'll start by marking all my lines in yellow.

APPARITION: *(Reading)* "A sexually repressed doctor heals a mad girl..." You're the doctor, and Liz Taylor is the girl? What fun.

MONTGOMERY: I'm up for the secondary role of Brother Holly. *Fip! Fook*

APPARITION: Oh, I don't believe that. *(Laughs)*

MONTGOMERY: When I finish marking the script, I'll count my lines.

APPARITION: What's the smallest number you'd do? *Zep seep zoo.* *(Pause)* As a boy you were so closed so condensed like you were trying to make yourself smaller. Suddenly you are much smaller. *See sap soap.* Do you want a tiny role? HA!

(A doorbell rings offstage)

MRS.CLIFT: *(O.S.) (Screams)* I'll get it.

MONTGOMERY: They're not offering me the lead.

APPARITION: But you could maneuver that. Turn Liz on to it. She's in love with you.

MONTGOMERY: No!

APPARITION: Liz ignited you in *Raintree.* Together you had the flawless physiques, the perfect temperament, this sluggish sensuality.

MONTGOMERY: That was acting, idiot! *Feep fook fuck.*

APPARITION: You were melancholy, cruel like cats. Her marriage was rocky.

MONTGOMERY: I'm turning all the lights on. You're not real.

APPARITION: FESS UP AND I'LL GO--Pretend I'm Liz in *A Place in the Sun* and you're George Eastman and you say—

MONTGOMERY: *(As George, angry)* "I love you...." *(Pause)* All right! *(Touchy)* I fell for Liz--just enough so it didn't cause an affair but when we got on screen we were so psyched. --The only time we had to kiss was in front of people *(Reckless, laughing)* And Liz got nervous and she'd pull away.

APPARITION: You had your fingers under that girl's skin. Why not *demand* the lead *(Hisses)* so you can fondle her! What can possibly harm you, because you've been harmed through and through.

MONTGOMERY: *Skep ske skeook!* Look I may have... I don't even know... if I've got the cameo. Or if I want it. I need to see what scenes I'm in... *Rop reep rope rou!* I did some fool joke and *promised to AUDITION. FEEP SOOK SAP.* If you have any power, give me some peace, so I can... get a handle on this script and get my senses back.

(APPARITION exits. MONTGOMERY puts on dark MUSIC, sits with the script. Lights up on waiting area. DR. BILLY reenters. SUNNY takes his coat. SOUND of rain.)

DR. BILLY: *(Flimsy excuse)* I... couldn't get a cab.

SUNNY: Your clothes are too tight *(Rolls her eyes, knowing)* Doctor Neuter! You're married, but I suspect you have a "friend."

DR. BILLY: Are you curious about my relationship with Monty?

SUNNY: Not at all. *(Pause)* Let me make that clear. *(Pause)* Your tight pants say a lot.

DR. BILLY: *(Pause)* May I use your phone? *(Into phone)* Send a car to 31 E. 61st.

(Hangs up phone. Crash of lightening.)

SUNNY: Will my son's face improve? *(Pause)* Ever? So it won't... fine... Have you told him? *(Pause)* Are you going to? He watches you, listening for every little tick of hope-- He won't listen to me. We used to have a relationship of mutual specialness. Now we rarely communicate about anything. In the morning, we sit at the breakfast table reading the paper without saying a word. Will you at least encourage him to vacation with me in Florida?

DR. BILLY: And rot among the brain dead?

SUNNY: He could create his own theatre family there. The little theatres would be kind—

DR. BILLY: I won't let you turn him into a remote, surface-talking actor. *Totemesque.* Using the proclamation method. A public speaker pretending to be an actor.

SUNNY: But--His body can't withstand all these drugs. Deep periods of morbidity ending with rash scenes of violence! In *Raintree* he was running a high fever, stuttering, confusing his lines. But still you let him be beaten to a pulp. His face is worse... Kindly stop fixing him...Dr. Neuter.

(Tooting of a car outside.)

DR. BILLY: My car. *(Looks about)* Where's my androgynous coat?

(DR. BILLY exits. Lights up on the bedroom where MONTGOMERY drinks and scavenges about. SOUND of heavy rain. SUNNY enters with a tray.)

SUNNY: The door was unlocked, so... Could you eat something?

MONTGOMERY: *(Violent)* Have you seen my acting journal?

SUNNY: Why keep obsessing on that?

MONTGOMERY: I've been reading--Tennessee Williams. Dialogue tastes nice. It's got all that marvelous subterranean stuff going on. If I could--

SUNNY: You're going to burn yourself out.

MONTGOMERY: *(Vomiting up his anguish)* I won't do it from my soul.

SUNNY: Have some milk--You need rest.

MONTGOMERY: *(Pounds a table)* English actors act from their bodies—

SUNNY: You're going to implode--

MONTGOMERY: Copying surface gestures: Lawrence Olivier--

SUNNY: You're eight pounds lighter on an already lean frame. You could almost wisp away. I breathe a sign of relief when I go to bed each night because you're still alive.

MONTGOMERY: I know what to eat to put the weight back on.

SUNNY: *(Pleading)* Can't you... start another career?

MONTGOMERY: *(Outburst of rage, pounds table)* Acting is all I know. I feel indebted to that--that—

SUNNY: Summer camp in Connecticut?

MONTGOMERY: To the universe. God. The calling.

SUNNY: Teach! In Florida--

MONTGOMERY: I've a lingering distrust of the classroom and--Florida--

SUNNY: Garbo retired gracefully. She's a year younger than you--

MONTGOMERY: *(Scared)* I'm not going to dry up or careen down another canyon-- I'm going to stay sane, stay alive, and stay working.

SUNNY: But the stamina to withstand hours of filming has diminished to a pathetic level--

MONTGOMERY: (*Holding up his glass*) Presbyterian gin… Water and tonic. Don't worry, bitch. I'm going to succeed. I'll add something in-- something from my head that drives me. (*Punching a fist into his palm*) The auditioner will feel this "unsaid!"--(*Pause*) After the accident, I could barely get out of bed. The second I stepped on the set of *Raintree*, my jaw, ear, weight problems all went away The adrenaline and the joy of acting pushed the illness away. I wrote down all I did and felt, so I could stay in that place of commitment. Now I can't recall what I--. I need AIR!

(*MONTGOMERY flees to the roof where the BARONESS waits with a large umbrella.*)

BARONESS: (*Frenzy of passion, Austrian accent*) I hope you von't mind me buying zee brownstone next door.

MONTGOMERY: Actually I need to be by myself to *focus* on where I put some--

BARONESS: But vhen I learned zee 2 roofs connect and ve had view of East River--Oh, say some riverboat line like in *Raintree* and I'll go—

MONTGOMERY: (*Indulging her*) "I like your river. I really do. It even smells good."

(*BARONESS responds in LIZ'S role, dramatic approaching with umbrella*)

MONTGOMERY: (*Stopping her*) You said you'd leave?

BARONESS: Eet's steeel drizzling. I don't vant you get vet. Vone day I marry you! Vhy you come here--eef you don't vant talk to me?

MONTGOMERY: Pardon my directness but--Being frank-inadvertently, somebody gets hurt in the process. The roof's where I go to hear myself think. (*Laughs*) It's the only place Mom won't come. She has an alert spiritual antenna. She could beam and find you. But she has a fear of heights. I can study or drink here--(*Pointedly*) alone.

(*Takes out a flask & the script. BOBBY-SOXERS yell from next door.*)

ALL GIRL FAN CLUB: (*O.S.*) Montgomery! Let us take a picture. Snap a shot.

BARONESS: *(Screams at girls)* Stay on my roof. Back!

ALL GIRL FAN CLUB: *(O.S.)* We love you, Montgomery.

MONTGOMERY: *(Laughs, manic)* Those girls are staring at me. Grwwl. I'm still hot. *(Concedes)* It's nice to have a few fans.

BARONESS: Yes. Eeef you don't have admirers even eeef you pretend you don't need zem, you lose confidence. *(Bursts into tears)* I'm relieved you talk to me. I study naturopatheec medeeecine and medeeetation to--Silence your pain. Be carefree. You get less vrinkless. *(Worried)* Vat's vrong, darlink.

MONTGOMERY: *(Clutches his head)* There's this ringing inside my ear... I need my journal to try to figure out other times when I overcame that...

BARONESS: Vhat zis boook loook like?

MONTGOMERY: It was 9 by 12 inches, black. Sometimes I brought it up here... when I felt positive and strong and confident. *(Gasps)*--I live with a panic, which I never felt before. I move about quickly but morbidly. ...It feels like I'm balancing an elephant on my head.

BARONESS: Vhy you act crrrazy?

MONTGOMERY: Because I'm going to have to leave this film business... If I can't find some... Some anchor...After so many years... I started at 13. It's been 300 years... Early on I saw myself as a character in a story. I was fortunate enough to have questionable lineage. To walk into the past and have missing relatives. I was an orphan once removed. They didn't know what category to put me in, so I found my home in the theatre. I still see my imagination as my real parent.

BARONESS: You've been een a place vhere zee vorld fell in love vit you. Everyvere zere are zese adoring eyes vich terrify. Everyvone zink you genius. Vhere can you go from zere?

(THE FAN CLUB girls creep in)

ALL GIRL FAN CLUB: Mont-gom-ery! Can we touch you.

BARONESS: *(To FANS)* No closer. *(To MONTGOMERY, worshipful)* You must express your dark feelinks through vorks of art. Zen you von't mind zee roses of zee profession and zee thorns. Come leeve vith me and I make you happy.

MONTGOMERY: It would be nice to have a constant oasis.

ALL GIRL FAN CLUB: Sign our autograph books--

MONTGOMERY: *(Deeply Moved)* Maybe I could sign a few--

BARONESS: *(To FANS)* Back girls! *(To MONTGOMERY)* Zey are fascinated by details of how you tink. Save yourself for me.

MONTGOMERY: You really love me?

BARONESS: *(Obsessed)* Zere is a mystical closeness, even zough vee are deeefferent-- Remember zee same forces zat distinguish you, disconnect you from zee group. But time vaits for you. You are a man. You don't have to be zee fifteen-minute star. Ven you remove zee bandage, you unhappy. You don't have zee same face. True. But, none of us can keep zee face ve had.

MONTGOMERY: When I act, I don't want to become a caricature of myself. But if I stop acting. I'm afraid my soul will... dry up.

BARONESS: Now you hurt so much eet feels like your heart's been halved. Embrace zee desolation. ...Vhen you are bored, I'll entertain you with quotes from your films. We tink of scene that makes you proud that ve can do.

MONTGOMERY: I want something separate from all this. Something intangible.

BARONESS: Lo-ve.

MONTGOMERY: Yes.

BARONESS: KISS ME.

(HE is about to kiss her when the phone rings. HE retreats to the bedroom where HE picks up the phone.)

(On a distant phone MARILYN moves about agitated as SHE speaks. HE yells into his phone.)

MONTGOMERY: Marilyn? Is it you, gorgeous?…Talk louder, honey…

MARILYN: *(Breathy, scared for him)* I know you think I should want you to audition but, Lee and I both agree you're not ready for public exposure--

MONTGOMERY: But! If. . .if, tell Lee --*(Pacing)* if I find my book.

MARILYN: You might try to copy what you--Keep all your mirrors covered--Only allow your dearest friends to talk to you--Go back to the Actor's Studio. You can feel scared and strong there.

MRS CLIFT: *(O.S.) (Shouts)* Mont-gom-er-y… .Rest!

MONTGOMERY: *(To MOM)* Did you find my journal?

SUNNY: *(O.S.) (To MONTGOMERY)* No.

(SOUND of rain; static on phone)

MONTGOMERY: *(Into phone)* Awful weather. Can you hear me, honey? *(Obsessed, loud)* I was infallible till I had that crash.

MARILYN: You can't do hard scenes--Like those in *Raintree*. *(Breathy)* Your body's too weak. It won't know you're acting. It'll sweat as though your emotions are real. Your psyche won't understand-it'll just know that every day on set--You're so sad. You can't do that without the Benzedrine from the studio pharmacy. *(Desperate)* You can't be naked on film now!

MONTGOMERY: But-- I may be auditioning--

MARILYN: Slow down. . . Become an observer at the Studio.

MONTGOMERY: Watch others do what I can't?

MARILYN: I observed for months--under my raincoat and scarf; no one bothered me.

(SOUND of thunder)

For now, take pills and breathe in sleep. Lose yourself in the florescent moon outside. Maybe you could land the lead in this new film *Miss Lonely Hearts*. I thought of you when I read the script. *(Laughs)*
This horny woman is after this reporter. And the man's just average looking. He writes a woman's love column.

(MONTGOMERY hangs up. Alone, HE lines up his pills, lowers the lights, and bursts into tears.)

(A brief pause, then the lights flash up. ROSTOVA enters followed by SUNNY. MONTGOMERY rises, scavenges around the bed for his journal.)

SUNNY: Sorry for crashing in. I hoped you were napping—

ROSTOVA: Sweetheart! *(Urgent)* Time's running out, prrrecious.

SUNNY: I told her to leave but she lurks about. --Stalking the library.

MONTGOMERY: *(Still searching)* Move back, Ma. *(To ROSTOVA)* Hello, honey!

SUNNY: *(Jealous)* She does one Chekhov scene at the studio and--she's a master teacher.

ROSTOVA: *(Defensive to MOM)* I guard him. I protect his solitude and journaling work. *(Yells)* Without me, he gets abused! *(To MONTGOMERY, laughing)* Don't keep hunting for book-- You look like you tip over mirrorrr with your walking and pacing.

MONTGOMERY: I want to sacrifice, do what the hell I want and not worry-- Commit myself to finding--

SUNNY: Relax. Don't distress your face. Your feelings appear on --

ROSTOVA: We have to decide if you want last audition slot. 6 pm?

SUNNY: People don't talk about plastic surgery and retiring even if it has a good ending.

ROSTOVA: *(To MONTY)* Did you look at script?

MONTGOMERY: *(Sarcastic)* It's just like the play. Brother has one slim scene. *(Stops suddenly)*

SUNNY: Montgomery can't film anything--

ROSTOVA: *(To MONTY)* The picture would prrrove to producers, you insurrrable--*(Pause)* What you doing?

MONTGOMERY: Looking for inspiration in this journal, honey. Here's a postcard from Dürer's book on Human Proportion. *(Reads)* "*Constructed Head of A Man in Profile* c. 1512. At one-eighth the height of the entire body, the head is the key to ideal classical proportion.

ROSTOVA: *Focus.* Do you want audition or not? As your coach, I'm seriously concerned insurance people destroy your future, if you don't take final audition slot.

MONTGOMERY: I'll set my Russian watch to remind me, sugar. *(Laughs)*

(SUNNY takes ROSTOVA into the waiting area.)

SUNNY: You've got to call off this audition. Did you see Monty? He's exhausted from all this. He looks at you and all he thinks about is—

ROSTOVA AND SUNNY: Intentions and subtexts.

SUNNY: He failed in *Raintree*--Though he and you labored all night on--bits of nothing--for each line. I don't want him … quivering from your suggestions--scribbling in some notebook.

ROSTOVA: We follow mission larrrger than ourselves.

SUNNY: I dare not mention the crow's feet or the wrinkles on his forehead. His agent ordered you to keep away-- Even when he did nothing wrong, in *Raintree*, hearing your words, "the scene is such a disappointment" made him believe he was bad.

ROSTOVA: How do you know?

SUNNY: Something went wrong with him during *Raintree* and he lunged his car into a tree and--

ROSTOVA: You rrread his notebook!

SUNNY: Pushing my son to master something extreme for each role… Bucking a bronco. Subjecting himself to incredible beatings--And for what? For who? For…Rumor is you sleep with him.

ROSTOVA: We work closely together. He's not marrried. He doesn't have children. He's alone. I understand his insomnia----And his fear of going bed by himself. He cuddles against me. And in morning we have pillow fights and laugh. I'm like "abandonee," that overripe cheese. I'm always ready for him.

SUNNY: I see.

ROSTOVA: I don't find his *(Pause)* loneliness--aberration. I always down-play your illegitimacy.

SUNNY: Thanks… They say Russian acting teachers are the uglies who can't land the parts. Monty is such a big figure in your life, I fear you exaggerate your role.

(Lights cross fade to the bedroom where something like Bach, Concerto for Violin and Oboe in C Minor *plays on the Hi Fi.)*

(SOUND of footsteps on fire escape. Rear window opens. Wild sleaze. DOCTOR bursts in.)

DR. BILLY: *(Panting)* When I got in that car… I just turned around and--decided I had to see you. I thought it'd be romantic to climb the fire escape. Actually I feel weak about being so--

MONTGOMERY: You're soaking wet.

DR. BILLY: You don't wanna know how much I paid for this suit. Can I borrow some clothes?

MONTGOMERY: You're not staying… I don't mean to be rude, but I'm working.

DR. BILLY: *(Yells)* We haven't talked… since your mom came. Now I see… The reason she's successful with you is because she's large. By the time I'm done talking to her I'm looking at moving to New Jersey. She's got too much *machismo*…

(HE eyes a photo of him and MONTGOMERY)

Can I have this photo or you and me for…safekeeping. I'm glad we're friends. I don't really like film people.

MONTGOMERY: Come back in the morning? I've got to call on music-

(Watch alarm beeps. Looks at his watch)

I'm searching for the perfect sounds for Saturnalia to decide whether I should audition in 30 minutes.

DR. BILLY: *(Laughs)* A Baroque Adagio? Can't you let our story decide what shape it is going to take. Feather in good fantasies about us.

MONTGOMERY: Oh god, go. *(Grabs head)* There's a privacy of sorrow and of feeling in music that's hard for an actor to capture. *(Clutches skull)* There's so much energy in the oboe and violin you don't need to go more deeply.

DR. BILLY: Do you want something for pain? A pill to ease you to sleep? Or put you out?

MONTGOMERY: *(Defiant)* No! I gotta live hard. I gotta live true. In the end I hope there's something more than your prescriptions.

DR. BILLY: You're odd. In all your sartorial splendor—

MONTGOMERY: I'm trying to be an actor; not a star, an actor.

DR. BILLY: Why not take a break with me. Go to Malibu. You're still alluring I even find myself trying to touch you when you're physically damaged. It's hard to keep worry in check. To think you're good looking enough, talented enough, young enough. To realize you're old. You're not twenty-five!

MONTGOMERY: Quiet! I need to try another record.

DR. BILLY: Couldn't you just enjoy LA. Seeing the sea sky, hearing the waves, strolling the beach.

MONTGOMERY: Go silent inside the ocean and sky?

DR. BILLY: We'll party a lot. When someone comes to town, boom, we'll party. *(Pause)* Just enjoy being alive?

MONTGOMERY: As opposed to what? Having an audience, being onset with actors, hearing them breathing.

DR. BILLY: We were close before--.

MONTGOMERY: Shush. Before I didn't need to pull the form from the sound. Find the trigger to the iconography. In Tennessee Williams, it's the handling of the black, there's this sense the sun is leaving the sounds. They've a darkness like falling down a—

DR. BILLY: You make no sense. Let me help you. Worse case scenario: You go to Los Angeles, your face gets worse, your concentration, foggier. You die. Best-case scenario: You meet a producer at a Hollywood club who finances you in a big project. Relationships don't have to hurt! *(Pause)* When people want things from you, you've got power.

MONTGOMERY: I want something from you. I want the old face I had.

DR. BILLY: And if I can't give you that, I'm dismissed?

MONTGOMERY: You don't know what it feels like to be a leading man, to be the head of a film--

DR. BILLY: You were rewarded even when you were a fiend. Now you've become inhuman because you are in inhuman circumstances. SHOCK. But I still care for you and will do all I can to see you improve. You want to change something before you self-destruct, don't let it be our friendship.

(The phone rings. DR. BILLY: exits.)

DR. BILLY: I'll leave you to your noises.

(LIZ TAYLOR appears on a distant hotel phone.)

LIZ: *(Into phone, elated)* It's me! How was the surgery?

SUNNY: *(O.S.)* *(Screaming)* Who's on the phone!

MONTGOMERY: *(Into phone)* Liz? We've a bad connection. If it's you, use the nickname I gave you—

LIZ TAYLOR: *(Highly wired)* Bessie Mae.

MONTGOMERY: *(Into phone, adoring)* Bessie Mae! You always sound good but now you sound gooder. *(Suddenly panicked.)* Did I leave my... *Raintree* book with... you?

LIZ TAYLOR: Why are you gasping? Did you take... I still burst into tears every day because--

MONTGOMERY: *(Nervous)* I can't talk.

LIZ TAYLOR: *(Urgent)* You are auditioning?

MONTGOMERY: *(Into phone, chuckles)* Yes... No... I'm afraid if I play a small role, I'd be too resentful of--the leads. *(Suddenly mad)* I need to get away from you... from you, from people taking photos of us, and talking about our next picture, and from us being cruel to each other because we're subtly competing with -- *(Contrite)* Sorry Bessie Mae. You're part of me... my other half. But, if you care, stay away!

(HE hangs up. LIZ hangs up. HE picks up his miniature trumpet used in his film, From Here to Eternity and plays a few notes sadly. ROSTOVA enters.)

ROSTOVA: *(Ruthless)* Ah, sweetheart. Columbia wants complete rrrreviews of *Rrraintree*--to make sure they're not doctored. Liz said--

MONTGOMERY: I changed my mind. I won't do anything she's involved with-- *(Quoting from Prewitt)* "If a man don't go his own way, he is nothing." James Jones.

ROSTOVA: People already forgot *From Here to Eternity*, prrrecious.

MONTGOMERY: *(Furious laugh)* For which I almost got an Oscar?! That's an insult!

ROSTOVA: Insurance people need most rrecent rrreviews--

MONTGOMERY: I WAS NOMINATED 3 TIMES FOR BEST ACTOR--

ROSTOVA: Study *Suddenly* script, love. Collect notices. And think about playing tennis!

MONTGOMERY: For a cameo part? *(Angry)* I'm being jerked around because I belong to the collective insanity of theatre.

ROSTOVA: *(Flamboyant)* It's 4:45. You've got half hour, sweetie-pie.

(ROSTOVA exits. MONTGOMERY grabs his tennis racket. SUNNY enters with a tray and sets the table. SOUND of rain.)

MONTGOMERY: *(Defiant)* Pow. Pow. Pow.

SUNNY: *(Pushy)* Put down that racket. Sit. . . You didn't notice the yellow rose on your tray--

MONTGOMERY: *(Belligerent)* Where is my *Raintree* book, Sunny? With the reviews? I know you have it. I was pushed to the front of the audition line but, I'd a long string attached to me... I need to remind competitors of who I am.

SUNNY: *(Scared)* You can't audition when you only eat raw meat and milk. It's pouring outside!

MONTGOMERY: *(Anxious)* I'll check under the bed.

SUNNY: You're not the Montgomery whom eighth graders fell in love with.

MONTGOMERY: Out my way.

SUNNY: You're not god no matter how much the fans scream. You think it's talent but it's beauty that got you where you are. I remember waiting for the review of *A Place in the Sun*. It was broadcast on national radio. Tons of teenagers crowded theatre to see the most beautiful couple of the century--

MONTGOMERY: Isn't that what you wanted. A son as a badge of victory.

SUNNY: Leave acting before it leaves you.

MONTGOMERY: But acting's how I feel most alive in the world. With other people and with... history.

SUNNY: You're still the great-great-grandson of Francis Blair, adviser to President Jackson.

MONTGOMERY: I'm an ACTOR. Who else I am remains speculative.

SUNNY: I tore up your book! I dumped it in the trash can along with those ... notices. Stop comparing yourself to someone who's gone--It's a death for me too! After all the glory.

MONTGOMERY: *(Looking in can, stunned)* Oh God, no. It's like a filo dough of work. Layers of pages, clippings, photos. *(Reads scraps)* "The New York Times applauds Clift's portrayal of the sensitive young private..." "Clift's love scenes with Elizabeth Taylor represent a new standard for romance." *From Here to Eternity* contains the best performance delivered by an actor of any gender on celluloid." You just gathered this up and... destroyed it? Well, I'll mutilate these pages even further. I'll go through these and cut my face out. Mount debris on the walls-- The closer we come to the negative, to death, the more we blossom. Go, BITCH... WHORE. *(Loud)* Go, Go, ...(Louder) Go, Go, Go *(till SHE backs off)*

(SUNNY exits. HE puts on a Gregorian chant like Missa Nigra sum: II. Gloria, *and a Roman Collar from his priest's role in* I Confess.*)*

(HE cuts up his notices and mounts them while HE says the Priest's Confession from the Latin Mass.)

(SOUND of wind. APPARITION appears in clerical garb.)

GHOSTLY COMEDIES

MONTGOMERY: *(Filled with self hatred) Confiteor Deo omnipotenti, beatae Mariae semper Virgini, beato Michaeli Archangelo,Beato Joanni Baptistae, sanctis Apostolis Petro et Paulo--*

APPARITION: Let me help you... !

MONTGOMERY: No *(Using their secret language) Da foi deep dan dop deep-*

APPARITION: I learned early to deface my photos.

MONTGOMERY: *(Enraged)* AWAY! *Kaw keep coop doop!!(Returns to prayer) Omnibus Sanctis, et tibi Pater: quia peccavi nimis –*

APPARITION: Pretend you don't care. Give me the scissors.

MONTGOMERY: *Nimis cogitatione verbo, et opere: mea culpa, mea culpa--*

APPARITION: I said, let me destroy that! *Fak fik mook!*

MONTGOMERY: *Mea maxima culpa. Ideo precor beatam Mariam semper Virginem—*

APPARITION: The scissors, please! I don't want you cutting anything—

(THEY fight. Alarm beeps on his watch)

MONTGOMERY: *(Checking watch)* 25 minutes till--I can't stop my . . alarm.

APPARITION: *(Encouraging)* Take my hand; pretend we're walking up the endless stairs of the *Campidoglio* in Rome--

MONTGOMERY: But I--I must finish the service--

APPARITION: At the top are the heavenly twins, Castor and Pollux, Apollo and Diana--Helen and Polus--Romulus and Remus who sucked at the teats of a wolf--

MONTGOMERY: *Beatum Michaelem Archangelum, Beatum Joannem Baptistam--*

APPARITION: Stop hiding, Father.

APPARITION: GIVE ME THAT ROMAN COLLAR AND LET ME HEAR YOUR SINS. I'll be the Mother Confessor. Plead guilty! Or I'll make sure you never act again.

MONTGOMERY: Here--take the Roman Collar.

(HE kneels: SHE puts on the collar)

MONTGOMERY: Bless me Mother for I have sinned... I'm seeing... a married woman...

APPARITION: Continue...

MONTGOMERY: Bessie Mae... Liz Taylor.

APPARITION: GO ON!

MONTGOMERY: I love her in the purest most complete sense-- but-- kissing in *A Place in the Sun* and touching her in *Raintree* I began believing she's mine.

APPARITION: Have you committed a mortal sin?

MONTGOMERY: No ... yes... Oh god... We began doing everything but—

APPARITION: For your penance... Destroy all mementos, say 3 Our Fathers and 3 Hail Marys, and act like the priest in *I Confess*.

(APPARITION vanishes. MONTGOMERY goes to the roof with the trash bag, and hurls his notices joyfully about.)

(The BARONESS enters in a wedding dress and his FANS rush out.)

BARONESS: *(Obsessed)* I bought a vedding dress. Skin-tight vith-Hundreds of brilliants zat shimmer and glitter--So bright zat my body ees clothed een light--

MONTGOMERY: *(Aggressive, insensitive)* Back! I'm celebrating! Turning my notices into airplanes.

BARONESS: But eet's so damp.

MONTGOMERY: *(Suddenly mad)* Creating a shower of paper. Want to play? I can stay in the present now. I've found my notebook and tossed it.

BARONESS: Vat ees thees picture with zee face cut out? Oh darrlink! You're arrren't on zee gallows alone. Vee cry for you- Zere's always suffering from life. Vee can't divorce ourselves from death.

MONTGOMERY: *(Gently)* Don't be kind. I need you to be hysterical so I can stay focused.

BARONESS: *(Championing him)* I've a complete set of notices zat shows you are very, very beautiful. Like in *Zee Search* when you teach zis boy zis Auschwitz survivor who search for his mother. Here's pictures of you at a railway station with homeless children in Würzburg.

MONTGOMERY: I don't want to see those notices. I'm trying to stay in the present... clear my head. Leave the past!

ALL GIRL FAN CLUB: Montgomery we love you. We'll always remember.

BARONESS: *(Calls out to FANS)* Go get all zee books girls and zee bunches of flowers. *(To MONTGOMERY)* Zese vill geeve you energy. You can know about zese, and not be vorried about zose.

MONTGOMERY: I put too much importance on this acting thing. Talked about it too much. I'm not going to cry for... something that made me miserable. I had to lose that face eventually. I just didn't think it'd be over night. *(Forcing a laugh)* Help me celebrate being struck down as I am. It's been a breakthrough. No one should need a book on themselves to say who they are. It's a kind of release to just be. Here's a scrap. *(Reads)* "In Italy. The statues of Roman soldiers and emperors dug up from the ruins of dead cities are set out on pedestals in the Borghese Gardens or the Doge's Palace. Their scarred profiles contain life. Even without noses and only holes for eyes, those statues dominate space." I'll do that in acting.

ALL GIRL FAN CLUB: Can we have your pictures?

MONTGOMERY: If you'll give me your enthusiasm and--. I don't want to be that person in the photo. I want to be someone stronger, more solid. How can I tell if I'm changing for the better? I'm sure this is some bad dream or surgery. Am I on an operating table?

(FANS leave. BARONESS turns on tape recorder)

BARONESS: Let's practice zee Vedding March.

MONTGOMERY: I'm sorry if I confused you. I do care for you but I've sworn off women. I've got to do penance. Say my Our Fathers and Hail Marys--*(Laughs, thinking)* Lets see--*Ave Maria, gratia plena, Dominus--*

BARONESS: Your body vill come alive vith me.

MONTGOMERY: *Sancta Maria, Mater Dei, ora pro nobis--*

BARONESS: Marry me; only act for me!

MONTGOMERY: No. *(To self) Pater noster qui es in coelis, sanctificetur--*

BARONESS: We could have a *marriage blanc*, a sexless marriage. Play games in vich you reject me.

MONTGOMERY: I've got to give myself to the priesthood of acting. Purge myself from my last film so I can be totally present without women like I was in *Red River*.

BARONESS: I just vant to sleep with you. Touch feets. Hands. Cuddle like zee polar bear. Act out a scene.

SUNNY: *(O.S.) (Fierce calls out)* Montgomery!!!Son!

(MONTGOMERY descends to his bedroom where SUNNY waits for him. HE puts on something like Dvorak, Symphony no. 9 in E minor, paces about searching.)

SUNNY: *(Hates music)* Turn off that violence.

MONTGOMERY: *(Hunts about)* I've got to review this script—

SUNNY: Rest. Take your medication.

MONTGOMERY: If you need to do something, bitch: line my pills up alphabetically: Amphetamines, barbiturates, Belladonna, chloral hydrates, Milltown, tranquilizers, seconal.

SUNNY: I was wrong to scare you… Here's the REAL notebook with all your reviews… I destroyed the copy I kept in reserve.

MONTGOMERY: Wait!… You're one screwed up BITCH… You did what? *(SILENCE)*

SUNNY: If you must act again, I'll help—

MONTGOMERY: How can I work with… someone who's a LIAR. Raised by degenerates. The FOGGS. YES I SAY THEIR NAME WITH CONTEMPT. NAMED FOR DR. MONTGOMERY SOME CLOWN WHO BIRTHED YOU AND HID YOU FROM YOUR REAL MOTHER… *(Triumphant)* I'M GOING TO PUT ON MY HAT AND HOLSTER AND MOVE INTO A BIGGER PERSONAGE. PONY UP AND PULL THE TRIGGER.

SUNNY: You don't need to show off with that costume…

MONTGOMERY: *(SILENCE)* I'M GOING BACK TO THE FAMILY OF MY IMAGINATION. TO THE ARMCHAIR GENERAL MONSTERS OF THE FILM BUSINESS. I'M GOING TO BECOME AN ACCOMPLICE IN A PROFESSION THAT IS OUT TO DEMEAN ME EVERY STEP OF THE WAY. *(Crazy language, jeering)* Blab, bleep, feek, fack. Fleep! Flup! Fly! NOW HOLD UP YOUR HANDS AND WALK OUT THE DOOR. *(MONTGOMERY takes out a pistol.)*

SUNNY: DON'T AIM THAT GUN.

MONTGOMERY: I NEED TO BE ALONE. NO INTERRUPTIONS, DIVERSIONS. *(Checks watch)* LITTLE DISTRACTIONS EVEN SUBTLE THINGS CAN BE A BIG ANNOYANCE. PREPARING FOR AN AUDITION IN 20 MINUTES REQUIRES TOTAL CONCENTRATION.

ACT TWO

AT RISE: (Lights flicker. Howling rain. MONTGOMERY puts on music box sounds like Vangelis, L'Apocalypse des Animaux. Thunder outside. ROSTOVA enters followed by SUNNY.)

ROSTOVA: *(Loud)* Montgomery, sweetheart.

SUNNY: *(Furious)* Who let her in. I should fire the downstairs maid. She conks out with that radio.

ROSTOVA: *(To MONTY)* Good news. We no longer need rrrreviews. Bad news. You've got to audition--with a <u>classic</u>. It's pretentious but--. But-- Take off hat and gun, love.

MONTGOMERY: Why not a classic Western like— *Red River*?

(Acts out a cowboy sequence)

ROSTOVA: No, Let's start with Hamlet. *(Dramatic)* "O, that this too too solid flesh would melt?"

MONTGOMERY: That line alone drops me to my knees. *(Sarcastic)* But I was hoping to wear blue, and I've never seen Hamlet in a color. *(Laughs)* And the role has strong side effects. One of them is death. *(Shoots self)* Pow! Pow! *(Adjusting his hat)* "Or that the Everlasting... had not fix'd His canon 'gainst self-slaughter! ...

ROSTOVA: Off with that stetson. Do Hamlet to my Gertrude. *(Theatrically)* "O, speak to me no more; these words, like daggers, enter in mine ears; No more--"

(Lightening/thunder. Pounding at door. DR. BILLY enters.)

SUNNY: Shush. Montgomery is working----

DR. BILLY: Go ahead. *(Romantic)* Get into the freedom of the character. Let something big come through.

MONTGOMERY: *(Refocusing)* I'll place... Hamlet in the Wild West and use my revolver. *(Spins the gun and shoots)* POW... POW

"To be or not to be– that is the question:
Whether 'tis nobler in the mind to suffer
The slings and arrows of outrageous fortune,
Or to take arms against a sea of troubles--"

ROSTOVA: Stop. That speech is overrrused, dear.

SUNNY: Go on, but remove the hat and—

DR. BILLY: Pistol. Depressing material--

MONTGOMERY: I like it. I thought it--

ROSTOVA: Honeybunch. The casting dirrrector said avoid—

MONTGOMERY: It's famous for a reason--it strikes a nerve. I've something you lack--talent-- And if you can't latch on to it, you'll kill that.
Taking a soliloquy I do brilliantly and making it wrong. I can't speak without your intrusions. I've a tiny life with too many people in it. Everybody.
Out. *(Laughs)* Gun's loaded. Hands up, or I'll shoot.

*(HE scares them out with his gun. Goes to the mirror to examine his face.
Mounting wind. APPARITION arrives through mirror.)*

APPARITION: I fly overhead, parachute into crisis situations and resolve
them.

MONTGOMERY: I'm not auditioning. I changed my mind.

APPARITION: Forget this Hamlet. You've traveled and acted from
Connecticut to California. Do an improv on a seminal moment.

MONTGOMERY: Oh god. My cheek looks bad.

APPARITION: Act out the worst event in your life—

MONTGOMERY: My jaw's blue.

APPARITION: Master the extreme emotion.

MONTGOMERY: There's a bruise on my neck.

APPARITION: Relive the night of the crash.

MONTGOMERY: I don't want anyone to know about that... that--

APPARITION: Give me that Roman Collar. Kneel. Pretend I'm your Priestess. We'll title your monologue, The Confession—

(His watch alarm goes off)

MONTGOMERY: 15 minutes till the audition!

APPARITION: Hurry! Say, "Bless me—"

MONTGOMERY: For I have sinned. It's been 6 months since-

APPARITION: That awful dinner party at Liz's. *(Mean)* What happened.

MONTGOMERY: My ear's hot! Liz and I--were... were...

APPARITION: Had you made love--

MONTGOMERY: No it was all... all, all that painful--

APPARITION: Did you go to first, second, third base?

MONTGOMERY: We dry humped off set-- I wanted to make love to--*(To self)* Ave Maria, gratia plena--

APPARITION: LIAR. Why did Liz throw that party?

MONTGOMERY: *I wanted to marry her.*

APPARITION: People say you... you got drunk coming face-to-face with--

MONTGOMERY: I didn't drink. I was--flying on a trapeze between how it was and how I wanted it to be.

APPARITION: You were happy being her boy toy?

MONTGOMERY: No, I was determined to confront her husband...

(Intense) Rock and Kevin—discouraged me, but Mike --

APPARITION: Who?

MONTGOMERY: Her husband. They quarreled intensely--

APPARITION: And you were his friend too. Traitor.

MONTGOMERY: No. I disliked him. I comforted Liz. Our attraction grew as her marriage died.

APPARITION: Liar. You used her as camera bait. You're 37. She's 25. *(Pause, waxing poetic)* She wanted to go beneath the mist of your mighty eyes inside the "ruins" of Monty Clift and you couldn't--

MONTGOMERY: I wanted her. People thought I had made love to her. Her husband sneered at me, faked a back spasm on the couch. "I know you're bedding my wife," he said. I wanted to bust his mouth in half... Instead, I dove for my car and the quickest way off the mountain--I knew I could make it because my house for *Raintree* was on Dawn Ridge Road 20 minutes away. But I don't drive much. I'd given my chauffeur the day off.

It was about 11 o'clock and the canyon drive was lonely, snake-black. What the hell. My head was spinning with--"Follow Kevin, it's dark," Liz screamed. "And there's some sharp turns down the hill!"

I floored the car. Tailgating Kevin. Laughing at how I might be scaring him by careening down that pitch black road. But--Holy Mother the brakes went soft. The car waffled. Tilted on its side. I thought, I'm going to smash into Kevin. What. No. I'll slam into that telephone pole ahead. Stop myself.-

APPARITION: So you crashed on purpose? Saving Kevin.

MONTGOMERY: I was sure I'd die. I woke up crunched beneath the dashboard. Blood squirting all over my face-- I felt stones inside my mouth. It was my teeth. Kevin yelled, "Oh God. Monty's dead. I--I--door's jammed." He rushed off.

ROSARY HARTEL O'NEILL

Soon Liz was pounding on the car, screaming, "Open that door."…
"Don't," I whispered. I was lucid. "Let me die. Fade into...the heat"… Rock
ripped the door open and Liz lifted me from the steering wheel.

Let me die, dammit! "There's a tooth hanging from my lip, pull it off.
It's cutting my tongue." The ambulance got lost. But the photographers
arrived. Liz yelled at them, "You bastards. If you dare take one photograph
of him like this, I'll never let another one of you near me again."
God I loved that woman!

APPARITION: But you couldn't be her.

MONTGOMERY: Yes... No. That day I had a strong hangover; that's why
I was so quiet at the party. I was drowsy and stupefied. I had taken pills to--
Oh God, I miss Liz. What do I have to do to get her back?

(Blackout. APPARITION vanishes)

Oh! The lights went out! *(Cries)* Sister? Anybody!

APPARITION: Work with Liz again. AUDITION!! Navigate the deepest
sections of your soul.

*(HE goes up to the roof. BARONESS and FAN CLUB come out dressed in white
with leis. SHE wears a garland of flowers.)*

MONTGOMERY: Do you have light?

BARONESS: No but - *(Shrieks)* Ve practice for zee vedding. *(Triumphant)*
Ve have zee moonlight, Beluga caviar, grapefruit gimlets--ruby red grape-
fruit, vodka, lime. Pretend eet's Havaii on zee eve of Pearl Harbour. You're-
-Lee Previtt and I'm-- Alma 'Lorene' Burke--een *From Here to Eternity*.
Now we plan for our --veddding.

ALL GIRL FAN CLUB: *(Excited to MONTY)* We'll dress you! Aloha shirt,
light colored pants—

MONTGOMERY: We aren't getting married.

BARONESS: Believe vat you vant. I believe vat I vant.

GHOSTLY COMEDIES

(MONTGOMERY's watch alarm goes off)

MONTGOMERY: I've an audition in 10 minutes.

BARONESS: Engagement ees important; eet'll keep you from getting seeck. Problem ees you're too smart. You see tings only God should see. Zee limit of vone group clappink is vat you need.

ALL GIRL FAN CLUB: APPRECIATION!

MONTGOMERY: 5:06 I've got to go!

ALL GIRL FAN CLUB: Let us watch you rehearse.

MONTGOMERY: I can't act if you gawk at me.

BARONESS: Ven you get fame like you zee king, eet's like everybody ees your mother. Ve vill vork for your vish to come true. Even if you are deeefficult, ve vill help you. Even eef you trow a tantrum, ve vill love you.*(Pause)* Ven you get seeck, ve cry. If you die, ve vould vear black all our lives and send roses every day. Ve feel for you becauz you are a grrrreat artiste and your sufferink is too beeeg. You vork too hard; you're explodink. Take zee vedding candles. You trip in zee dark!

(HE fumbles toward the bedroom where SUNNY enters with supplies)

SUNNY: *(Joyful)* I brought flash lights. Your lanterns from summer camp.

MONTGOMERY: *(Chronic pessimism)* The flashlight works. Out my way.

SUNNY: I'm just the mother.

MONTGOMERY: I'm not ignoring you. It's just there's a lot at stake, freedom, comfort, sanity. I'm waiting for you to leave.

SUNNY: I called the electric company? A tree's down. --Columbia phoned. You need to audition with a musical instrument.

MONTGOMERY: What the... ?! Go. I need to warm up *(Hums)* Uhmmmmmmmmmmmmmm.

SUNNY: Rostova suggests your miniature bugle from--*Eternity.* —

MONTGOMERY: *(Depressed, loud)* It has a tiny ding on the bell's mouth but *(Hums)* Mee Mee Mow Mow Moo.

SUNNY: Can you still play Taps? The film's about the death of a--.

MONTGOMERY: I'm not going to repeat myself. *(Hums)* Ba Ba Bai Bee Bo Boo!

SUNNY: Do one or two bars.

MONTGOMERY: *(Hums)* No---NNNNNNNNNNNNNNNNNNNNNN NNNNNNoooooooooooooooo.

SUNNY: I put the headshots with the glasses in your portfolio. I checked your blazer; everyone is getting so superficial. They are thrown off by a stain. Remember to smile!

(His watch alarm goes off)

MONTGOMERY: 2 minutes.

SUNNY: You need ointment for that fever blister.

MONTGOMERY: No. *(Rebellious)* You nursed me through the accident and that was far worse than the accident. It was like pealing back a scab. I've lived every bad decision you've made. Get out!

(Breaking down) Oh Ma, we've come so far from those 5 sentence auditions and most of it was a pretty good ride. Broadway at 13. Best Actor Nomination at 23. I was so happy to make you proud. I wanted to convince you of your greatness. To defy those Blairs and Anderson's who wouldn't claim us…

You did everything for me, Ma. I appreciate it. You're like a Pelican. A pelican is thought to pierce its breast to feed its young with its own blood. Please go now and let me fail.

(SUNNY exits. HE locks door. Walks to the mirror. The room is bathed in light. APPARITION arrives to sound of angels/harps. SHE holds a newspaper.)

APPARITION: The improv won't work… You must do a love scene … with Liz. Let her powerful self cut its way into your-- This paper claims she's in New York at the audition site now.

MONTGOMERY: *(Terrified)* Oh no. Liz came. I'm not auditioning! With Liz--I never chose what--I wanted. But what I dreaded least.

APPARITION: Liz is playing this sexpot, who seduces her doctor--

MONTGOMERY: I won't read for that! I got all the adultery out of me in five months of therapy. *(Angry)* Liz and I approach scenes differently. *(Groping for words… awkward)* Liz's… instinctual. She has no--limits. She goes with her fingers.. I … want a regular audition. To make sure I… I want to…

APPARITION: I'll stand in for Liz. *(Screams as Liz)* Hurry. My body is on fire. I've no skin. My clothes burn.

MONTGOMERY: Don't take your clothes off—

APPARITION: I need to touch you, feel your whole being.

MONTGOMERY: *(Backing off)* But I'm the Brother!

APPARITION: No you're Dr. Sugar!

MONTGOMERY: STOP! What kind of audition is this. I'm an actor. I have to jump to that bad "what if." What if Liz and I touch faces, let our bodies go sweaty? What lunacy is in store? What if I--breathe Liz in, destroy her hair, inhale her flesh?

APPARITION: Audition for the doctor. Don't be a coward. Let the wild world of Liz Taylor open before your eyes. *(Pause)* The questions you're facing won't ever be completely clear. You don't have to answer them. Just satisfy yourself that they've all been explored.

(APPARITION disappears. Sound of helicopter. MONTGOMERY goes to roof. Looks about, carries the real notebook.)

(BARONESS sits under an umbrella by the ledge with a basket)

ROSARY HARTEL O'NEILL

MONTGOMERY: *(Obsessed with his lost sister)* Did you see someone? My sister?

BARONESS: *(Delirious)* A helicopter flew up to zee moonlight.

MONTGOMERY: *(Apologetically)* She's a withdrawn type.

BARONESS: Zere's nobody. I make "picnique" and vait to show you zee sky.

MONTGOMERY: I thought I didn't need it but, I have to search the original notebook to see how to handle certain love scenes—*(Smiles)* Ma had the book all along.

BARONESS: *(Yells)* Girls bring out zee martinis.

BARONESS: You've two fever blisters. You vant ice?

MONTGOMERY: No.

BARONESS: In Hemmingvay unpublished draft, an expatriate's grief ees eased only by a 3 martini lunch. . .

MONTGOMERY: I can't start that now.

BARONESS: Look troo zese binoculars, make a vish on a star.

MONTGOMERY: I wish. I wish--I haven't missed the audition. *(Checks watch)* It's 5:15.

BARONESS: I can't believe you must audeetion. Perhaps zey postpone eet because of veather.

MONTGOMERY: But how do I deal heroically with all these...

BARONESS: Act brave like een *From Here to Eternity*.

(ALL GIRL FAN CLUB arrives with martinis and a notebook)

ALL GIRL FAN CLUB: Have 3-2 ounce martinis, olive twist and onion, Chopin vodka.

BARONESS: Here's the big notebook.

MONTGOMERY: Thank god it's still in tact. Here's something. *(HE reads, haltingly)* "In his sketch, Dürer paired Adam and Eve's flawless physiques with emphasis on their perfect temperaments."

BARONESS: You have other options. Don't get depressed.

(MUSIC wafts up from next door)

MONTGOMERY: *(Identifying it)* "*The Pathetique*" Tchaikowsky's final symphony. He lived on the edge of a nervous breakdown. It's uncertain if he died of cholera, after drinking a glass of unfiltered water or of suicide. But, he never saw the success of his last symphony.

BARONESS: You von't find zee key to zee future in zee past. Lets rehearse zee vedding dance. *(Putting a lei and sash on him.)* Put on zee flower lei. And zee colored sash.

MONTGOMERY: No. I just need a flashlight--I didn't mean for us to go this far--

BARONESS: Zat girl is our officient. God put out zee lights just een time.

MONTGOMERY: I care for you but-

BARONESS: Ve got zee Havaiian Vedding Song-- Zen you vill be renewed! I put museeec on tape. Zat's right.

MONTGOMERY: I can't dance now.

BARONESS: Some say ven zee vind stirs, zee ancestors are pheeesically absent but surround you vith love. I tink zee grrreat artists--Shakespeare, Chekhov, vill come like vind to help you at zee audition.

(HE takes her cheek and is about to kiss her when all three phone rings in the bedroom. HE goes there and finds the DOCTOR)

DR. BILLY: *(Awkward, still adoring)* How are you?

MONTGOMERY: *(Angry)* Miserable, mean, normal. I'm working pretty well with constant interruption.

(One phone rings on)

DR. BILLY: Don't answer that phone. It won't be the first time electronics took over the mansion.

(MONTGOMERY picks up a phone. LIZ appears on a distant phone.)

LIZ TAYLOR: *(Into phone)* Terrible tornado. You hear me... I've gotten your audition moved back till 6:30. You've one hour more. But be on time. People want to go home...

MONTGOMERY: *(Urgent)* Speak up you're fading. Are you in New York?

LIZ TAYLOR: *(Slow, loud)* Do something from Chekhov. The director loves that. Call if you have any questions. *(Static)* Can you--

MONTGOMERY: Hello... Bessie... Hello... Phone's dead.

(To DOCTOR, hyper) Check that cord. Why are you still here?

DR. BILLY: *(Moody)* Bad traffic, bad car service, no parking spaces. Should I go on? I've been roaming the house. It's so spacious-all the beds I slept in before--

MONTGOMERY: Is that cord connected?

DR. BILLY: I need to look at your jaw. This won't hurt.

MONTGOMERY: Check the phone line.

DR. BILLY: You'll work yourself into an infection.

MONTGOMERY: *(Wipes, mouth, fearful)* People are waiting for my audition.

(SOUND of rain crashing.)

DR. BILLY: Let me touch your cheek. Hold my hand there a little too long. I can get away with it because I'm balancing the prerogative of the doctor.

MONTGOMERY: Go next door and see if their phone is working.

DR. BILLY: Hold still. Does this hurt or this. You feel warm.

MONTGOMERY: I need to call a car.

DR. BILLY: It's like the earth rushing through if you give me a look. You should do well on the audition. Your eyes shine even in the darkness and it's difficult to not fall in love with you.

MONTGOMERY: Look, I see the error in my ways. I break off with people when things start closing in. The corruption of this lifestyle is so deep, so interior, so wild.

DR. BILLY: Can't we just leave things open. Don't shut it off.

MONTGOMERY: Part of the struggle is trying to keep my tender side. Wondering if it was ever really there.

DR. BILLY: *(Urgent but nonchalant)* Can't I be the soul mate you want? I like quiet… thought, the rain. I just want to be in the room with you. Giraffe's don't talk. They have sonar communication. Knobs on their heads.

MONTGOMERY: Most relationships confuse me… I end up hurting some--

DR. BILLY: We won't burn bridges. It'll just go quiet for a while.

MONTGOMERY: You're a dear friend, but I've no time now. I've just enough energy to work this--

DR. BILLY: You're at the end of your rope and I'd shorten the rope?

MONTGOMERY: I can't stir up the old feelings. When after this audition there's maybe the final departure… when I knock on the door of my talent and it's gone. Is that phone connected? *(Screams)* Check, please.

(DR. BILLY checks the phone cord)

DR. BILLY: No. We contradict ourselves by doing what we say we aren't going to do while we're doing it… Without you, I lead such a discreet, impoverished life. I just want to watch you practice. Give me a couch and a book and I'll wait… and watch… hoping for the singular moment when our lives could come together. I'm a simple person. It doesn't take a lot to make me happy. You smile at me, I say "Ooh."

(SUNNY enters with food, followed by ROSTOVA)

ROSTOVA: Ve're on board for 6:30, sveetheart, a 2 person scene--

MONTGOMERY: From Chekhov, yes. *(Nervous)* Can I audition with you…

ROSTOVA: Of course love.

SUNNY: She's not pretty enough for a scene partner. Embarrassingly masculine--I told her-- Any assistance needed, I'd do.

MONTGOMERY: Quiet, bitch. *(Scared)* I won't do a love scene.

SUNNY: Eat your raw steak, your egg yolks in milk.

MONTGOMERY: Stop. I'm feeling more and more entrapped

ROSTOVA: *(Dominates)* We'll do *Seagull*--Scene where son, head wrrrapped from his self-inflicted wound, asks his motherrr to change his bandages--*(Urging him)* Use your infirrrmity, lovie.

(MONTGOMERY eats, chokes on meat)

MONTGOMERY: But the son's suicidal there--*(Coughs)* the scene … requires deep… penetration… into his… subtexts and he's so delicate *(Choking pounds chest)* and--

ROSTOVA: Trrrue, opening night in Moscow same scene was disaster, sweetie.

MONTGOMERY: And… I can't *(Coughs)* recall all… the motivations.

ROSTOVA: Imagine grrreat Chekhov covering backstage in Moskva. *(Orders)* AND fo-cu-s.

MONTGOMERY: *(Coughs)* But so much subtext... inner images--

ROSTOVA: We won't score your lines--

MONTGOMERY: *(Coughs)* Back story, beats, events--I've got to cut myself off from fans, rehearse in the moment, personalize the elements.

ROSTOVA: Fixate on soft moment between-- Motherrr and son. *(Dramatic)* Starrrt with--"Motherrr, change my--".

MONTGOMERY: *(As KONSTANTIN)* "Mother, change my bandage. You do it so well."

ROSTOVA: *(As MOTHER)* She gets new bandages, imitates gun to head, says: "And no morrre click-click while I'm away?"

MONTGOMERY: *(As KONSTANTIN)* "No, mother, that was a moment of insane despair"

(MONTGOMERY's choking gets worse)

(As self) I can't do this--this way. I need to brood over feelings. *(Coughs)* Spend time imaging--break down the beats--

(Chews steak) It's happening to me lately. *(Swallows. Waits. It didn't go down. (Pounds chest)* It's too much... Ma, brandy!

(To ROSTOVA) It happened to me in Santa Monica. It won't go down. There's an obstruction.

(Screams) Brandy! I don't need to *(Gulps)* complete everything... finish all.

SUNNY: Here's some Irish cream! Drink. Rest.

MONTGOMERY: Give me my book. I need to check Mozart...

SUNNY: Rostova come outside!

(SUNNY and ROSTOVA exit. MONTGOMERY puts on a record. Music box sounds like Vangelis, La Petite Fille de la Mer. *He opens his* Raintree *book and reads:)*

MONTGOMERY: "Mozart was baptized as Johannes Wolfgang Amadeus Mozart. He played before the empress of Austria at age 6. Died at 1 am on Dec. 5 at age 35. Mozart's *Requiem* which he was desperate to complete was left unfinished at the time of his death."

(HE throws down book goes to mirror)

(Touches lip) 3 fever blisters are helping themselves to my skin! God there's pus. Time to quit when 50 facial muscles retire. Even championship dogs snap and have to be shot.

(To self) Okay fool. You're not auditioning .Turn back your sheets, pile up your pillows, gulp down your meds--and-- No, first "Mu-sic."

(MONTGOMERY lifts on a sad record like Brahms, Lullaby: Berceuse Op 105. *HE lines up pills, puts on a sleeping mask, gets in bed.)*

(SOUND of phone ringing. We see MARILYN on a distant phone. HE fights to hear over the static & music.)

MARILYN: *(Bubbly into the phone)* Hey there star. Come talk to me and we'll walk in a cloud of dreams.

MONTGOMERY: *(Into phone, confused)* Marilyn. You sound adorable, but… I'm napping.

MARILYN: Wake up! Pretend my Italian maid's cooking and--

MONTGOMERY: I can barely hear you… so much static…

MARILYN: Lets talk about pills and shrinks and auditioning.

MONTGOMERY: Stop *(Static)*… Liz called you--

MARILYN: *(Into Phone)* That dyke? No. *(Pause)* This famous British astrologer told me you must act today. Crazy huh? Right after surgery--

MONTGOMERY: I challenged these bozos to let me do a general audition for Liz's film... It was a joke. But I've decided--

MARILYN: *(Breathing quickly)* --I know how you feel... when facing an audition for Liz. You get so physically worked up you get sick over it. You've got to act like ... you don't care. *(Urgent)* The more you want any role, the less attractive you are. *(Static)* But, do audition, if that's what it takes.. No potion can make you feel as alive as acting. Get a makeup artist, do breathing warm-ups, and don't forget the Benzedrine.

MONTGOMERY: Hello! *(Cries)* Mar-i-lyn. Phone went dead.

(HE hangs up. Lights down on MARILYN. HE turns on melancholic music like Bach, Concerto for 2 violins in d minor. *Starts to relax, rolling head, neck. HE spots pills, pours a handful, starts to take them. APPARITION arrives)*

APPARITION: *(Flabbergasted)* Give me those pills!

MONTGOMERY: They open my mind, help my breathing warm ups-- *(Inhales, exhales)* 1,2,3,4,5. . .

APPARITION: Are you going to audition on pills? I'm 18 minutes older. I demand an answer. What are—

MONTGOMERY: *(Angry)* I'm trying to restore my stamina--progressively. *(Exhales)* 6,7,8,9--Get into a restorative pose that allows my body to relax into trance.

APPARITION: To act opposite Liz?

MONTGOMERY: Let my eyes close so I tune out the visual distractions from around me. Sometimes I need a boost.

APPARITION: Kill yourself. I'm not the evil sister who wants to inherit your money.

MONTGOMERY: The worst that can happen is getting sick and vomiting-- *(Exhales)* 6,7,8-- Go! *(Waits. Pause)* Okay. I'll ignore you. *(To self)* "Mother, change my bandage. You do it so well... *(Catches breath)* "No, mother, that was a moment of insane--"

APPARITION: You're doing that for the Liz audition?

MONTGOMERY: I don't know why the fugg--I'm doing it. I got myself in a prison trap *(Laughs)*.Look, I can't go like a sheep to this audition. Watch all these idealistic kids salivating toward getting a few lines. Plucking their eye brows, getting their head shots, and dreaming about a--

Film is a cool industry. I just hate the people in it...

(Smiles) The smallest pill makes all the difference.

APPARITION: Why not meditate: go inside the inner sanctum of the audition space. Float along the rim trail of the room for a bird's eye view of her. Then bite into courage, go face to face with the goddess.

MONTGOMERY: I'm not doing a love scene. I may not even audition

(HE grabs some pills.)

APPARITION: *(Laughs hysterically)* It's so funny all the actors that died of drugs. They call it "an accidental overdose." Why don't they say--They were druggies, wanted a bigger buzz and they killed themselves.

(APPARITION unrolls endless scroll.)

Here's a list of artists who'll probably die from morphine, heroin, codeine, seconal, barbiturates, and vomit inhalation—

MONTGOMERY: Out! You shouldn't even comment on actors seeing as we accomplished more in life than you'll in-- Let me warm up.

APPARITION: *(Reads)* Pier Angeli, Natalie Wood, Judy Garland, Nick Adams, Dinah Washington, Marilyn Monroe.

MONTGOMERY: But I just talked to her?

APPARITION: Did you stop her from her pills for--sleeping or waking? Or did you pet, feed, play with her? Let her take you on a trip down sugary lane?

(Removes a death certificate)

Read Marilyn's pending autopsy.

MONTGOMERY: No. No. Go.

(His watch alarm goes off)

5:25. I may be auditioning. I've got to collect my--

APPARITION: *(Reads)* External examination: "The unembalmed body is that of a 36 year-old well-developed, well-nourished Caucasian female weighing 117 pounds, measuring 65-1/2 inches. The scalp is covered with bleached blond hair. The eyes are blue."

MONTGOMERY: *(Shudders)* Stop. I need to focus.

APPARITION: Don't be the next big person to die. Don't let your notice read: "Montgomery Clift(37) - actor. Death officially certified as 'acciden-tal-suicidal and undetermined.' High levels of sedatives found in his blood." Give me those pills.

MONTGOMERY: I can't. I promise not to gorge myself... pump myself with ... .Sometimes ... ! I need just one . ..to remind myself I'm a great-- To get the courage... to master a role--

APPARITION: Music has the same aphrodisiac affect. Alive and unleashed, Mendelssohn lifts the feelings. Dance with me. Enjoy the sounds moving through music. Take a leisurely swing or a spectacular sidestep. Relax in my arms.

MONTGOMERY: You're truly amazing. Someone everyone should know. I grew up with a script in my hand and I loved creating people from paper. But I was always going apart. I was always freezing during the day so I could thaw onstage at night. Forgive me. I let family fade into obscurity and my twin into someone I hardly know.

(APPARITION puts on romantic music like Mendelssohn, Symphony no 5 in D minor: Reformation. SHE and MONTY dance. Helicopter buzzes above.)

MONTGOMERY: *(Looks out)* Oh Gawd the helicopter is back!

(APPARITION vanishes. HE goes to the roof where BARONESS in flight gear looks out through binoculars.)

MONTGOMERY: *(Oppressive fear)* Did you see my... my--sister?

BARONESS: *(Cries distraught)* Vhy you von't marry me? Ees it because of-

MONTGOMERY: Liz. Yes. She's in New York. *(Throat dry)* Do I dare... act for her. *(Gasps)* Touch her *(Gulps air)* Liz... my... Tell me quick-You're the serious one whom all my fans agree with... I'm so distracted by the minutiae of Liz's moves... I don't know if *(Gulps panic)* I can pay attention to the world of the film and the actors around me.

BARONESS: *(Powerful, wise)* Look at zee sky. Ven you fly, eet's a ragged climb; not a strrraight ascendant.

MONTGOMERY: Dare I do a lead with Liz--I've boxed myself into a screwed up general audition.

BARONESS: Tell me about zees doctor role.

MONTGOMERY: He's a brain surgeon--but his hospital's broke-

BARONESS: I know zee play. A rich vidow vants him to say her niece crazy-

MONTGOMERY: And lobotomize her. But he falls in love.

BARONESS: Vith zees girl who vent to zee Encantadas--You've been to zee Galapagos Islands? Seen zees strrrrainge buzzards vaiting for newborn turtles and zee soft-bellied tortoises –

MONTGOMERY: *(Looks at watch)* 5:28.

BARONESS: Laying eggs in zee hot sand? You feel for zem?

MONTGOMERY: Yes. *(Breathes deep, straightens his back.)* Should I--

BARONESS: Tink of zee turtles and you play zis doctor--Pretend you fly. Eeet takes away zee illusion of control. *(Pause)* And be meesterious ven visiting zese powerful castink people!

(Helicopter sounds. BARONESS straps on helmet. Sound of ringing phone. HE bounds across the roof, and moments later appears on the bedroom phone.)

MONTGOMERY: *(Into phone)* Hello... Liz. Bessie Mae... Does... your phone work... *(Slow)* What scene--? Bessie Mae! I can't hear you... Call me back.

(HE hangs up. Lights blink on)

(To self) Oh. We've got lights! *(Looks up)* Stay kindly ones!

(SUNNY enters, followed by ROSTOVA. There are some signs ROSTOVA is imagining herself on stage.)

ROSTOVA: *(Pushy. Speaks in monotone,)* Allo, musckin.

SUNNY: *(Angry, referring to ROSTOVA)* Rostova seems docile--But she has a steely side--I... I can't let you work with this lunatic. Given her track record of destruction.

ROSTOVA: *(Jealous)* Your mom should play egocentric motherrr actress.

MONTGOMERY: Don't fight please. I've just 30 minutes to prepare my-.

SUNNY: I'll get your audition suit.

(SUNNY hurries out.)

MONTGOMERY: *(To ROSTOVA)* Explain, again why I can't read from the script?

ROSTOVA: Luvvie. You wanted generrral audition. Now they demand it.

MONTGOMERY: It was a ruse. I didn't think they'd--.

ROSTOVA: Sweetheart—

MONTGOMERY: Put me through the humiliation of a beginner's—

ROSTOVA: I TOLD you. They make rrretaliation. You're uninsurable-

MONTGOMERY: Is this a nightmare? I'm Montgomery Clift!

ROSTOVA: They say you got bad seeing, hearing, moving. You weak--.

MONTGOMERY: Surely they have audition sides from *Suddenly?*

ROSTOVA: They want you do classic audition and fizzle… They don't want another *Rrraintree* with big hospital costs, film delays. But we win. You'll do Chekhov like starri. Act with motherri because we've no time for perrrsonalizing role, and she bring out meanness in you… I put on sense of humor, velvet gloves and go out door. If audition succeeds, I move you to private studio for preparrations and rrrehearsal.

(ROSTOVA gives him an abrupt kiss and leaves, flipping her scarf and not wait-ing for an answer. Lights blink and stay on. His watch alarm beeps.)

MONTGOMERY: We've got lights! *(Checks watch)* God, it's 5:30.

(SUNNY enters with his suit and toiletries.)

SUNNY: *(Urgent, hurried)* Recite your lines while I fix your face--

MONTGOMERY: *(As KONSTANTIN)* *(Rattled, recites from Chekhov)* "She loves me, she loves me not, she loves me, she -- "

SUNNY: You've 4 blisters on your lip. I'll fix them with makeup.

MONTGOMERY: *(As KONSTANTIN)* "You see, my mother doesn't love me. Why should she?"

SUNNY: Hold your head up. We don't want that double chin.

MONTGOMERY: *(As KONSTANTIN)* "She wants to live, to love, to wear pretty frocks; and I--"

SUNNY: Is that a bruise expanding? You should have used ice-- Did you cover your bald spot? Change your jacket. I'll turn round while you switch your slacks.

MONTGOMERY: No just get out.... *(Annoyed)* You never cared for-- My acting was a way for you to be-my supposed savior, stay a rich aging still beautiful woman who has a close bond with art... *(Pause)* Okay I'll change in the closet.

SUNNY: How can you say I never cared. I was fascinated with you and your sister. I wanted to walk in with you both like earrings. Twins were a victory for me, the highest score a mother could get. Two beautiful-- And you were perfect. I'd see you move like Adonis and I'd write down everything you did. You're mad at yourself for ruining your career, don't blame me.

(HE comes out dressed in audition attire and escorts her to the door)

MONTGOMERY: Out Bitch. Sister is the only one who didn't kow tow to you. To SHE who must be obeyed. I've seen the men you've helped, me, brother, father, meaningless fossils in an alien universe... Our instability isn't normal. Keeping to ourselves like royalty. Waiting to be finally accepted. Were we ever recognized in a court of law?

(Starts to rip up the Chekhov script.)

SUNNY: Don't destroy that!

MONTGOMERY: Making me memorize a page from the dictionary each day... Cut off from friends. Keeping... Keeping 15 monologues ready at all times for an audition. The only way I could bear it was to grit my teeth and be temperamental and sullen! I think I should take all these pills. Right in front of you.

SUNNY: Stop! You don't mean that!

MONTGOMERY: *(As KONSTANTIN)* *(Quotes from Chekhov)* "No, mother, that was a moment of insane despair, when I couldn't control myself. It won't happen again. *(Kisses her hand)* You have magic fingers. I remember a long time ago-- "

SUNNY: Do you really son—

MONTGOMERY: No bitch it's Chekhov. *(Guilty, sad)* I've had a lot of distractions, what with the fever blisters. Somehow a germ got in my lip and it stopped the skin's ability to breathe. I'm glad I have a mother who can treat an infection. Could you put some ointment on my lip, Ma, then I know I'll be able to go.

(SHE does so. HE kisses her hand)

MONTGOMERY: *(As KONSTANTIN)* "Lately, these past few days, I have loved you as … tenderly and as completely as a child. I have no one left but you now. ." *(As himself)* I can't go on. *(Coughs)* My throat is caught--I think I've a fever.

SUNNY: Rest. You shouldn't audition in a storm. People are too resentful to have to be at work.

MONTGOMERY: *(To self)* How can I liberate myself when people keep nagging saying I need this or that?

SUNNY: Do you have your bugle? Eat--

MONTGOMERY: Am I dead? Do you hear what I'm saying?

SUNNY: Your steak's from the Barberry room at the Waldorf.
(HE gulps down meat, choking.)

MONTGOMERY: *(Swallows)* Look I'm trying to feel inside myself. Repair the gaps. Challenge myself. *(Panicked)* MMMMMMMM I can't breathe!

Acting is alone, going out of your mind and staying inside it-- *(Gasping)* Chopin disliked playing for audiences--He wrote 140 piano pieces for intimate settings.

SUNNY: You don't have to try out!

MONTGOMERY: Yes, I do. When you're sifting for gold in a stream you have to be in the stream. Bitch.

SUNNY: Don't curse.

MONTGOMERY: Well, listen, whore!

SUNNY: Stop! *(Annoyed)* You're the son of never enough. You just have to show up and life degrades. You stumble into talk that makes you explode.

MONTGOMERY: *(Suddenly contrite)* I'm sorry Ma. *(Breathing with difficulty)* I care for you… It's just that it's my audition, and I've more invested to feel slammed by.

SUNNY: I'd rather have you alive than famous.

(Throws himself on the floor)

MONTGOMERY: I'm such a jackass… Forgive me. Sometimes I feel I'm a kid… *(Pounding chest)* I look up and I'm amazed that I'm me in a room of grown ups. Other times… when I fail, I jump straight to panic. I do not pass go. As a boy I used to love looking at your feet and wish I was your shoe twin. You have such baby infant feet, Ma.

SUNNY: In my day, girls wore shoes two sizes too small just to have tiny feet.

MONTGOMERY: Oh, there's dust on your shoe. Let me get it… *(Clearing his throat, nervous)* Without acting, I'm pretty much a nobody, Ma. I'm not slick. I'm not college educated. I say that as an observer, as someone who's near the powerful. *(Laughs)* It's all about contacts and hormones. *(Pounding chest)* I'm as confused as anyone else. Hold me, Ma.

SUNNY: Don't fuss at me.

MONTGOMERY: Let me kiss your hand at least.

SUNNY: *(Withdrawing)* Act sensibly. Go read a book or--

MONTGOMERY: I was proud to bring the awards home to you. For a brief period we had this interrupted reality. This fake sense of coziness and grandeur. That's why I've got to audition. I'm a loser iconically, *(Coughing)* but I'm still a good actor. *(Pause)* Where did I put that script?

SUNNY: *(Fierce)* You can't audition now. You'll show everyone you're a failure.

MONTGOMERY: *(Pounds chest)* Breathe 1,2,3.

SUNNY: Look at you! You have no capacity!

MONTGOMERY: *(Gasping)* Breathe 4, 5, 6.

SUNNY: Of course, no one will tell you.

MONTGOMERY: *(Gasping)* 7, 8, 9. --It's always great to do a passionate audition even when it's bad.

SUNNY: They'll just look into their hands. I've grieved you as much as I loved you. I beg you.

(HE holds hands over his ears and vocalizes while SHE talks!)

MONTGOMERY: *(Covers ears)* MMMMMMMMmmmmmmmmmmmmm mmmmmmmmmmmmmmmmmmm

SUNNY: Save what's left of family pride. Don't audition. Why beg people you don't know for a role you care nothing about. You don't even want to do this cameo.

MONTGOMERY: I'm an actor. Do you know what that means? *(Yells, furious)* I've got to be on because everyone in my family is off.

(Sound of helicopter from roof. MONTY runs up. ALL GIRL FANS point above.)

ALL GIRL FAN CLUB: *(Hysterical)* The Baroness has gone.

RUBY: *(One of the fans)* She got rather bubbly. And flew off in that helicopter!!

MONTGOMERY: No! I've an important question to ask her. I thought she'd never leave—

RUBY: *(Groping)* That's because she's never left you before.

VIRGINIE: *(Another fan)* *(Uncertain)* She's... always ... been there.

RUBY: She's in that pinky sky area and when you look up—

VIRGINIE: You can feel her as a force of nature.

MONTGOMERY: Is that her, way up there... But why did she go?

VIRGINIE: *(Emotional)* She's off to the airport.

ELLIE: *(Another fan)* To go back to Austria.

ALL GIRL FAN CLUB: *(Sad)* We must disband the club. Go into the weeping!

MONTGOMERY: But why?

ALL GIRL FAN CLUB: We've no leader...No purpose.

(MONTGOMERY runs and gets his Raintree book and gives it to them.)

MONTGOMERY: Don't cry. Take this with you. I haven't found anything in the past that's really been of any help in the present.

ALL GIRL FAN CLUB: Whooeeeeeeee. Thanks. Kiss us!

MONTGOMERY: I'll kiss whoever makes the least noise and talks the lowest.

(HE kisses all the fans. Shivers. Blows on hands)

Brrr. It's getting cold. Did the Baroness have any parting words?

RUBY: She says, to do what terrifies you most.

ALL GIRL FAN CLUB: We said you weren't afraid of anything.

(HE walks back and forth as if trying to decide what to do pauses, looks up, then paces more)

ALL GIRL FAN CLUB: You're a super star. You're not a scaredy cat.

VIRGINIE: Will you try for the lead?

RUBY: If not, you'll make a fool of us.

ELLIE: We've devoted our lives to you.

MONTGOMERY: Let me warm up a minute in this patch of light.

ALL GIRL FAN CLUB: We're rooting to see how you'll do *Suddenly Last Summer*. *(Singing)* "We love you Mon-ty; forever and ever!"

RUBY: We can't wait to see how you'll act with Liz--

VIRGINIE: We don't want you to marry. Not her not anyone.

RUBY: Audition for the lead.

ELLIE: How do we keep the fan club going if you don't star.--

VIRGINIE: We'll follow you every where.

ALL GIRL FAN CLUB: Say you can do it. We love you.

(BARONESS enters with flower)

BARONESS: Actually, I didn't go.

MONTGOMERY: Marvelous.

BARONESS: But I've unlocked my door and invited all the neighborhood *(Signals and we hear O.S. applause)* To vatch you leave--. If you don't go, I blow whistle and let zem up here. Vill you audeetion for lead?

(MONTGOMERY looks up, thrilled, moment of understanding)

MONTGOMERY: Yes. Advancement starts with humility. I've come a long way from Omaha Nebraska, and fluctuating finances to this New York City rooftop. I hate Hollywood so, I don't plan to return to do anything less than exceptional. I've a laziness to overthrow. My life is too easy. I need to go to a film set where I can live hard.

BARONESS AND ALL GIRL FAN CLUB: We love you! Mont-gom-ery!

MONTGOMERY: *(Looking about)* And--Success is in the people. I'll put on courage like a coat. Break through the wall of ice that surrounds the audition.

BARONESS AND ALL GIRL FAN CLUB: Hooray! You can do it!

MONTGOMERY: With so many strangers behind me how can I not succeed? *(Laughs triumphant)* The days will pass anyway. And life will end whether I audition or not… *(Looking up)* I'm going to fly when I act, not think. Run my career on serendipity.

(SUNNY, ROSTOVA, and DR. BILLY rush upstairs to the roof.)

DR. BILLY: The car's downstairs.

SUNNY: People are lining up all around the house.

DR. BILLY: Word has leaked out that you're leaving for an--

ROSTOVA: Won't you take one of us to the audition--

MONTGOMERY: *(Obsessed)* Interview. Lets call it that. Because I'll--come from the place it's me interviewing them-- --To see if I'll choose them to work with.

ROSTOVA AND SUNNY: Take us.

DR. BILLY: Don't go by yourself.

MONTGOMERY: I need aloneness to create. And… every time I'm in plays I feel like I've come home. *(Points to sky, triumphant)* Chekhov is buried in Moscow Federal City Cemetery, section 2. *(Points again)* And Shakespeare in Holy Trinity Churchyard, Stratford. But they are also *(Pats chest)* in here.

When I audition, I'll feel them… as a force. I'm going to take up their quest. Keep working till the day I don't. Embrace my new family of fearless strangers.

I'll audition for the lead. Enter the scene alone, And when all goes quiet and the lights come up, I'll say: "MONTGOMERY CLIFT, THE ACTOR IS BACK."

CURTAIN

MONTGOMERY CLIFT FROM "JUDGEMENT AT NUREMBURG."

The author's New Orleans homes. Clockwise
from above:

*2140 South Carrollton was the home of the author's
grandmother and where she was raised.*

*1437 South Carrollton was a family inheritance.
The author lived in this house while running the
Souther Rep Theater and teaching at Loyola University.*

*524 St. Philip, the author's current residence in
the servant's quarters of a 17th c. French Quarter
home.*

*54 Fountainebleau Drive: the author's parents cottage
decorated for Mardi Gras in uptown New Orleans.*
Photos: Mary Brent Anderson

ROSARY HARTEL O'NEILL

ABOUT THE AUTHOR

ROSARY HARTEL O'NEILL is the author of twenty plays, many published by Samuel French, Inc. and produced internationally by invitation of the American embassy in Paris, Bonn, Berlin, Norway, Tibilisi, Georgia, Oslo, Budapest, Hungary, London and Moscow. In 2010-11 she won fellowships to the Norman Mailer institute playwriting and screen-writing and the Ireland Tyrone Guthrie Residency in playwriting. Her play *Uncle Victor* won a signing at the Consulate General of the Federal Republic of Germany in New York in 2011. She was founding artistic director at Southern Rep Theater from 1987 to 2002 and has been playwright-in-residence at the Sorbonne Un., Paris; Tulane Un., New Orleans; Defiance College, Ohio, the Un. of Bonn, Germany and Visiting Scholar at Cornell. Her play *Beckett at Greystones Bay* a finalist in the Pen and Brush International Play competition, 2010 will be produced at the German Consulate, NYC in 2012.

Other fellowships include the Virginia Center for the Creative Arts (VCCA), five fellowships with Ernest Gaines, Playwrighting Fellowships to Squaw Valley, Dorset Colony House, Au Villar France and Wiepersdorf, Germany, and to the Playwriting Center, Sewanee University. Her acting text, *The Actor's Checklist*, is used worldwide and in its 4th edition with Wadsworth Publishers. Her directing text, *The Director as Artist*, (Harcourt) is a seminal text in the field.

She was chosen outstanding artist and awarded a Fulbright to Paris for her play *Wishing Aces*. She was a finalist in the Faulkner Competition for New American Writers; a finalist for outstanding artist for Louisiana 2002. Awarded 7 Fulbrights, she was a Senior Fulbright research specialist in drama to Europe, 2001-2006, and a professor of Drama at Loyola Un., New Orleans 1984 - 2002.

Recent awards include: membership in the Actors Studio Playwrights Unit, Columbia University Harlem Writers Project, HB Studios Playwrights Workshop, NYC. She is playwright-in-residence at the National Arts Club, where her recent work has been developed.

Author photo by DC Larue.

For more information about the work of Rosary O'Neill,
visit her web site at:
www.rosaryoneill.com

PRODUCTIONS AND PUBLISHING

FOR PLAYS:
ENGLISH LANGUAGE RIGHTS
Samuel French, Inc.
45 W. 25th St., 2nd Floor
New York, NY 10010
212.206.8990

FOREIGN LANGUAGE RIGHTS
The Marton Agency, Inc.
1 Union Square W. Suite 815
New York, NY 10003-3303
212.255.1908